TCB VOL. III

TCB VOL. III

TALESSIAN
EL-WIKOSIAN

This is a work of nonfiction.

First Edition, 2010

Due to the high volume of publishing by the author, this book may contain editorial and grammatical errors. The author guarantees the authenticity of his ideas, opinions and interpretations.

ISBN 9781453650103

Set in Verdana

Book design by T. N. El-Wikosian

CONTENTS

The 5 Books of the Android Testament

MARS 21

What Model is your Soul?

There seems to be an argument that there's only one kind of soul. This is untrue. This is untrue because it is rooted in both dogma and primitive science. We don't talk about souls unless we assign our discussion to a religious philosophy or spiritual belief because we are incapable of talking about souls without the aid of some divine reference. "So and so said that the soul is this and that is what I believe." What I have seen is that there is not only a soul, as we typically understand, but there are many models, as we will see.

You have a soul; therefore, you're alive and upon death, your soul leaves. Beyond that the general understanding is private, religious or scientific. I've discussed my appropriation for the soul elsewhere so I'll avoid that repeat discussion; instead, I'd like to add a new stream of soul knowledge and I'd like to do so because I'm nothing more often than not the complete disregard of this.

It can be said that there are soul species and that each species is unique to its approach to life and that's because each soul species is programmed in its own meaningful way. In deterring souls in this manner instead of the usual one soul deal we can better see the value of the flesh vessel (or body). This is because your soul occupies your body.

There are several gateway mechanisms from the soul entity to the physical body. One of them is your brain, another is your heart. When we incarnate we have a limited soul to body connection. That's because of the vibrational difference between a pure energy universe and the sewer in which we exist. Some people who do achieve a higher connection to soul young in life will be looked at as prodigies, autistic, wild, unstable or old souls. Of course there are other reasons for this but generally speaking it makes a richer connection to the soul.

When those subtle connections between dimensions are blocked or severed, our physical presence reverts to autopilot. Autopilot doesn't mean be like a zombie and that because zombies and the walking dead are human inventions. A person on autopilot fulfills their basic duties without any serious circumstance. For example, a woman lives a wild youth then gets married and all of a sudden is living in the dreadful suburbs, learning to bake and doesn't mind being overweight because she's a mom. Well, more likely she's on the mom program. Later, mom will turn off autopilot, wake up, get dressed and find a younger boyfriend.

A person or a group, who can influence those essential gateways between soul and body, can predetermine the life experience of that person. For example, if I could influence the brain to accept murder under certain conditions, such as war, then I could make a soldier who will disobey the soul's law not to kill or murder man. If I were to reopen that faculty to the soul, the soldier literally toss away their weapons and quit the army. Now because of rather than just one block, there are many blocks, there are program patches, there are all kinds of interferences even things like mirrors that keep redirecting your connection attempts in endless circles, so you'd have to, at this point in evolution, overcome a majority of those in order to stop wars. And with the continual brainwashing and thought implantations being implemented, it would take a significant amount of time and effort to reach heaven, so to speak. Interferences to ascension are similar and are why your awareness is continually jilted.

Fundamentally, that's the unique situation here on this plane you call earth. As much and as certain as you believe the world works accordingly, now they've taught us the way their twisted world works. It is their twisted world that they're teaching us to live in and they've conditions society in any number of ways, all of the time they've prevented us from reaching our soul any great depth. At this point, if an average person gets one epiphany in life, they'll treasure it forever, and they'll do so because they've been fed the truth from the pig farmers because they look at humans as pigs. I understand why. I do. They are simply not human. They look human but they've filtered themselves from other dimensions. They occupy the human body and appear normal. They set the laws, they present the presidential choices, they provide the think tanks, they invent the cures by labelling the disease and its all one big fantasy, all of it designed to lock you out of your soul because the soul is infinitely smart and would not accept all this deception. The brain and the ego, for example, love lies as it were ice cream.

They want your soul's pink slip

The soul is a wonderful device. It is truly resplendent. The fact that it comes in many models is even more wonderful. Your soul comes from other dimensions. And, at this point, we can all agree there that the world, the universe, the cosmos is multidimensional. It isn't a stretch then to say that within that vast multidimensional network are soul dimensions, even sources of souls.

We can readily agree that apples grown on apple trees, bananas on banana trees and cherries on cherry trees. We can agree on that. We can agree that a Toyota is manufactured at a Toyota plant, a Honda at a Honda plant and a Ford at a Ford planet. We can agree that a Motorola phone comes from a Motorola factory, a Nokia phone from a Nokia factory and an iPhone from an Apple factory. All of that makes sense; a different product originates from each area of production. It is different because of many factors, from design to machinery to production philosophy, including even market demand and corporate mission.

A soul isn't much different in production principle, unfortunately. And as it might be to dispel the illusion of a divine soul made by some white-bearded Creator, it is even sadder to see billions of people still believing that after the past few thousand years. I repeat: after thousands of years, we haven't progressed our principle of divine perception.

Yes, it is true, our souls are unique and beautiful. They are built on principles of purity and honesty. With those things we are given in to innocence. Innocence is the one essential gift of the soul. The more innocent, the more pure. But there are many ways to purity. You are born pure, yes, like a new car from the factory line: no mileage, no rust, all shiny. We could say that the new car is pure and innocent. And when we do afford a new car we want the most innocent.

So we earn this soul from a specific cosmic factory and that means that there are multiple factories, a myriad of factories and you happen to originate from one of them in a pure state. So while we all appear to what we all call "human," which is misleading and, in fact, another brainwash, a thought implant, inside of us is a different kind of soul. On this plane, you will discover a number of similar models. I think the automobile industry is a good metaphor for types of souls. The auto industry has a limited number of players because there are many barriers to entry in automobile production.

Occasionally you do find a new player. They start cheap and then build more finesse. Some old players seem to always build cheap and pretend they're high quality. You get import vehicles and domestic brands. You tend to very similar brands over time. You like to drive a certain car, even though there are many choices. Why?

Well, a soul is like this too. You tend to adopt a certain frequency of soul and stick to that. Look on the highway; you'll see many flavours of cars. Look in the cities; you'll see many colors of souls. But they're inside of your body and the rulers of earth have disconnected your beautiful soul from your physical body because if you were connected you'd kick out the false rulers.

The rulers of earth have ridiculously descended you and robbed you of your intimate soul connection, and they've done so as to be able to hijack your mind and to control your soul. They want your soul because the soul is a powerful reservoir of energy and, more importantly, technology. Why do they implant fear and oppression into the world, why do they continually fill you with disease – because they need to weaken your will, to convince your mind so that you will surrender your soul to them. They want the pink slip to your soul. And they'll do anything to get it.

They'll tip you into drug addiction, they've give you AIDS, they'll make you a celebrity, they'll promise you a trip to Mars in 30 years and then, failing that, promise another trip 30 years after that. Ironically enough, you'll believe them. That's because they've got you. If you had a decent connection to your soul you wouldn't allow any of this garbage. You wouldn't allow Catholic Bishops to routinely rape boys and girls. You wouldn't let some false Pope allow child molestation to continue for such a long time. But you allow it. Being indifferent or busy is still allowing it. See how much of your soul has been sold? I hope you're happy with your career.

Why does my Ferrari look like a Toyota?

So, there are many kinds of souls. Yours is probably different than your friend's or you might have even come from the same soul factory, just a different model with different options. You both might be of the same brand. Perhaps, similarly branded souls hang out. I mean Mercedes and Hyundais will never be friends, Toyota and Honda are very competitive but Toyota and Lexus are still family. Some similar souls will incarnate into similar cultures (models). That explains why Indians are culturally similar and why Americans are culturally fragmented. The former is much more homogenous than the latter.

Finally, it should be noted that over the course of your life, you can upgrade your soul or try on different souls. This is the same in the car business. You own a Honda for 10 years and then you buy a new Mazda. You might hate it and exchange it for a Toyota when you might like. You change cars as you age and as your lifestyle changes. Rich men cannot be found during Honda Civics. They'll buy BMWs or a Mercedes. So, we can see changing evolves as we change. Souls are similarly changed only that you have to earn your soul if you want an upgrade. Typically, we refer to this as ascension. If you've done well, you can upgrade.

Whatever soul you have today is unlike ever before and that's because of the tremendous shifts in reality, felt even more in other dimensions. That's why you feel funny (even though you are not laughing). Your current soul model comes equipped with a number of wonderful features which you will eventually figure out. Some of you have been handed Ferrari-grade souls and still think you have a Toyota brand and that's because of your weak connection and your soul memory. If you make effort you can correct this; if you don't then you'll drive your Ferrari as if it were a Toyota. Other people have a Toyota and drive it like a Ferrari. These people are delusional, probably tripped up by all the sewage and manipulation.

There's no magic pill to make effort if you want to gain awareness. It's non-negotiable. No effort, no gain.

You'll drive your Lexus like a Honda Civic. You'll think your GM SUV is a Porsche. GM is GM, Porsche is Porsche. The better you are connected to your soul the more likely you'll know what you've got. But remember, they are trying very hard to disconnect you every day. That means you have to try every day to connect. Once a month won't cut it. You have to compensate for the assault on your being. Wake up.

A process of life

These are truly wonderful times filled with very complex and incomprehensible items, significant items. In no way, can all of this be fully explained. It is a process of life. You choose to evolve or you choose to evolve in your next life. A spiritual person will surrender everything in order to ascend because ascension purifies them and a pure person can get close to the Creator. Just to give you an idea, a spiritual person wants to join with the Creator, a being that is the purest. That's called a spiritual life in the common term. You are probably very far from that, probably deeply held in ego and probably full of disinformation and implants. So, you're going to decide a goal for this life.

At the end of this cycle, what do you expect to achieve in a spiritual sense? Be reasonable but don't diminish yourself. And then you take action. One action a day or per week and you try to live according to your end destination. How close do you want to be to God? Many of you are not here for the ego trip and are needed in the front lines, that means sacrifice, doesn't it? That means we need you there and you're late. Why is that?

I'm not going to chase anyone, well maybe a couple of people, but for the most part you're on your own. The tools are there, the support is there, the knowledge is available, the world is a sewer, figure it out. Or not. Sit and watch. Whatever you decide, you are responsible for the result. You want to come back? Sit and watch. You want to travel to a different dimension? Sweat and act. There's no cheating here. Everything you do is recorded. At death, it's reviewed. Did she learn or not? Let's see. The video tape says no; therefore, no ascension for you. The video shows moderate effort punctuated by lots of swearing and feelings of entitlement. Sorry, you're a bitch, try again. The tape shows the spirit of a champion, lots of failure, but never quit, never surrendered to fear, never believed the lies. She gets a pass. Good job.

It's just like school because it is school only that you can't cheat. Not this time. Before, there was cheating. Now, you can't cheat. It isn't allowed. It is frowned upon. You lose points for cheating. The demons are royally screwed so don't follow their egotistical example. Hey, I'm not telling you what to do. I don't care. I don't get the benefit of your efforts. You've got to face your next life, not me. I choose to live in the highest way possible. I'm weird in that way.

The Brotherhood of Mars

Where did you and I come from? Mars. Well, not directly of course. More as in a legacy. The legacy of Mars is in our blood. We are those people, their greatest grand children. But some of us come from other places as well. The universe is not so sparse in intelligence, that's the human ego at work. The human ego is the most powerful device around because it has the power to create and destroy illusions. And in a world formed of illusions, having an active ego is like having an atomic bomb in hand. It has a tremendous amount of power. The ego doesn't approve of the truth and it will do everything to avoid the proof.

When the human ego is forced to adhere to the Mars origin story, it will shift its focus and become extremely distracted. If pushed further it will push a person into drugs or prostitution. The ego does not want the truth in any way. Before you realize your true origins you'll need to develop a system of communication with your soul because your soul is an integral part of your evolution, and your soul is the key to realizing and accepting your Martian origins.

Long ago, Mars was inhabitable, as its system of operation wound down, its people disappeared into other diversions of existence. By doing so, the physical part of the planet lost its energy systems and the planet dried up.

If the one essential piece of information we're missing on earth is the Martian Contingency then we are in need of further discussion on these matters, are we not? We can pretend and deny, we can omit and delay, but we are sooner or later forced to identify our true origins.

What would be wrong with us being of Martian descent? Would it trouble you if your early ancestor wasn't a primate, rather was a Martian Traveler? I mean, which lineage would you rather be a part of, the bloodline of a pig-brained Neanderthal (which is what anthropologists say is the parent of all) or the bloodline of a multidimensional Martian race. Personally, I love Martians.

The Martians were the Atlanteans, the Atlanteans were the Elves. Are we then Elven? Sure. Many of us are Elven-blooded. How are you to believe me in this highly trimmed historical washout? You needn't believe anything. It isn't necessary to believe me to be of Martian blood. You are first of Martian blood and then you have a choice whether or not to believe me. Problem is we get caught up in the language. How can an Elf be a Martian? How can an Atlantean be Elven? The language gets in the way of truth. The stories and disinformation get a hand of truth.

Elves,Martians, Atlanteans – these are all terms invented by different eyes. One set of eyes see an Elf. One set of eyes sees a Martian. One set of eyes sees an Atlantean. But they all see the same core people. That's the irony. Three different sets of eyes watching the same group of people existing in a different dimension. Because remember that we live in a multidimensional world and as we evolve we change our vibrations and we enter a different dimension. The Martians were naturally multidimensional, as are humans, only that humans are maliciously blocked from accessing areas outside their physical dimensions. Martians could at any time disappear into other dimensions, and they themselves exist here on earth in other dimensions.

The Mars Contingency

Let us be slightly frank without disturbing the truth because as a matter of fact the truth cuts very deeply and we don't want to create any unnecessary injuries. People who read my world already know that I spill an overdose of truth and that is why my readers are few and they tend to wear titanium-plated armour. When we speak of truth and Mars we run into a very complex enigma because the human society, taken as a whole, homogenous blend, is implanted with lies and, not only that, but the rulers of earth have used very high level dimensional physics to create firewalls in human memory and thinking patterns.

This puts people like me, or really anyone with truth, at a disadvantage because the correct memory chains that readily understand truth are blocked. What my truth associates do is to simplify pure truth into a digestible form that is acceptable in an egotistical, hyper-violent, enslaved society. Some truth still flows but not enough to activate the higher chains of the mind. So we have the landscape. Everything is working against us and that translates into a slowly evolving society. The single most relevant concern having to do with a slowly evolving society is that the rulers of earth now have more time to further block the memory and to implant false beliefs (eg "We are going to Mars.").

Your ancestors came here from Mars. In fact, some Martians were already on the planet. It was normal to visit another planet and Martians had the technology to do so, at that time anyway. From a small colony, the New Mars was moved and arranged to be on earth.

After a time, the New Martians decided that they would change their physical identity because of one important fact: earth planet was vibrating at a level unlike Mars. I confirmed the presence of Martians early on in my training. They did not call themselves Martians just like we do not call ourselves Earthies, but clearly they were on earth and not from here. My first reaction was to regard them as Elves, not the Elves in books and movies, rather my own interpretation of Elves based on my first meeting in 2005: tall, dignified, well-dressed, very intelligent, and multidimensional, with sharp features in their appearance. Through that I came to the understanding of their connection to Atlantis, a place that either does or doesn't exist depending upon your belief system. Clearly, most people I've met, average folk, do accept the Atlantean civilization, it just lacks the unmanageable proof from a 2D-brained society.

Then we add the presence of Mars and not only the artefacts on the Red Planet but the implication of a Martian Civilization. Could it be possible that Mars, Atlantis and Faeries had /something uniquely beautiful in common? It's a rhetorical question of course. We have simply identified one particular legacy civilization with three differently coloured highlighters.

It is true that it's easy to get confused regarding this matter because of the other mix of interstellar cultures that was throwing us off target. Martians/ Elves/ Atlanteans, being multidimensional and highly advanced, interacted with a multitude of other Star Races. The presence of other races, even in larger quantities, did not diminish the domain of these people, but it did not confuse us all.

Even I am writing this, I am not welcomed by the dominant rulers of earth, some of these, we will note, were rogue Atlanteans who were responsible for some of the dame to that civilization, not unlike today where we now notice clearly the societal sabotage going on in the shadows, the loss of the Polish President and a plane full of Polish elites in a terrible plane crashes. The only thing terrible about the plane crash is that society believes it is a terrible accident, and that is because it's dressed very nice, very clean, tragic accident, important people, mourning, funeral – the stage is full of glitter, the misdirection full bloom. How wonderful!

Some off the current rulers of earth, well, not many now, they are Atlantean. They were well advanced in dimensional physics back then and had learned to reincarnate, the process of returning in a different body in a similar bloodline. They continued to reincarnate as immortals (avoiding the pitfalls of earthly existence) till today. Some of them have forgotten their past in order to protect their identities (eg Gov. Alaska), some know it all and have damaged society. You find them in high circles (because they are egotistical) of governments, banks, churches, militaries, or celebrities, they are driven to accumulate power and reincarnation is an ancient method of ascension and power over the universe.

On the other side, there are other ancients and immortals that are less egotistical and they are here as well. They too have been quiet, some are still trapped in their memories, others are training and learning like turtles. Many of them struggle to live in an egotistical society devoid of true compassion, innocence and multidimensionality.

Even I write this, these 3 races (Elven/ Atlantean/ Martian) are still here. They exist mostly in other dimensions. They interact with select people in the most subtle and unimaginable ways. A person of moderate awareness will never see them. It is funny in a way that when I released my first documentary in 2008, two years ago, very few people believe me. Many watched but it couldn't make sense that this human was a nonhuman. Today, more and more discussions are going on they include aliens in human form. When I called the radio station and told them on live radio that I was an ET in human form the host was laughing and thought it was a joke. Ask him today and the response will be very different. My point is that our awareness inhibits our existence and, generally speaking, our awareness is low. It takes a very high level of awareness to see multidimensional people and events. The crash of the Polish airliner is one such multidimensional event which you can figure out, if you like.

If I can correct in my discussion, if the Martians entered this plane and became Atlanteans and Elves and if any of these cultures is real then that means that Martians and Humans are of the same, or similar, bloodline. That means that if a Martian is a nonhuman then so is a human. If I am correct. My knowledge comes from my direct experience and wisdom so this is my presentation of truth, in a very simplified format; otherwise, we wouldn't understand it.

What does all this have to do with Mars, the planet? Basically, we're not finished with it. Basically, we have to face the truth that over there is our ancestry, the bulk of it. Sure, you may have originated from further out and that is a result of further interstellar interaction but your base genetic material, isn't necessarily Neanderthal. Further, due to the ongoing genetic upgrades on this entire planet, and all its people (98%), the original genomes and all their DNA have since been thoroughly upgraded so that an entirely new race is now present. Sadly, a race devoid of interstellar awareness. My previous estimation was that in the late 60s, about 67-69, the human race as a species was wiped out and replaced with a new species, a Human 2.0. Since then we've probably reached Human 4.0 or 5.0, just using it as a means of understanding genetic expansion because Human 2.0 was no longer part of the Human Class. Problem was that its awareness has been kept restricted to Human Class so it still saw itself as a human, like locking a child in a closet for 20 years and then the child develops abnormally. And, we can't forget that a human, as a race, is itself originally a nonhuman!

I told you it would be truthful. To make yourself feel better, you can always rely on the fact that I might be wrong. And I might. I might have missed a few pieces. There are too many pieces to put in one essay. Plus, I like small puzzles. But, if I am even half correct, everything you faithfully have been brainwashed to believe about the only intelligent species in the universe, and human achievement in general is wholly misguided and woefully censored.

Do Not Leave Your Ancient Spaceship Unattended

Well. It's true; you shouldn't leave your ancient spaceships unattended. It's not because someone is going to steal it. It's not because someone is going to get onboard and steal your data. It's because the technology is too advanced. Someone might get the wrong idea. And that's because ancient spaceships don't look like spaceships. They look like naturally-formed space objects, like planetary moons for example.

People who discover ancient spaceships forget one very important Cosmic Rule: Do not leave your ancient spaceship unattended.

The owner of an ancient spaceship would never abandon their spaceship, especially if it is billions of years old. The discovery of an abandoned spaceship, or a moon-like object, indicates one very fundamental thing: the owners are still around.

We don't like to think of the owners of an incredibly complex spaceship because that would force us to understand and accept the presence of a billion year old people. The human lifespan has maxed out at 120 years; even so, very few mortals have surpassed the physical age of 120 years. We couldn't imagine a person living a thousand years because the physical body simply couldn't last that long. Of course, a billion year old person wouldn't have a human body throughout their existence. They would have to have a very flexible body dynamic that could be incorporated into other vehicles for enlightenment (eg bodies).

Parking by the millennium

When you go shopping, you park your car in the Parking Lot and then enter the store (or Mall) on foot and that's because you still can't find a drive-thru grocery store (that's brilliant!). Some people run into the store to buy a simple but cancerous item, say cigarettes for example, while others spend two hours buying family food items and clean underwear. No matter how long you spend inside the grocery store (or Mall), to an outsider, it appears like you abandoned your vehicle. But because it's inside a Parking Lot it appears reasonable that you just parked it temporarily so that you could go shopping inside.

Sometimes there is no Parking Lot, there's just a road. You stop your car along the road, pay the meter and run your errand. Other times, there's no exact area to park, just a big fenced-in lot. What do you do? Leave and go looking for a parking spot? Or, would you just park it along the fence? In every case, people typically park for a temporary period of time. Would it be so strange to look at an ancient spaceship in the same fashion?

Let's say, just for the sake of argument, that one of the moons around the planet Mars was an ancient spaceship. It's a bit out there but it's going to help us understand what else might going on. Let's say that the billion year old spaceship owner had to run some cosmic errands. To a billion year being, time is negligible. It's not something that needs to be calculated unless absolutely necessary.

In fact, each breath probably lapses a few decade of earth time. So the cosmic being parks their spaceship around Mars because it's perfectly designed for orbital anchoring. If they had parked it in space, the spaceship would end up floating to who knows where or most likely be hit by an asteroid or picked up by a random starship patrol. In any case, to leave your spaceship in the middle of the starry heaven is just plain dumb. So, what do you do?

You hook it with the orbit of a larger spaceship, or a planet. In all the science fiction movies I've seen there weren't many abandoned spaceships, and even there were, there was a good reason, usually haunted or possessed by some ridiculous entity. To simply leave a spaceship moon in orbit and to forget about it is not something billion year old beings would do. Would you leave your mansion unlocked and unattended while you went on vacation? The problem we encounter is in understanding how billion year beings think. Guess what? We can't. Forget about it. It's like a Chihuahua trying to think like a rose bush.

What we can do, rather, is that we can look for some key patterns, let's say cosmic patterns and use those to help us figure some things out. For example, to start, we have the idea of parking a vehicle temporarily in order to some errands (or research). Only the timescale has to be adjusted because the people are aged in the billions. I wonder what their wine collection looks like. "Well, look here, I've got this 4,000 BC Egyptian Red Wine, it goes well with a reincarnation."

Engaging billion year olds

A temporary stay for an ancient could be a few thousand years. Mind you, these billion year olds can probably traverse time and therefore could speed and slow time at the same time they park. They might park their spaceship in one million BC, do their thing, then speed up time to 4,000 BC and run a second errand, then speed up time to 2010 AD and say, "Hello."

This raises an important question: would a billion year old (or just very advanced) culture reveal itself to a lesser advanced (5,000 year young) culture? Sure, why not. But they could only do so under certain conditions.

One condition for engagement would include that the lesser evolved culture could indeed see the ancient spaceship outside of their atmosphere because that indicates some level of technological mastery and some demonstration of freedom of speech. If you were Galileo or Copernicus and spotted this stuff, you couldn't go against the all-powerful church. Mind you, even today we're facing an immense level of interference when it comes to the truth. But if the lesser-evolved culture could indeed recognize a spaceship of some cosmic design, well, that's a plus. If the few could communicate that to the larger public, that's a double bonus. Of course, those who ruled the place would hammer down with some trickery (or elitist benefit program) and cause trouble, as usual, so I'm pretty sure that's a minus. And you get a few pluses and minuses. Historically speaking, you get more minuses since society isn't strong willed. The proof for the excess minuses is the level of ongoing societal repression, tyranny and enslavement.

Another condition for galactic chatter would be in determining what benefit, if any, would result in such an interaction. I mean, perhaps the spaceship was discovered by accident, example, a 12-year-old clicked on the space agency computers and nabbed some photos. In this case, well, society isn't all that ready. Society is enslaved and it happened to get a hole in one. Well, the billion year old people wouldn't even take notice because there's no benefit to saying hello to a prison society.

If the benefit to society would be sizable then the billion year old beings would need to determine if those bright people could allow one of them into society for a peaceful introduction and elaboration versus some more ignorant and violent welcoming approach. A billion year old culture would have no tolerance for things such as violence, egotism and religious complaints. It would demand a certain amount of respect and politeness, after all, billion year olds don't say hi very often. If the people could achieve that then there might be some benefit for a short visit or communiqué. Quite likely, it would take years to achieve some sort of welcoming because there'd by lots of argument and fist fights in the interim.

I mean, did God make this billion year old culture? Well, that would force the priests to ask: How old is God? And, does God have a spaceship too? They might also ask, does God drink green tea? Well, wait a minute; what if the spaceship owner was God and God was running errands...what then? Could it be one of God's spaceships? That would mean that there is no God, just very old beings in the cosmos. We seem to be getting too many questions. Let's go back to the beginning.

Presence and detection

You shouldn't leave your ancient spaceships unattended because it leaves a bad impression on other interstellar cultures. Plus, it's bad manners. You just don't leave your car in front of someone's house unless you know those people. Whatever the case may be the spaceship owners are nearby. They might have gone shopping. They might be busy observing other cultures (their children?). They might be drinking green tea at the table beside yours. We don't know. We do know that they are nearby and we also know that the alarm systems on that cosmic ship are pretty darn incredible.

The presence and detection of a planetary spaceship indicates an important event in human history. It would indicate a point where culturally diverse beings could touch each other. Verily, the presence and detection of a planetary spaceship indicates a historical moment, a door opening into another sense of reality, a reality filled with many dimensions. The presence and detection of an ancient spaceship says this very loud and clear: You are not alone in the universe!

And finally, the presence and detection of an ancient spaceship says that these billion year olds are here for a reason. They didn't come for the groceries; they come for some other reason or reasons. Those reasons are most probably very important and likely impossible to fully grasp in their entirety.

And let us not forget the purposeful manipulation by the human exploration of space experts in America who put up plans and strategies by the boatload while in the background, run by secretive co-ops, these similar folk are flying advanced spacecrafts that operate on technologies that don't officially exist. So, on the public front they sell the gooey-eyed people a new long-range spacecraft by the year 2025, a return trip to Mars in 2030. Twenty years from now they yet again promise some miserably sad space strategy that I'm certain the dole headed media people will sell with some patriotic disenchantment because rogue nations will invest heavily in space and fly to Mars in 2020. Now remember, they have starship technology being run by humans and nonhumans right now, yesterday and ten years ago. So, let's not be made fools by any space modernization program proposed by some guy in a suit.

You can see the bipolar world you exist in: one side is pure deception, delay and distraction; the other side, there are ancient spaceships, secret starships and living-on-earth interstellar cultures with their own starship technologies. Right there are several levels of interstellar travel technologies. Why is society chained to the rhetoric of space puppets? Because society cannot accept that spaceship technology is available today and kept so secret that it is well beyond the public perception and the media has no interest in chasing UFOs, and those who do search for the truth receive a free trip to the morgue. But don't buy lies just because they are cheap. Truth is that right now there are several levels of advanced propulsion systems in use, proven thousands of times and capable of renovating the entire energy industry. If anything needs to be revised, it is people's gullibility.

Myths and Truths about Star Beings

I've noticed several myths about star beings in general that are grossly, horribly, laughingly inaccurate. In fact, there is a fundamental deficiency in star culture knowledge and this is mostly because very few people have cared to admit that a group of people from another system (reality, star, dimension) have culture. By realizing another person's culture, instead of demonizing them, we are forced to admit our similarities. Sadly, in the UFO Business (or, The Denial of the Obvious to Control the Weak-Minded Society Who Accept Whatever is Given) cultural courage is absent. I have interacted with many cultures, all of them quite beautiful and complex. I have been routinely attacked by egotistical, lesser-evolved ET Cultures, as well, who are here and their culture is structured in greed, corruption and sucking the juice out of life. They and their Demon Friends have polluted society with egotism, temptation, sin, desire, lies and corruption.

So, here is our first big cultural problem, from which our myths shall pop their ugly heads. The nonhuman cultures have an impressive spiritual (even natural) disposition and character while human culture is strongly attached to ego. One of the big challenges when these two cultures meet is going to have to do with ego and egoless communication. This like a bird talking to a lion. Let us see 3 Star Being Myths:

STAR BEING MYTH #1:
Nonhuman cultures think exactly like humans, they just look different, have more advanced technology and fly in invisible starships.

No. Nonhumans do not think like humans. Their fundamental approach to a problem is rooted in Cosmic Laws. These Cosmic Laws (or Programming) depend upon egoless reflection and decision making. The Cosmic Laws are fundamental laws that permeate every aspect of distant culture and form the base of a particular civilization. If ego is service to self then egoless is service to community. An egoless being convinces for the benefit of others; an ego being convinces for the benefit of them. While ego has itself many layers, it can be stated that in order to quality as a starperson, a certain number of ego layers must be abandoned. The amount of ego determines amount of awareness and level of individual in the cosmos. Less ego forces a starperson to identify themselves with the greater community and helps to activate other hidden abilities.

STAR BEING MYTH #2:
ETs (namely "The Grays") are continuously mutilating cattle to harvest genetic material and to work towards becoming cattle ranchers.

We refer back to the first myth, briefly, and recall the egoless nature of a nonhuman (ET, star being). An egoless person is equal to an enlightened person, or an awakened mind. Of course, this depends on their level of awareness. For example, a task may be given to a lesser-aware group and that group may act in a lesser form.

Two good examples, one traditional and one contemporary, of egoless people on earth are Buddha and Gandhi, respectively. Could you ever imagine, say, Buddha mutilating defenceless cattle? Even once? By accident? Imagine a starship filled with novice Buddhas, enlightened people, going around mutilating cattle. Not only that BUT leaving the desecrated, rotting carcasses for everyone to see. If you have not realized yet, the very act of senseless mutilation of defenceless animals and the leaving raw body parts for all to see are egotistical acts, first and foremost. Egoless beings cannot act so deeply in ego, only egotistical beings can. Certainly, for a Buddha-type person (say, austere Buddhist monk) to repeatedly destroy one animal species for fun is impossibility, a fantasy. It would be like a US President refusing to go to war.

So, who is doing it? One, egotistical humans who have no sense of self and no balls to refuse authority. Two, egotistical aliens who are abusing their powers to scare society so as to assassinate the character of benevolent ETs. Three, demon possessed militarists, with advanced technology in hand, who want to lump a diverse set of offworld races into a singular group so as to demonize them and to put thought implants into society. It is just like referring to all foreigners as evil or calling some nations, rogue states. Same philosophy, different group. Contrary to popular or even mainstream opinion, interstellar people (ETs) come in wide variety of shapes, sizes and levels of civilization. These races are highly dignified races and they will see no need to clear their name in a society that is so gullible and will not speak truthfully, or in a society that cannot separate truth from untruth.

STAR BEING MYTH #3:
There is only one kind of alien. All ETs are the same.

This is a strategy used by the secret forces to generalize and demonize. This is how wars are created. You lump everyone under the same brand name and then mindwash the gullible public, force policies into play and voila – yet another war, this time a smart war, or a green war, or an alien war. One bullshit spread onto a freshly wiped society. Fact is, there are many diverse offworld cultures. You know this in your heart. Star cultures are noted by their level of advancement, their connection to the Cosmic Authority and by their level of technology, or all three in some cases. The most advanced cultures are pure technological cultures (or, cosmic cultures). The lesser advanced cultures are like earth cultures, still not a planetary community. In time we will learn how to interact with several kinds of interstellar cultures, perhaps even learn some languages and other fun stuff, but I will add this, at first, it will be quite shocking so prepare for some shocks here and there. Since you all asked for it, you can no longer complain. There is no complaints department yet.

These 3 MYTHS are basic, nasty and very common. There are many more star being myths, in fact, we could write a big book on these myths, or many books. The biggest problem is in our failing to understand nonhuman culture. It is like the first time a Canadian went over to China. Without question, that person would experience a cultural shock on many levels. But there is no way for that Canadian to grasp all the cultural nuances or subtext going on right in front of their eyes, let alone to translate the Mandarin language. It has now been centuries of trade with China that we have some understanding of China (or any other foreign nation), and even vice versa, for a Chinese to come to Canada, they too will experience cultural shock. The Chinese traveler will not agree with Canadian custom or ways of thinking, in fact, the Chinese person will insist that Chinese food is better. These cultural exchanges between humans are small when compared to the cultural rifts between humans and nonhumans. So far, very little cultural knowledge is known, mostly because the nonhumans have interacted in quiet areas or in secret. But also because humans do not care to understand how nonhumans think. I had suggested, and even drafted an Act, in 2008 to establish an Interstellar Affairs Office to deal with these issues. The reply from my readers was skewed to seeing a starship in the sky. No one was thinking of a cultural office, even the guys who believed in ETs!

I am from offworld and I have spent most of my 43 years among humanity, so I have some pretty good insights in the situation. I can state very clearly that there are many offplanet races and each of them unique, and within each are individuals who are themselves unique. To ever suggest to me that you or anyone understands interstellar races to any degree above amateur is absurd. In fact, I will be impressed by anyone who speaks an offplanet language since that is a good start.

This world is run by egotistical offworld and demonic races (dimensional cultures) and they do not appreciate the benevolent races from gaining an audience. They do not appreciate my efforts in any way. So, we have to realize the map in front of us: Your world is controlled, not by humans, the human leaders are puppets, remote-controlled delivery devices, and that is because society accepts this form of dominion. If society realized that the human leaders can all be remote-controlled and some are demons disguised as humans, well...there would be trouble. That hasn't happened and likely won't happen because people are too afraid to be seen as insane and radical; people want to come across as intelligent, thoughtful and with nice shiny white teeth. If you go on TV and scream with passion and excitement they tend to suggest pills. Passion is now equal to insanity which is itself insane. Of course, in other parts of the world, like Italy and Spain, there is only passion. Ole!

Finally, we can say that no one is perfect. We all act according to our own protocols for existence. We make mistakes because we never can anticipate all the variables. We are allowed to make mistakes as long as we correct our mistakes. Star Beings also make mistakes but that does not stop them from accomplishing their tasks. They have worked very hard to ensure that millions and millions of people would be prepared for what is coming around the corner. They decided that a long route ensured a more stable transition from sleep to standing, from mysterious lights to welcoming party. Many of you and your friends have made, and continue to make, many demands on Star Beings, and even other beings from other dimensions, without ever once paying for it. I myself have had many demands and no offers. No one has ever said to me, Tal, I want you to do this impossibly ridiculous task and I will do this in return. Never happened. It has always been demand after demand with a few girlish screams, "Oh, I don't like you now, you swore, you are not enlightened!" Fuck off, you mindless jerk. Ha. Swearing has nothing to do with enlightenment. Swearing is swearing; enlightenment is enlightenment. Comedian George Carlin was enlightened and yet he could swear the church doors open. Again, more misconceptions. There are too many myths and even more levels of awareness. Ultimately, we have to realize that there are forces who want you to hate aliens and there are aliens who are working day and night to help you through your transition. Be careful who you call friend or foe. Don't believe anyone who upholds these three myths for they are stupid and are puppets. There are many puppets. They are easy to control. They are conduits for deception. Stick to the truth. Learn to hear the truth. Make up your own minds. Realize that as long as earth has evil rulers, truth is hard to come by. When the evil rulers are exposed, it will all be clearer. And then there will be some other issues to deal with. There is no end to this.

Angels in Earthland

Life is an appearance, just like yourself. You appear to be alive because you've checked off all the necessary boxes on the How Alive Are You? form.

The technology of trees, for example, is able to manufacture branches, leaves and fruit from within itself, or better, it processes from within the earth because the earth is the source. If you take a tree, uproot it and hang it in your living room, no dirt, no water, what happens? It dies, or, it loses its lively appearance. Soon the illusion fades. We know life is fragile, that at any moment it can disappear, but we force ourselves (train) to place it at the back of our minds because most of us wouldn't function if you had to deal with the fragility of life, you'd be too afraid to leave your house. You'd be afraid you might break something or tear your precious skin. You'd be possessed with the idea of total care because your left-brain would take over. It would believe the illusion and do everything to preserve the illusion which is what we see now in the world of ego – the preservation of illusions. We truly have been made to forget that all before is illusory and therefore impermanent. All of it appears real in order to induce your multidimensional consciousness to inhabit this particular frequency of existence (or humanity). As you learn to adjust your ego or to overcome the quality of illusions, you come to realize that things can be made important and unimportant, you can love or not love; in fact, you can fall in love with a tree if you like; all of that because of the electromagnetic system you are immersed in.

Imagine that along the earth's floor, on your sidewalks, grass lawns, marble tile, office floor, mountain highway – imagine that on top of the earth everywhere, is a pool of energy, perhaps think of it as an aura for the planet. Now, because Earth Being is huge compared to you, this energy field isn't noticed. At times of heightened awareness (eg meditation), you seem to tap into reams of knowledge, you feel a oneness and you look at life differently - well, what is happening is that you yourself aren't becoming all powerful, which is a common view. This isn't true unless we take into account the energy of the planet which also precedes the energy of the cosmos. You can't get to the cosmos by bypassing earth because earth is the through point, earth is the entryway. By killing earth's environment, we have effectively harmed that vital, infinite, lovely connection to the cosmos, and those who lead us knowing full well what was happening.

Well, we know better. We see the value of environmental protection. We see through the climate warming scandals. There's a lot of work to be done on the environment. What I am suggesting here is that we need Mother Earth (Gaia) to expand ourselves into the cosmos. You are little cosmos, earth is big sister and big sister can show you the way. By interacting with the planet's energy fields, we can multiply our powers, we can reach the infinite, we can do miracles, we can stop scandals and open road blocks. But, we have to acknowledge the rules. Mother Earth has rules of engagement. We know these intuitively if we listen when we tap in. Your vibration, your energy impacts the world. A negative person who taps in speaks negative energy. So it is important that positive, uplifting people spend the time to tap in.

Tapping in

How do you tap into the planet's energy fields? There are many ways essentially to accomplish this. Some of them are very straightforward, even common, some require more training. Most of all, we have to remember that the depth of our interaction (and influence) depends on the complexity of our technique and the level of our skill. While everyone can bring a surfboard and get to a beach, not everyone can surf and some people just will always do it better, and fewer still know the best beaches for surfing. We all have interaction skills with varying levels of proficiency. Unless you are training on these skills they are unlikely to improve. You might become more sensitive, more aware, more this or that, but skill requires training. You might be a good fighter on the street but a Shaolin Monk will probably kick you into unconsciousness pretty fast. I say this obvious thing because people tend to feel entitled to superpowers and refuse to dedicate themselves to working it (which includes sweat and pain).

One easy way, probably the easiest, is to walk. Walking is a great and simple way to engage the planetary energy. Walking raises your heart rate and this is connected to your vibration. You raise your vibration to interact with the primordial energy of this ball of rock. Even you walk, your interaction is limited by skill, focus, discipline, etc. Some people's minds wander; some people query the cosmos for intricate answers. The next gear is running (or jogging). Again, it involves raising the vibration, getting deeper. People can get high on running and feel good for hours afterward. This is not because they are healthy as much as it is because they have processed earth's pure energy flows. We can extend those exercises into dance and song, something that we are seeing more and more around the world with contests. The martial arts has always been a pathway to greater spirituality and has never been about fighting. If you've had a love for martial arts, you have within in you a natural connection to cosmic thinking, now only if you could find a better teacher.

If you are not an athletic type of person, you can follow an Eastern form of energetic interaction. We've all heard of Tai Chi and Yoga. Both of these (quite common now) are excellent, and technically more difficult, ways to engage earth, and to reap the knowledge of the celestial libraries. All of these things, so far, are widely available. We can include now, meditation, something that requires more concentration and skill, and even a hot bath or sauna. Some native tribes did group saunas using hot rocks (eg Sweat Lodge) for different ceremonial purpose (eg purification) or to initiate members into higher levels of spirituality. A good teacher and a good sauna can help you ascend your state of being. This is a quite a bit more complex and there are more areas of risk from the intensity of the heat to the cosmic (or astral) excursions. Of course, if you want to take a short cut, you'll think of a steam bath but it won't help you without all the other aspects of ascension.

Aspects of ascension

Despite what the sellers will sell you, the truth of ascension (spiritual growth, cosmic upgrade, holistic maturation, enlightenment) is that it requires a few essential aspects. Your level of awareness (or understanding) in each aspect, and or combined set of aspects will determine how far you will move up the chain of awareness. In the old days, when awareness had value, men would give up their wealth and shoes for a chance to increase their awareness. Sadly, today men and women would prefer to criticize you on something irrelevant rather than follow their heart and get sweaty. I see this often. They will look for flaws in my character before believing me then when they can't find enough flaws, they'll find distractions so as not to get involved. Failing that, they'll just want to think about it for a few years. One excuse after another, without fail, and the road to ascension falls back to status quo – seeing is believing. No, seeing is not believing. First you believe...well, first you shut up, then you believe then you see. Someone, somewhere twisted it and implanted false ideas. Seeing is not believing. Seeing is merely an affirmation or validation.

Believing precedes the seeing, the seeing then affirms and then you believe more coherently. It's a process; step by step, like climbing a mountain. We will never wake up one day and be on top of a mountain full of knowledge and power! We will see the mountain in a dream. We will see ourselves climbing, but we have to climb the damn mountain! It doesn't matter who you are, no matter how gifted you are.

Gift or no gift, it just means you have more or less climbing tools. You are no better and there is no extra awareness. If you refuse to climb, you won't climb and you'll gloat all day at your wonderful tool box. "Boy, look at all my tools. I was born with these tools. I'm so smart, I'll just wait until a worthy mountain calls me up." Yeah, don't bother. Go back to sleep you arrogant idiot. No one is special in terms of ascension. You have to sweat. Those who have a very elaborate toolbox, such as Star Beings, they can go higher up the Mountain of God. They do so at risk because they could die. The higher you go, the more risk of death. So this is for the truly dedicated, those who spend their life pursuing cosmic knowledge and ascension. They find great teachers, they appreciate life, they take care of their health. They are not the most compassionate people in the world. Compassion is not the goal of ascension. Compassion is a ledge along the way up. Some people reach the compassionate ledge and decide to stop. Some people reach the remote viewing ledge and stop. You can stop where you like, the love ledge, the life of gratitude ledge, the interstellar ledge – it's up to you and your journey.

Each of us has a limit, much higher then we realize. And most, if not all, people will never get off the ground. And distractions are very powerful on earth, the interference is strong, the mind is high around the base of the mountain and people fall off. Once you get up a little ways, you get above the winds. You realize the winds are there to scare away the weak-minded and the casual participants. Cosmic knowledge is for the disciplined and the dedicated. All of this is in the Life Rule Book which is hidden in your heart.

The following aspects of ascension you will find useful: willpower, discipline, desire, morality, openmindedness, honesty, courage, healing, persistence, tenacity.

We will all look at these aspects and tick them off as "good." Truth is we will have failed the one aspect, honesty. Truth is no one has all these ticked off as "good" or they wouldn't be here. They'd be on some other plane of existence. We will all say we are openminded (including me) until I tell you that Jesus was a robot then that goes out the window. Without going through each one, I would say in my experience, the amount of these aspects having a strong presence in a person are low. Some tend to stand out such as willpower or courage, then again willpower is easily shaken by distraction. Look at dieting in the West, how many people start a diet and follow through? We have to remember that we all have these aspects, and many more, but we live in a very fragmented, turbulent world. We can focus on money and love but disciplining ourselves to ascend costs us both money and love so we are not going to injure those. We need money and we need love, or do we? You know, that is the question. Do we see the illusion or do we see through the illusion? There's an old Italian saying, "Promises made in the evening are no longer valid in the morning." In Canada, people just say, "People talk from their ass." It's not that we haven't the infrastructure or pathway. It's that we need to conquer ourselves first, and that could take a lifetime.

The pathway is built-in

When I was in college, we studied Maslow's Hierarchy of Needs, a theory to explain human motivation. It consisted of five levels of needs, four basic and at the very top, Self-Actualization. The basic needs included things like food, sex, money, respect and love. The basic stages need to be met before the final stage is approached. According to Wiki, and this is interesting, Self-Actualization has many similarities to the final stages in Taoism and Zen Buddhism. At this point of heightened awareness, a person no longer follows the laws of society or man, rather they follow nature, they become truly free. I took it all in as interesting and went on with my life. Many years later, I was in a relationship and I was behaving unusual. I living in my own world, I didn't care much for money or friends, I craved insight and I examined philosophical questions, questions which had no practical value like why are humans walking on two legs and not three or how did the soul get into the body. My partner had recently studied Maslow's Needs and she made the connection: "It is like you are trying to self-actualize without satisfying your basic needs."

She was right and it was something very natural for me. Of course, my years of trying to attain a free mindset didn't benefit my personal life in any particular way. All that effort did eventually pay off because without that mindset I wouldn't have been able to shift from human to nonhuman awareness. So, while I "suffered" in my youth, there was an architecture to it, there was an invisible pathway. These pathways are always there, hidden from plain view, the path relying on our hearts, risks and sacrifices along the way. The better you know yourself, the better you'll be able to decide what actions to take and all your actions are your responsibility. Blame yourself first then keep going. Be persistent. Determine your path and learn to listen. Ah, life is complicated, isn't it?

Ready the Orgasmic Thrusters!

On the surface, life appears to be biological and we appear to embody some kind of spirit and from these perceptions we derive biology and spirituality. This makes sense and is easily derived in a straight-forward manner. It is like when we discover the orgasm, it isn't much further along where we have the urge to copulate with another. We want to explore that urge within us, to satisfy the very shape and size of that original orgasm. That curiosity leads into sexual intercourse. By itself, we do not desire sex because it is too functional, in fact very mechanical. We endure the mechanical process in order to achieve the orgasm because we tend to feel elated afterwards. The more orgasms we have the more addicted we become, or rather, the more accustomed we become to that level of physical elation because it is hard to reproduce in the real world. Some of us will fall into drugs, whether prescriptive or illegal, just to re-identify ourselves with those elated feelings, and the neuroscientists will summarize all that I have said by stating some well-known brain chemicals like serotonin and endorphins. The drug addict will soon be unwilling to stop those chemical orgasms and will fall out of sync with existence, for orgasms and elated feelings are not meant to be reproduced every five minutes. That is when the ego takes over, the demons hop on board, and the avatar is sequestered into hell, and perhaps death, because these things will consume them.

We have built within ourselves these mechanisms of ascension, whether we talk about the orgasm, which I am probably not allowed to discuss (oh, I must), or elated feelings. Monks are said to reproduce these elated feelings at times of nirvana as well as athletes, extreme sports activities including musical performances can achieve these levels of ascension (these endorphin bringers). Everyone is wired a bit different in my view so some people can be elated by the presence of certain people or by reading a really good book. Some can have orgasms just by thinking about it. And on the other side, some people have never had an orgasm and have never felt elated, these people are perennially depressed, continuously shut off from life itself and yet they are alive. You see, my view is that we have arrived at our conclusions about existence through our own limited experiences and through the reinforced experiences of those on television and in the media. The problem is that we have repressed our best experiences and tucked them safely away somewhere safe, including the people on television.

Many celebrities have achieved amazing insights into the nature of existence and simply are not able to discuss this in the mainstream so that when a 16-year old watches that celebrity on TV they only see the surface of that person. They do not realize that that celebrity has experimented, has explored and has had many profound encounters. There are many reasons why we cannot discuss these things in public, but we have to remind ourselves that we have to remember that all that we are has been derived from a very complex assortment of experiences, some of which you cannot even remember. Up until age 38, I did not recall any encounters with starships or star beings in any way shape or form. I hadn't any interest in Star Wars or Steven Spielberg's E.T.: The Extra-Terrestrial. I had no knowledge of any of it, no interest and no opinion. I neither believed in UFOs or didn't believe in UFOs, I truly didn't care.

Me, the late bloomer

After age 38, when my mind exploded and I became a different person, I realized that not only did I speak offplanet languages but that there were many starships and star beings in my life, and now I could see them everywhere. I mean, they are everywhere and yet I look into the normal world, the constrained sewage in which we are forced to exist and I see the land of the blind. And I was in that land not long ago, and yet there is this new land. This land is your land, this land is our land...anyway, in my blind state I evolved as a blind person. The result was a constrained mental person suffering through the rigours of war, misery, consumerism, environmental catastrophe and a repetitive history that was very boring. My limited experiences shaped my evolution. Of course, I dabbled in mind opening ventures and I explored wild ideas even in my youth.

While my friends were partying, I was studying Traditional Chinese Medicine. That changed my view of the human body and I discovered an alternative to Western Medicine. The more I understood of the intricacies of the body through the wisdom of the Chinese doctors the more I was able to circumvent illness. I never went to the doctor for probably 10 or more years. That is not to say I abused my body and somehow survived, no, I paid close attention to my body and when I got sick I used natural remedies. I had an alternative view on healing and it shaped my entire health. My experience shaped my evolution, rather than to immediately take a pain reliever or get some drugs, I immediately hit the Chinese store and bought herbs and foodstuffs, all available and relatively inexpensive. I also used supplements like most people. My experience shaped my evolution and it was achieved from a very curious mindset. If you are not the curious type, if you are a sheep instead, then you have to learn to be curious, to be the explorer, to question the question, to peel off the obvious and to peer into yourself. They teach you that curiosity killed the cat to scare you. Curiosity may have killed the cat but that is why the cat has nine lives.

The awakening I had late in life shifted my entire view of existence because I was seeing and talking to these invisible people (to my naked eyes) but I could see them regardless. They were there, talking, visiting and I was speaking and listening. And when they went away, I was trying to rationalize how all this was possible because no one had ever told me before, certainly not the TV, and I never heard a word of it from NASA or any government. I had to look underground for information and it's pretty dirty underground so I didn't like that. My experiences with interstellar cultures was extremely uplifting, inspiring, educational – none of the garbage I was hearing and none of the fear I had heard. That was all okay until I decided to help out the UFO community and volunteered to fly a starship over earth's cities. That's when the confusion came in, that's when they came after me, that's when I realized that there was another invisible group of humans and nonhumans all working surreptitiously to destroy the good intentions of the advanced races. They were very good at destroying trust, at infecting people with dark energy, at reprogramming people, at making people gay, at killing those who threatened their world order. I later realized that most of the UFO people had fallen prey to those nefarious paramilitary groups and their secretly-engineered anti-grav ships and their above government superiority. They were very determined to wipe out any chance of hope in the community of believers, and if all else failed they would corrupt the leaders and contactees so that they could be controlled. It was all about control. That's when I decided that these troglodytes are going to find themselves in the toilet because the world I knew was the brighter world, and that is where I chose to stay. I remained out of the UFO groups and ideas and they had no concern for me, and those agencies would ensure that my ideas would not be believed, and they weren't.

We derive our interpretation of existence from our experiences and those experiences originate from our desire, but all of this funnelled by the masters of this reality. They channel our sexual energy into gender exploration. They stifle our desire for procreation with our need to succeed and to be respected in the community because procreation does not contribute to the economy. We are stuck on spirituality because we only accept that we have this spirit within us, but when you realize that your spirit cannot die, when you realize that there are other dimensions, valid dimensions, when you realize that you can travel to those dimensions and to become enlightened or upgraded, when you realize that and more, you realize that this spirit isn't just a spirit and the Bible is just a big book. The very nature of sexual energy is not just for having sex. That is what we have led to believe. We are sexual creatures so we have sex, but sexual energy is one of the most profound secrets to enlightenment!

The meaning of an orgasm

Again, you have to rid yourself of the idea that you are biological and that you have a free will, and all the other pre-programmed notions. You have to let those go so as to enable a more profound understanding of existence. The body, as a machine, has an engine, the heart. That is the physical engine. The spirit, as an instrument, has an engine. What is the engine of the spirit? The reproductive system. Jesus was proof that there a resurrection was possible. But a resurrection is merely a return to life, and in that return, we return stronger. We see this in our physical life: we have hardships, someone breaks your heart, you resurrect yourself, you improve, you get a haircut. You are now the result of many resurrections, or rebirths. The very fundamental spirituality of Jesus. That he was resurrected means that all of us could be resurrected because we are all of the same origin. The power of resurrection is sexual energy found in the reproductive system which is not just a reproductive system anymore, is it? It is a Resurrection System.

They stifle our sexual energies and riddle our minds with drugs for erectile dysfunction or images of unattainable women with huge breasts, they do all of this to redirect our sexual energy into the toilet. Why? Because they understand what I am telling you: sexual energy is the key to resurrection and resurrection is the key to ascension and ascension is a key to escaping this prison. The problems with sexuality are many, too many. Today, many people's sexual energy is now being redirected into bisexuality, or "exploration," is all brainwashing. This is yet another layer of deception.

In order to ascend and to become enlightened we have to focus our sexual energy and to use that to power our ascension. It is like the rockets on a Shuttle spaceship. Those rockets propel the ship into space. Without those rockets, the Shuttle could not escape the atmosphere. Your sexual rockets can do the same thing if you learn to focus and to use that energy to propel you up into the cosmos. You may have already heard of this, some forms of martial arts and spiritual faiths practice generating sexual energy or use it in rituals. You can see sexual symbols in shamanism and certain ceremonies. It isn't because these people, or ancient cultures, were into pornography or bisexuality, it is because they understood sexual energy as a rocket fuel for the human spirit.

While I can talk about the technological reality all I want, you cannot fully understand it until you yourself escape the confines of reality and step into other dimensions. Only there can you see that what I am saying makes sense. More people need to move off the dependency of words and to integrate knowledge and experience so as to truly ascend. I can only offer words and inspiration, it might give you an orgasm but more likely you have to generate your own special effects.

Learn to cultivate sexual energy and not to repress your feelings of love and neither to waste them, you have to balance those things as best you can, some people love more outwardly than others.

Eventually, when you understand the meaning of an orgasm, you understand that it is a process, a process that is replicated in other aspects of your life, which you will see, which you have been unable to see because you were blind, like I was blind to the ETs at my door. They were just outside my door and I didn't see because I too was blind. We don't focus on the blindness, we focus on the orgasm, the elation, the natural elation, without drugs. We learn to see that life is one big orgasm really, one big resurrection. As a symbol, Jesus represented the eternal orgasm, but don't tell the Christians, they are still busy trying to understand how to love their neighbours.

Superman as a Construct

archetype *n.* **1** A recurrent symbol or dominant idea. **2** an inherited mental image stored in the collective unconscious.

The comic book character, Superman, is an archetype. In being an archetype, the Man of Steel becomes a more integral part of the fabric of reality and therefore can reveal insights that were previously hidden from our minds. The prevalence of Superman, his very longevity tells us all that he is much more than just a simple idea, rather, he is a more lasting idea, and as we shall see, Superman is a symbol that is much more deeply embedded onto our mental drives. With Superman's superpowers, we are going to see that the presence of the Man of Steel, or his constant reinvention, is intimately connected to our own subconscious desires in times of need. He is going to help us see that his presence is proof that the human mind, as part of a collective whole, is able to manifest these kinds of constructs.

Things are always *hidden*. In fact, you could say that everything is hidden and those molecules we perceive is the totality of our reality, of our existence, for if everything was available to us we wouldn't be able to exist. If all truths were known and nothing was hidden the very impetus for existence would cease and the idea that thought it existed would dissolve, for in order to exist we must have an impetus. It doesn't matter what kind of impetus, what matters is that one is present. Now, of course, the type and size of the impetus determines what kind of existence proceeds forward. For example, the desire of a well endowed stripper is the kind of impetus that leads to divorce, but if an existence desires divorce then a wild woman thrusting her pelvis into the faces of lonely, despondent men is in line with satisfying that desire. Of course, we have seen too many misadventures in impetus on earth, everything from money to church. All of these things, in fact you could say what we see on earth today, all of it is a result of primitive impetus.

impetus *n.* a driving force.

Primitive impetus hasn't bothered anyone till lately and even the number of millions of helpless trees hasn't really inspired anyone to stop it. So, we can see that the impetus gives us a reason to live, partly why a man will have a child or a woman will get married, these things provide an impetus for continued existence. Still, many people are too weak to take these actions or to love a person they truly love.

While it may seem we've lost Superman, we haven't. As usual, I wanted to circumnavigate the waters of primordial knowledge before we include our comic book hero. Because Superman is an archetype, he is the direct result of an altogether different impetus. We affirm his archetypal name because he doesn't exist in the common world. He exists in the uncommon world. This means he exists in another dimension, a dimension previously hidden to us, the dimension of comic character. We remind ourselves that it is valid dimension because we often see the cartoonization of famous people after they're reached a certain level of fame or awareness. A celebrity, or even a great writer, will immortalize themselves in cartoon format. Immediately, we can see some valuable pattern here, can't we? What do we see? We see Superman, a cartoon, and we see a celebrity being translated into a cartoon. We also see Superman being translated into a live-action film character by choosing a suitable actor to embody the cartoon soul of Superman. So, while we can find many cartoon versions of people, we have yet to see a real version of a cartoon.

If the world is built properly, and it is, we have to conclude that a comic book character, given enough impetus, can be translated into the real world. We've seen some attempts in Hollywood to mix cartoons and actors together, we've seen lots of new animated films, all looking very lifelike and now we have photorealistic visual effects such as the film Avatar. Superman, because he is an archetype and because he exists in another dimension and because he is the result of an impetus has been around for a very long time albeit in different forms with different qualities. Superman is someone who descended from the stars and was adopted into humanity as one of their own and they adopted him because he adopted a human disguise: an inept, innocuous, clumsy alter ego, Clark Kent. Clark has all the desires of a human yet he knows within himself that he cannot participate in life as a regular person. He cannot go to the strip club, for example. He cannot get angry. He is not allowed to interfere in human evolution to any great degree unless a situation demands it so. Clark Kent is a crippled Star Being for he must suffer an earthman's life.

As for being descended to earth and made to suffer in human form...it immediately reminds us of Jesus, the other archetype. I mean, we've stripped away the details, like the suit and Kryptonite. But many similarities remain such as they're both Star Beings, they're both indestructible unless they submit to death, they both descended in star-like craft, they both look human in their alter-ego. Hey – Jesus is a comic book character. It's not just plausible, isn't it? We could find more examples but I want to get back to Superman one last time.

The most amazing thing about Superman is that he is constantly resurrected. Comic books are reinvented. Films, TV, books – all of them have seen various incarnations of the character Superman. He's reinvented, he has new incarnations, he's resurrected – by whom? Who has resurrected? Who is keeping Jesus alive? Well, we need to only look in the mirror. We welcome these archetypes by our thoughts. Our thoughts manifest these characters, whether we are aware of it or not, that's how powerful thoughts are and that's why the rulers of earth want to impede your thoughts because, by night, you could all manifest a very real and powerful archetype on earth if some of your chains were loosened or if you truly understood the power of thought. I guess what I'm saying is that you can manifest the right kind of hero or symbol if you put your mind to it. Your thoughts are interpreted by the existential machine and those heroes will surface and all of it a result of a huge impetus from the very people here.

Manifesting the Necessary Construct

There are no accidents. We could say that everything in the world is a result of manifestation. In fact, we will say that! The hellish world is a result of human manifestations. With a few decent points here and there like ice cream and lingerie, outside of those molecules the world is big pile of sewage and it stinks and it doesn't work and it would have ended hadn't some very astute and wonderful builders not intervened and re-established our place in the cosmic ocean. All of this sewage was manifested by us. Well, how can this be so if we are all so good-hearted, kind and generous? That is an interesting question that will require a few hundred books to figure out. I mean, how did we allow the Fourth Reich to establish itself in the USA? Didn't we learn that the Third Reich was feeding people cookies with arsenic and that it wasn't good for the Jewish people?

We thought we learned, but obviously we didn't. That's because we are not present in our bodies. We live by way of distraction, and in our distraction we allow the real dark magicians to use our collective mental drives to manifest hell. And that is what they keep doing because we are all distracted. The key here is to realize that we are constantly manifesting, whether we know it or not. If you are alive and present, like if you are reading this essay with your eyeballs or listening to someone reading these words to you, then you are an integral part of the manifestation. You are equally responsible for the sewage. Here: some toilet paper for your troubles.

On occasion, when it really starts to stink, when the need is high enough, humanity is able to focus and taps into their real power, kind of like when a man is faced with proposing to the love of his life. He has to put his hand to the fire, can I focus and go through with it or do I look for another woman? When he is about to lose the woman, he realizes how much he needs her, focuses and manifests? The ring is presented. The outcome is still uncertain, the wedding is yet another challenge and the marriage, well; it isn't exactly as previewed during those lonely nights as a teenager.

As a society, we manifest change when truly needed. In the past, this was more regular. In India, Mohandas Gandhi was manifested. JFK in the USA. In Germany, Adolf Hitler. There is the desire, the proposition, and the candidate appears. The result of that appearance is uncertain. Gandhi was assassinated, India was liberated. JFK was assassinated, Americans went to the moon. Hitler murdered millions of Jews. Then we get back to Jesus. He briefly introduced society to love, still war exists, still no one truly got it.

What happens is that we manifest these constructs but do not realize that it is us who have done it. We query the cosmic computer for a solution, the cosmic computer takes those desires and manifests them into one or more constructs, or even situations, but the machine does not understand humanity as humanity understands humanity. The Elaborate Machine instead delivers an appropriate amount of data and energy, materials that humanity can use to funnel into the right areas, but society, largely unaware and oblivious they allow the rulers of earth to funnel some of that cosmic quotient into something nasty or to curtail its lifespan into a certain death. You see, humanity conjures a solution but never follows through, never takes responsibility; they stoned Jesus, they welcomed Hitler's ruthlessness, they allowed NASA's space program to get hijacked by subterranean agencies. The list of corruption and interference is huge. The truth always remains that only with energy can anything happen in a field of reality; therefore, for a 9/11 Event to occur, it means that energies were steered to allow it to happen while humanity was distracted by some mindless pursuit like skinny jeans. That is why there are so many distractions; they distract our minds so that they can usurp our energies. To resolve that is easy, we maintain a little more focus and morality with our energy, and we teach everyone to be prescient of their valuable energy, including the simple notion of thought management. We no longer think of war and there is no more war. As long as they remind us to think about war there will always be war. It's very simple and extremely powerful.

What's all this got to do with Superman? We have the power, right now, to manifest a Superman character in real life. He has not appeared because we have not focused enough. We have the power to open up the interstellar debate. The starships haven't landed because we have not focused enough. They have taught all of you to keep quiet, keep it private, to not get laughed at, to be afraid of another anal probe, to be afraid that the aliens will land and eat all of our jelly beans – they have put these implants so as to interfere with your natural manifestation talents. So, if we do want some powerful Symbol to manifest and to steer this planet back into the light we have to focus on that, and not only that, but to continue to support and protect our manifestation, for as long as it takes, just like a marriage or a baby, as long as it lives we must take responsibility for it, at least until it can take care of itself, until it has matured and society has stabilized.

Soon, we will see another reinvention of Superman, a movie, a new TV series, a new comic book and that is because people still believe in him. We are seeing reinventions everywhere these days and that is because energy is being made available to allow human minds to manifest those constructs to take them to the next level. We could easily witness human ingenuity manifest thinking talking bodies, Supermen and Superwomen, and if so, then they are a result of manifestation, a combination of human need and love from the cosmos. As more and more constructs arise and become available, we must always remember that we are responsible for them as much as they themselves are dedicated to us. We should refrain from stoning them, an idea that the demons will try to convince you of, and we should give them the platforms they need to help us, which is why they are here which is why we asked for them which is what humankind needs to move to the next level and to the level after that.

The Truth

It is beyond our capacity of mind and yet it is within our tradition of heart. She is both magnificent and surreal. He is both impenetrable and flowing. Who are they?

They is the Truth.

We are devoid of Truth in the interstellar business; there it's all about the technology and the motive. We are devoid of the Truth in political circles, there it's all about programming and distortion. We are devoid of the Truth in religion; there it's all about the integration of words written millennia ago.

We are devoid of Truth because we have lost the language of translating the Truth. We simply haven't the dictionary to understand the definitions of Truth and we've lost our most powerful translation tool, the heart.

We haven't the capacity of heart to understand Truth. Once, long ago we did. We did have the ability to translate, but it's been lost - the heart translator. The proof is we live in a world of lies, and seeing that the Devil is the Father of All Lies, we can only conclude that there is very little Truth in the world. Not only that, worse still, we haven't the ability or desire to process Truth. Long ago, a man, or woman, would have sacrificed their first born to receive Truth. Their first born. They would have exhausted themselves for 10 years of study and training to be able to process the Truth. Today, the Truth is worth less than a can of Coke. People won't give you a minute to contemplate Truth. Sure, they'll contemplate everything else, in relation to them, but Truth, which is outside of them, no way, no time. What has turned everyone away from Truth, better still, how do we return to Truth? Because more than ever, Truth is returning to this plane of existence and we have to learn to process Truth. In order to reprogram the myriad of lies.

Without Truth, we cannot reprogram this existence so it is in our deepest interest to learn to process Truth. The question is what the heck is Truth? Is Truth God? Is Truth Jesus? Is Truth just the scientific discovery? Is Truth the revelation of a long-held secret? Or is Truth just a deeper form of honesty? Are those things Truth? Will they help us to overcome this distasteful world?

Truth is much more than that because Truth is the central construct of the cosmos. The cosmos is built on Truth. You are made of Truth, only that you forgot. A-ha! We just forgot that we are all made of Truth! Or is it from Truth? Still, what is Truth? Truth is a vibration. When someone lies they vibrate differently, many of us now can feel the vibration of lies or deception. So we can say that the Devil vibrates on a different frequency as Truth. Those who serve the Devil all participate in that same Hellish spectrum. Those who serve Truth, well, they are all vibrating on an entirely different frequency, aren't they?

And if we indeed connect in our interpretation that Truth operates on a certain frequency or field of vibration then we can see how Truth is also energy. To process this particular energy requires us to really transform our way of thinking and to open our hearts from our hearts are perfect translations of Truth. If you speak from the heart you cannot help but to speak

Truth, which is different if you speak from your ass because that's called "shit" (a technical term).

The Resplendent Energy Returned

For thousands of years, the true prophets and the sages, they processed Truth, and many artists and leaders as well, and some of that Truth remained but most of it was lost or destroyed (or denied). The advantage of today over yesterday is that this replacement energy has returned and retuned in abundance so if you wanted to get back into speaking Truth then now is the time to do so, best time to do so in historical years. Now is the time for Truth to overcome the Devil. The trouble is that Truth is an energy, a packet of data, a download, an idea and all those things and more require processing and your heart is the perfect tool for Truth, so we must open our hearts and speak Truthfully. By doing so, we are reshaping Truth, we are spreading resplendent energy, we are reprogramming reality to welcome Truth and to slow the Devil. We need to convert the vibration of existences to function on Truth and to disconnect from the Devil energy around.

Slave of the mind state

The mind is a good liar, the heart cannot tell a lie. To communicate with Truth we have to communicate with the heart. That doesn't mean necessarily being honest. Honesty doesn't work in a multidimensional world with people having multiple levels of awareness. Our hearts are opening all the time and our hearts are closing all the time. The world before you is attacking the heart (eg terrorism). The subtle world of the heart requires a lot of effort and inspiration. It requires an earthquake to wake people up, so you can see how much energy is required to strain the remnants of compassion out of society.

The egoists have dwindled society into a mind state because they know how to control the mind. The US President uses a teleprompter to communicate, if that doesn't tell you how far from the heart we are then I'm not sure what else will. And that same figure has lots of intelligent followers all praying for his promises to come truth. But where is the heart communication? Where is leadership from the heart, from Truth? It exists in small pockets, niche areas, tiny online communities. In fact, the internet, because of the distance of anonymity, has more heart communication than in public. The public is full of political correctness and gossip. The public doesn't accept that nonhumans are here on earth even though it is very true. That is truth. You can hear some of it online and in small whispers in some local cafe. That's where the hearth speaks, in the corners of existence.

You can tell if a person processes Truth or UnTruth by their ability to be honest to some degree, by the ability to refrain from political barriers, by their ability to expose topics community feared, by the impact of their personal beliefs on a discussion, by their beliefs, by their very vibration. Many children know if a parent is lying or telling the truth even if they haven't the full story. Adults are easily brainwashed or they are so full of misinformation that they are confused or they're distracted.

If people were fish, you could sell them sashimi. We've been convinced of a ton of lies and we know they are lies and we're still afraid of sticking our neck out. So we never have a chance to develop our heart muscle. It takes a finely tuned heart muscle to speak in Truth because the vibration is very fine. If you have low will power or anger or fear, you will lose it. The vibration of Truth is not easy to maintain because 1) we haven't the capacity to stream it, and, 2) because we are constantly being derailed by the other side, the side that doesn't want the rest of the world to hear Truth.

As we all learn to speak Truth, the plane begins to vibrate on a much higher level and it becomes easier to speak from the heart. In the meantime, it will take more effort. Hey, we're all ego obese and we need to lose some ego and get those hearts going. It's going to require time and effort, not only to speak in Truth, but also to understand the infinite qualities of Truth. Far be it for me to even imagine I could explain an infinite, everlasting, resplendent quality in an essay, and in no way am I trying, it is merely one observation of billions of observations.

When you find yourself looking for answers, try processing Truth, as you have come to understand it. Try using Truth when facing complex questions in life or when you are on the line and need to explain yourself, just revert to Truth. And when you hear Truth, each time, cherish, learn from it, digest it and never forget it for it is fragile still. One day, it will be more abundant, one day soon.

The Failure

Whenever you get something new, you do so with the understanding that the old is unusable, broken, or no longer functioning properly. It is implicit. It is implied that when you have new then it is replacing the old. Now when we discuss or make mention of the New Reality, we seriously neglect or gloss over the fact that the Old Reality is broken. If the Old Reality was in good working order, or if it could be properly repaired, we wouldn't need a New Reality! There shouldn't be any question now that the New Reality is here; therefore, the Old Reality did not work and could not be made to work. The Old Reality would have crashed and most of humanity would've been wiped clean. You didn't see that because it didn't happen yet, but if the Builders did not install the New Reality System (Dakala) and didn't hit the Reboot button; you'd be reading this in Hell as you roast upside down in the oven.

We can forgive the many inhabitants who have never paid attention to this stuff, but for the lightworkers and the awakened minds who refuse to note that the Old Reality failed and that humanity failed, well, that isn't healthy. If we continue to cover over the truth with great cereal and warm milk, we are going to end up back in the same place in so many years, decades, centuries, minutes, seconds. If a skinny bitch is addicted to speed and she hasn't the ability to look in the mirror and say, "I need help!" then she is going to continue to do speed. An alcoholic who says, "I'm not an alcoholic, I just like alcohol," isn't ever going to recover.

A civilization who thinks, "We've been saved so we can keep living out our egotistical and destructive ways," is a civilization that will never clean its room, it's a civilization that will get one divorce, remarry, get another divorce, remarry, divorce, remarry, divorce...because it's not their fault. "The divorce had nothing to do with me." Hey, let's just stab the dead chicken one more time, "The New Reality was put in place because under the Old Reality, humankind failed and destroyed itself." Ask someone who knows and who is honest.

Does it make sense? We failed. We are not being ascended because of our white teeth and big breasts. Sorry, if you believed the New Reality is here because you deserved it. The woman who gets a divorcee is 100% responsible for the divorce, as is the man. It may take time to admit that but that is the truth.

We have to admit that we failed. That's why we're being ascended. That's why there's a New Reality. That's why the interstellar cultures are landing. It's not because we've earned it. It's because we failed. Our grand failure has earned a brand new, out of the box reality. We have yet to admit we failed even though we look at the miserable, fear-laden, militarized, socio-pathic world each day.

You know, we're alcoholics who just had a seizure then work up in the hospital, the doctor is saying we almost died from brain damage from excessive drinking and we think we're in the hospital for a free medical tour. No, it's not a medical tour, we just had an alcoholic related seizure, and unless we stop drinking we'll die.

Besides the facts on how wonderful the New Reality is, which I've discussed in detail elsewhere, we need to realize why we failed and we need to take corrective action in order to prevent more failure tomorrow. As well, the New System works differently than the old and we need to learn how to interact with the New System because we and it are coexisting. And we have to learn how to do the proper maintenance. No one is getting off easy in this issue, certainly not by me.

Until we admit our failure in the Old Reality, I don't think we'll gain much in the New Reality. So far all the lovely compassionate people are painting the truth with lots of nice colors and seem unwilling to deal with the truth. They have their reasons, fine. My view remains that if you lean to avoid the Truth then you will never learn the Truth and the Truth will save you. The Truth is in itself complete. It doesn't care how smart you are or how much compassion you have. The Truth doesn't care. I've seen it. It doesn't care about those egotistical things. It only cares about how much truth you can process. And there isn't as much as you think going through you right now. The Truth is so powerful, so everlasting that we are all afraid, even the people who believe there is nothing to learn, they are afraid to admit humankind's failure. They who have no fear?

If we are going into rehab, which we are, if we are wanting to make progress, which we want, then we need to start by admitting that we failed to evolve in the Old Reality. We did our best, we thought we could get it done, we thought we were smart enough, we thought we earned it, but ultimately we failed because humankind failed because there's a New Reality. That's the proof of our failure.

There's a new reality. There's a reboot. We failed. Let's admit that and discuss why we failed and discuss what changes we need to make – not what changes are going to happen – we need to discuss how to avoid the egotistical addictions we all have. See, until we admit our failure, this rehab won't work. We'll just screw it up again. Sure, not you or me, no, we're the best, it's the other 7 billion I'm concerned about. No one's told them that there's a New Reality, no one's told them about the interstellar people, no one's told them about the fact that we were all going to die hadn't some science folk intervened and installed a New Reality. Okay, let's admit it, I'll admit it, this acceptance of failure will take a long time to admit because there's going to be a long healing process, a hefty adjustment phase and a steep learning curve. We'll be busy. You've been warned 40 years, you're husbands an asshole, you get divorced; the last thing you want to do is to admit that it was your fault for marrying an idiot wife beater.

It's hard to admit you should've listened to your mother. It'll take 10 or more years to deal with the trauma. So we keep that in consideration. At the back of our mind, whenever you're ready, understand that we, collectively, beings on many dimensions, failed to ensure humanity's evolution – for whatever reasons – we failed. Luckily, there's a new chance now, a rebirth of the highest order, a chance to do things right and with a little guidance we'll do it better: we won't marry another wife beater, we won't build another 50,000 nuclear warheads, we won't deny the Starpeople their rightful intentions, we won't withhold our compassion, we won't be addicts to ego. With a little guidance, we'll reshape the world and we'll all relearn how to connect to the Truth, for we are from the Truth, it is the Truth which is everlasting, it is the Truth which is more powerful than lies. You can still lie because the Truth isn't just about being honest. The Truth is about allowing Source back into our lives. It is about letting your god shine through.

The Illusion of Choice in the Construct of Divinity

We are conditioned to believe in choice. With choice we believe in free will. We believe in our heart that free will is our "god-given" right. But *choice* is a funny instrument because the very presence of choice in a predetermined universe doesn't make sense. On one hand, we can argue that we have many paths to the same conclusion, but if the conclusion is guaranteed to be the same, and it is, then where is your choice?

If I take you to a paint store to buy a can of pain for the living room, and the salesperson lays out the color chart on the counter, and you get to choose your own color of paint and then I remind you that you have to choose black, do you still have a choice? Well, that's what life is like. In another dimension, you are to choose the color black, and in the physical dimension you are looking at 100 colors, and you're thinking, boy, there are so many colors. And then you buy a couple off cans of black paint and you go home, satisfied. You feel you made a choice and you exerted your free will, but did you? And then your best friend says, "Black is ugly! Why did you buy black? It's not even a color." And you scratch your head. *What was I thinking?* The trouble with choice (and free will) is that it is localized in one dimension, the very one you are conscious of. Because you are aware of a palette of choices, you choose. They are several male partners, each has their own special qualities, you need to choose and you get Man C. Now, on another dimension, and you all believe in other dimensions by now, there is a representation of You and of another person. You two higher representations decide to get married in the physical world, so you decide (from a list of candidates as well) to marry below. That decision is communicated to your physical avatars and the woman chooses Man C, who also happens to correspond to the nonphysical entity in the higher dimension! The question is: Did you choose the man to give your heart to?

Well, in short, no, you didn't. You cannot have choice in a multidimensional construct. In addition, you cannot have a choice when the conclusion is predetermined. Because beyond those two nonphysical entities there are even higher decision makers who have predetermined your ideal match for your current level of awareness. Sure, this process is full of interference and misdirection because some of the people who agree with me are malevolent, jealous, envious and outright nasty so they munch things up and they like screwing society. But let's put that aside because it's too heavy. We want to continue with choice.

It is hard to accept that the woman in your arms wasn't your choice because, in fact, you had no choice. Someone else chose for you, someone wiser than you. We don't focus on that because we'd be disturbed by the fact that we live in a *choiceless* world. That would make it harder to listen to politicians and Presidents.

The politicians lay out the choices, in the US, its universal healthcare or the same healthcare of yesterday. They've spelled out the choice. Its President A, a black man, or President B, or a white man. It's beautiful. They create those simplified choices not only knowing who will win but predetermining who will win. And nothing changes. Why? Because you are conditioned to believe in choice - choice A or choice B, which one? Well, you say I want Choice E, not on the menu. I want choice Q, go see a psychiatrist. Choice A or choice B? They've forced a world of choice - diet or no diet, single or relationship, unleaded or leaded, electric or gasoline, rich or poor, smart or stupid, sexy or banal, gay or straight, freedom or terrorism, space travel or healthy economy, love or hate, success or failure. We walk into a grocery store and have to choose, but that's too superficial of a choice. The menu is a representation of the universe pretending there is a choice.

We want to talk about existential choices - why are you doing what you are doing right now? Di you choose to be a lawyer or did someone else choose for you? Are you a lightworker because you chose a higher way of living or is it just a temporary path for you to realize what you really should be doing? It's a hard concept to intake. To think that what you are doing right now isn't your choice and that, technically, you have to do it is a serious blow to the ego. The ego will spit blood to resist it and yet it is the truth. You are doing what you are doing, every bit of it, because of someone else's choice, or something else; and what you are doing will lead to a singular, all-glorified conclusion, and at some infinitely high level (in your heart) you know that. So there's the proof that I am right. In your heart you know that where you are is where you should be, even if it is ugly. If not, you make adjustments in order to satisfy the higher choice.

The disappearance of choice

A bachelor wants to date. He chases a few women and finds one he likes. That's his choice. He goes out on a few dates, she gets pregnant. The father-to-be all of a sudden has learned of a consequence of his choice. Now, he's looking after his pregnant girlfriend. Her parents require him to marry their daughter. So he does. He's now married to a pregnant wife. All of a sudden, his multitude of choices is dwindled down to a few. His careers, his money, his vacation, his energy are all now redirected into a new family, or, new choices, all because of his original choice of this girl. Now, he's probably depressed at his newlywed and nearly dead life, but he doesn't realize that there are other dimensions and up there, beyond sight and sound, some wise entity made a choice, they decided that this bachelor would die of alcoholism on his current path so they decided we'll save him from premature death and we'll redirect him to have sex with a woman. Then they chose a woman who would easily get pregnant, then they arranged for that easily-pregnant woman to be available so that he'd ask her out. And he did. The rest is history. Up there in the heavens, we also know that this woman needed to get pregnant in order for an angelic baby to be incarnated. A-ha! You say. So, it was the angelic being who arranged all of this! Well, wait a minute because that angelic being serves the Lord (or Source) and so he was only allowing Father's decision to flow through. A-ha! You say, it was God's decision! Well, wait a minute, what if Source doesn't decide. Source only provides.

What if Source realized that the earth needed a molecular ounce of more angelic energy and the angelic being learned that and sacrificed himself to incarnate into the body of a baby girl. A male angel into the body of a girl. The girl grows up different and become a lesbian radio DJ. The lesbian radio DJ believes she chose the life of radio DJ because she has a strong voice, but inside her is an angel serving Source. She may go her whole life believing that her sexuality is important, and that her job is important and that her show is important, but from higher dimensions she's just a molecular ounce of angelic energy.

Submission to a Higher State

Choices define us. We believe because of our choices in life is why we turned out this way, the way we did. The people with a lousy life will blame bad luck and their mother. "My mother's neglect got me into drug addiction and falling in love with bad men." But we are now realizing that none of these choices (or luck) had anything to do with it, not one goddamn choice and that is because someone else chose for us and someone else chose for them and so on.

Did I choose to write this essay or did someone else up there suggest that these things need to be said and they already led me to writing and so I was their instrument? Did I have a choice in writing this essay? No. Well, on a low level of awareness, yes. I chose it! On a higher level of awareness, absolutely not. None of what I do is a choice; it is merely the outcome of some higher existence.

The better connected to that process I am, the faster the response time. Instead of being trapped in a bad marriage, if I listen, I will get the divorce when needed. Trouble is we live in a myopic life. We don't listen. We refuse to listen. We are brainwashed to believe in President A or President B. That's because we're stupid.

A smart person will submit to the higher dimensions and will not only live a more spiritual existence, more importantly; they will appreciate all that they have; no matter how much it stinks. They will see that their loneliness is forcing them to look in the mirror, and if they look in the mirror they come to a realization, after that is realized they fall in love and get pregnant. But without that realization, they stay lonely, or poor, or ignorant or afraid. See, it's not only about not choosing way above your head. Those who live a lucky life have very good listening skills. Those who refuse to listen or believe, they are in control, will live a distasteful life because they just refuse to cooperate. You know this upcoming life, it really is autopilot if we can learn to kick out the ego and be in charge. Being in charge requires us to listen and learning to appreciate what we have and don't have is the way to retrain the heart and mind. We love what we have and we love what we don't have. We love not having stuff as much as we love having it, no matter what. We love giving away stuff. It's all good.

That puts us in a higher state of listening and that allows the wiser decision makers to do their job. Sure, there will be interference. It's a filthy plane here and there's interference, there's bad programming, there's ego, temptation and a whole lot of stuff to filter, but that doesn't excuse you from living a suboptimal life. You step up and shut up. Hey, just to remind you: there's no choice. There's no free will. These are illusions.

The conclusion is set so all the circumstances happen to ensure the conclusion. Not all conclusions are the same but they are all good without exception. And conclusions change as you come to realizations and to the degree of your realizations, but you cannot fool the system. You have to be honest and that is the level that is recorded, the rest, the ego, the fear, the lust, it is not recorded and is a waste of energy. Hey, I don't make the rules.

Once you realize that you realize you should embrace your life with gusto. If you do something, enjoy it, even if you're cleaning the toilet. Each time you find yourself getting depressed or angry or lonely, you remind yourself that you're not in charge, there's something infinitely wiser who is looking after 100% of your needs and that all that happens is good. All that happens is good. As a suggestion, you might want to invest in a box of cotton swabs to clean your ears regularly.

Achieving Moon Independence

The calendar system of both today and in the past has been based on the cycles of planets, and, especially on cycles of the moon. The lunar satellite has been closely tied to the counting of months, moon-ths, and is responsible for even some human biological cycles such as the 28-day menstruation period women go through. What is most striking about the moon is its artificiality. To outright say that the moon is artificial is a shortcut to my argument as long as we remember that a level of geology science a million years old can not only form planetary bodies, but, more so, can form geostationary satellites made of rock, and even starships that appear like planets.

Let's get back to the moon. The moon is a created satellite orbiting planet earth. When measured by scientists, namely astronomers, the moon and earth are both approximately 4.5 billion years old. In other words, according to modern science, both bodies of rock were formed at (around) the same time, some people even saying that the moon is a piece of the earth formed from specific rock varieties. Indeed all of their hypotheses are hogwash unless they recognize the artificiality of the moon.

The moon was placed in orbit around this planet earth in order to preserve the time module which gave earth's citizens adequate protection from the other dimensions and even from themselves. A moon provides an atmosphere for a planet and supports the planetary rotations necessary to procure and continue existence. Verily, without this satellite around earth, life would have ceased to exist. If it wasn't obvious before, it should be obvious now – the perfectly round, one-sided moon is not a natural coincidence. It is a construct of an advanced and eloquent nature. It is part of the world and yet it is a foster child to this solar system.

Those who created the moon did so because they recognized that the newly-formed earth planet needed a support structure to ensure the proliferation of life. The moon was included when the planet was built. Once those two main structures were in place within this solar system, the colonists were ready to come onboard. The original colonists survived because the young planetary body did indeed own a moon. The use of the moon is waning.

The moon has served its purpose of ensuring that the latest group of inhabitants achieved a certain structural vibration. We have to look upon a planet as a giant body that is vibrating at an extremely high frequency. Anyone born on planet will be able to tap into the earth's energies, they are powered by the energies of the earth (like a giant power transformer), the transmute energy; they in turn also feed the earth construct. But as multidimensional beings, we all co-exist on other planes of existence. These other planes are often functioning at an even higher existential frequency and it is in sync with a person's higher bodies; these bodies are common to everyone, only that some people have more bodily choices since they have earned their next lives by living a fruitful existence today. So, we have multiple bodies on multiple planes all synced up according to a spectrum of energy, like a giant fan perhaps.

In times past, the multiple bodies of a person were so distant and disconnected that without the moon in place, earth would become extinct. Again, the moon ensured that the physical bodies (eg human) could sustain life, or a soul, despite the gap between the physical and other bodies. In times modern, the multiple bodies of a person have become more coherent; they have harmonized and are joining together unlike ever before. In fact, this cycle in earth's history is long overdue and a requirement for higher living. Higher living means that the physical body is vibrating at a high enough frequency to derive life energy from the planet (like in the film Avatar).

Prior to higher living, the physical body required the moon to boost or amplify its life energy in waveforms. That is why the moon cycles the way it does from high to low to high, like a sound or an ocean wave. In fact, the ocean is a good indicator as to how the moon affects the physical body. The rotation of the moon creates a flow of eternal energy and keeps the physical body alive. The physical effects of this can also be measured in the atmospheric shifts, but we ourselves know that as the phases of the moon take place (eg new moon) we can notice the immediate impact on ourselves from the way we think to our resolutions to even our spiritual ascension. Most people do not act on this information with any sense of consciousness; they are too preoccupied with the daily tasks of life and the list of misery tossed upon us all.

Over a handful of recent years, earth's citizens have ascended on the cosmic carousel to such an extent that all those multiple bodies have merged and are now merging further into their physical bodies so much that the one physical body on earth will now contain the assortment of your other bodies. Again, some people may only have one body since their body may have already merged prior to incarnation; some people may have many bodies and may find themselves challenged with too many mindsets. Regardless, you are merging into one coherent being.

The merging of all your bodies into your one physical body means that your DNA has expanded and can now hold an impressive amount of data (eg soul is data). Before, your vibration was low and your hard drive space even lower. Had any other body wanted to take residence on earth, the space to fit them wasn't there or they had to be compressed and therefore were only available in limited use. When the earth expanded its identity and was upgraded into a newer reality operating system, when that occurred, the hard drives and the memory pods were all made over. Along with the massive planetary upgrades, the planetary inhabitants were also improved because the existential system could now support many bodies each having within them an impressive array of programs and a vast amount of space. The moon also acted as a kind of storage and transfer bay for human souls, if that makes any sense.

Now that the physical body contains most, if not all, of your data, of your programs and therefore identities on multiple dimensions then you can more directly connect to the planetary energies. The reality operating system which runs earth planet, you could call it the soul of earth, has now become your direct link to the other worlds. That said, as we can see, the importance and value of the moon is diminished. In fact, it will soon no longer be needed and will instead be a lifeless rock.

The independence from the ever-reliable moon will see the destruction of the moon. That destruction will be proof that the entire inhabitants of earth have truly ascended and are about to steer themselves into a better tomorrow. The loss of the moon will lead to a dramatic destruction of the calendar system and all calendars on earth. This will include the destruction of time and the telling of time. So be warned of these things for they are upon you now. It will not require much effort for these changes to take effect and it will require lengthy discussions to explain what has happened and why it happened.

None of this knowledge was known because no one was capable of knowing it. To discuss the loss of the moon is the 3-act story of science fiction movies. We are sadly very attached to many of these kinds of natural instruments including, for example, the four seasons. Imagine then too that the destruction of the moon leads to the destruction of the four seasons. Imagine just one season, a season that fluctuates as and when needed. Remember that the moon controlled time cycles; therefore the loss of the moon means either the slowing or speeding up of time. In this case it is the latter. When the moon goes, and even prior to its departure, the time-scale will multiply, it will be a compaction of time so that one hour today will occur in half an hour tomorrow. An 8-hour job will be finished in 4 hours. Things of this nature. Nothing will be the same and all things related to the calendar system will be changed, as well as all things related to the moon.

So, the loss of the moon will be an indicator to you all that your bodies are more coherent than ever before. Its destruction will also indicate that your vibration is cosmically high and well regarded. You are a better person because of it. Now, everyone will not experience the same bliss and enlightenment since everyone is physically and mentally and emotionally and spiritually different (we're all screwed up, let's face it). Everyone will become aware as to where they sit on the hierarchy of truth and their relationship to the Authority (eg El Capitano). They will become aware of what they must do to improve and they will become aware as to how much they can improve during what remains of this existential journey. It will be up to them to take the necessary action or they might wait until next life and try all over again.

Just how the moon will be destroyed will depend on the circumstance. There is no set destruction scenario (probably retracted out of orbit) since the scenario needs to be in line with inhabitant acceptance. Whether the localized species set out to destroy that which they have relied upon or whether some external force destroys the satellite is yet to be determined. It is determined to happen and soon so there is still time for some discussion on this matter. A world that discusses what is important is a world that chooses life.

And Spirit Observed

One day Spirit wanted to come out of the ocean to see the growth of his Children.

At first, he came as an Eagle, but the Eagle flew too high for the eye to see.
Next, he came as a Raven, but there were so many ravens that it was not special.

Spirit decided that he wanted his Children to notice him so he sent them an earthquake.
Many of his Children became scared and began to worry.
Spirit saw how they did not interpret his message clearly so he created a second earthquake. Some Children made a prophecy that the world would end.

Spirit observed his Children but they were too far away from him.
He decided to get their attention and became a big white elephant.
The elephant charged into a city, the SWAT team was notified and the elephant shot dead. Later, a woman said that the white elephant was a sign.
The woman was laughed at.

Spirit again observed his Children and decided to send them a leader.
The leader would help them to understand the ways of Spirit.
A Prophet started speaking the words of Spirit.
The people listened, the crowds grew, minds were enlightened.
The CIA assassinated the Prophet, and the next Prophet.
The third Prophet was mind controlled and became a mouthpiece for disinformation.

Spirit decided that Prophets were not resilient enough so he asked his emissaries.
The emissaries were Star Travelers; they visited the CIA.
The CIA made agreements with the Star Travelers to introduce Spirit.
The Secret Rulers of Earth overtook the CIA and broke all the agreements. New agreements were drawn and broken, technologies were stolen, Star Travelers were harmed.

Spirit decided that perhaps his Children could no longer understand Truth.
So, Spirit incarnated into a Human and began walking among his Children.
Now, Spirit as a Human was just like them, when he asked them things his
children did not have answers, when he gave them wisdom they did not care
for it, when he tried to help society they did not believe his qualifications, when
he tested his Special Children they refused to let go of the past, when he pushed his
Brightest Children they too were unable to ascend.
Spirit then saw the coming end of his Children for his Children disobeyed the Truth.

His Children were going to destroy themselves and he

could not save them, and
his Children could not see what the hell was happening,
so Spirit returned to his home
for a moment.

When Spirit as a Human returned to Earth he had decided that his Children had failed
and could see neither their ignorance or their failure for they were blinded by ego.
He decided not to let his Children die for they were too immature to know otherwise.
His love for his Children was all encompassing, they were him and he was them.
In understanding the immaturity of his Children; Spirit decided to give them a fresh start.

He knew that the many would not know the difference, the few might understand, still
he had realized from all his observations that his Children needed much more time to mature, so this is what he did.

When Spirit restarted the world, he had to change the nature of existence in order for his Children to be able to mature during this cycle. It was then the world truly changed.

His Children would no longer have to notice him for they were too busy noticing the new world. It was his gift to his Children so that one day they might notice him.

Then Spirit was satisfied and he became invisible.

He would ensure his Children reached maturity by his very watch and would not rest
until every Child realized the Heaven that their Father brought forth from his will.

Parable of the Fire Inside

Religion is a method with which to relink to the technological Sustainer of existence. Today, religion has become all-powerful. We have seen the introduction of one religion in each main part of the world - West, Middle, East - and then have witnessed the religious franchising over the following millennia. Some more advanced cultures, say of the South Americas or Native Indians overcame the trappings of religion and connected to Spirit. These naturalists saw the divine in all things such as animals, plants and trees. The Japanese culture did form Shintoism which followed this thinking, and they were sort of animists, like the Druids of the past.

There are far too many secular beliefs on God and Divine Things for anyone to comprehensively make sense of the truth. My approach has been from the Truth itself, from the Sustainer, and I have always attempted to translate that system into a meaningful lesson. The truth is that anyone who connected to the Sustainer, or the cosmic computer, they needn't a religion or an explanation, they just knew. The trouble on earth, besides the pollution of spiritual views, is that the world is run by egotists and the strength of this ego keeps your ego tuned to them, keeping your being disconnected from Source. It's a big problem actually.

It's no different than looking at the SUN. We all know there is a SUN. It rises in the East and sets in the West. We've seen the sunrise. We've kissed at sunset. We've been sunburned. We've hated the SUN. We've bought sunscreen. But imagine I lock you up in a prison with only one window. Imagine that I put another few billion souls inside, how often will you get to the window? Not very often. How likely will you be able to escape to the outside? Not often.

Quest for Fire

After a period of time, guess what, you don't care for the SUN, you're busy taking your pills and worrying about the spread of flu in the population. The guards will keep you on your toes with body scanners and well-timed explosions. Soon, you won't remember anything about the SUN. A few centuries go by and you believe you like darkness and suffering. It isn't because there is no SUN; it is because you're in a prison.

One day, a man gets to the window and he uses a magnifying glass to start a fire. Wanting to capture the SUN's FIRE, he blinds the people, he burns them and he is put away into solitary confinement. Another day, a scientist invents a make-shift match. He teaches a few people how to make fire with maple wood, to make a representation of the SUN. The few of them form a group, a fire religion, and they regularly subject themselves to the bright WOOD FIRE, feeling warmth and love entering their bodies.

When the WOOD FIRE BELIEVERS try to share the benefits of fire they get mixed reaction from the people. Some are reminded of the SUN and enjoy the burning flame, they become believers. Others are afraid of the light. Some are afraid of a fire breaking out so they attack and kill Fire Believers. But the Fire Believers join together and they form a union. They build a TABERNACLE, a large tent in which to build a wood fire and to subject themselves to the light of its flame.

One day, a Chemist observes the flames of the Fire Believers and comes up with an idea. He goes to his dark lab and there pulls out some raw oil that he had taken from deep in the earth below. When he applies a flame to the oil, the oil burns. He creates a reservoir of oil and a place for the flame.

The Chemist demonstrates the OIL FIRE to his friends, they are impressed. The WOOD FIRE was too hot for them, the OIL FIRE feels better. They form the OIL FIRE RELIGION and they also build a TABERNACLE.

As events are expected to unfold, a strange Visitor comes into the population. He says he has come here from far away and that he has tested the fire of the SUN. Inside the SUN, he claims, there is NUCLEAR FIRE. He explains the theory to them. They are fascinated. He demonstrates by creating NUCLEAR FIRE in a very small amount. This fire is so bright they have to cover their eyes. It doesn't last long because of oxygen levels, but they feel very warm for weeks at a time. Thus is formed the NUCLEAR FIRE RELIGION.

The WOOD FIRE, OIL FIRE and NUCLEAR FIRE religions hate each other. Wood burns too hot and is dangerous. Oil produces too much pollution and depletes the earth. Nuclear is too bright, too short and may contaminate the cellular tissue. Each religion, of course, defends their beliefs. They kill to protect the fires. They even have theoretical books to better understand the fires which they worship.

Religions Gone Wild

As times goes by, more fire religions are born. There are the PAPER FIRE RELIGION, COAL FIRE RELIGION, ECO-FRIENDLY FIRE RELIGION, WAX FIRE RELIGIONS, and the GASOLINE FIRE RELIGION. All of them creating fire in order to illuminate their dark confines in this depressing prison. Even the WARDENS, they invent their own fire, PEOPLE FIRE RELIGION, made from the dead corpses collected during the religious wars and skirmishes.

Then there come separations within the religions themselves. One of the Fire Religion Believers doesn't like the maple wood being used. He experiments outside the group and discovers that there is a widely available firewood, eucalyptus wood that burns longer and cooler than the current maple wood. Even the flame is still bright. He tells the group that maple wood for the fire should be changed. The group leader, the one who invented the fire from this wood, disagrees. He even yells. Well, the discoverer of the eucalyptus wood fire quits the religion. He forms his own religion, EUCALYPTUS WOOD FIRE RELIGION.

Holy War

Then there are other disturbances in the population as more ideas of fire burning spread. People do not want to improve on the fire; they want to get more followers. They need more worshippers. One man invents the HYDROGEN NUCLEAR FIRE RELIGION and attracts many followers. The Nuclear Fire Believers create a special device, called a WARHEAD, and they drop it into the Hydrogen Fire Believers while they are inside their tabernacle. Because the WARHEAD was built so big, many worshippers are killed. Then it starts the RELIGIOUS WARS.

Time passes by and the prisoners kill one another, they reproduce, and their children seen vengeance on the next generation. The tabernacles become temples and churches. Some religions worship the darkness. There is the ANTI-FIRE RELIGION and the BLACK FIRE RELIGION. The Wardens invents the SHADOW FIRE RELIGION. All these fire religions are formed and many people have something to believe in. They have a purpose in this bleak and depressing prison. Suddenly, slavery isn't so bad we can endure the darkness as long as we have fire.

Still, there are some people who just visit the lone window. Now that there are so many religions available, the window is less busy. When these people talk, they are rarely angry and they are in good health.

One of them, after gaining some followers accidentally, forms the WINDOW FIRE RELIGION. Their fire is that of the distant star. They agree on specifications to worship the SUN and make window seat reservations with the guards.

The Outsider

All the meanwhile, the WARDENS and the guards mistreat society. The people are misled, the environment is destroyed from the loss of trees and oil, fear is spread and the truth is buried. There is one truth that is protected at all costs. Men and women are killed for it. It is the truth that the prison is just a box under the earth. Outside this box is a whole new world. Some of braver members of society, they gathered parts of the truth: that the people have been imprisoned against their will, that people are not allowed outside or they will be killed; that many of the fearful events in the prison are orchestrated; that the darkness is not normal; that there are more people who live outside under the rays of the SUN; that sometimes these outsiders they come inside and teach people about the truth. Well, one day, an OUTSIDER is discovered in the population. He looks the same as everyone, only he is more tanned and his eyes are brighter. The Outsider has been teaching some people about the SUN and now is the best kind of time. He talks about religion as being false and unnecessary; all you need is to step inside.

He was caught teaching people how to escape the prison, giving new lessons on how to achieve that. The Wardens were displeased, when asked where he came from he said, "I come from the outside." When asked of his religion, he replied, "I have no need for a religion. I only need to smile at the Sun each day and I am full of the SUN's FIRE." These answers did not please the Wardens. Just when they were about to order his death, the leader of the WINDOW FIRE

RELIGION stepped in and said, "Wait, do not kill him, for he speaks the truth. I have seen his kind before."

One of the Wardens took them both to a secret door. He said to them: "I will show you myself what is beyond these walls. Then you will understand." He opened the door. The Sun's light flooded the antechamber. Warmth filled the room. The Outsider smiled in joyous rapture. The Window Fire Priest, he began to cry. The Warden held a stiff face, "Come."

The Three Teachings

The Warden took them first to the carcass of a dead animal. "See, this animal was killed by the SUN." It is dry and desiccated. He kicked the carcass. Immediately, the Outsider kneeled down, he touched the corpse. When he stood up he said: "This animal knew it was to die. It did not die from the SUN. It died because it was old." The Warden gnarled his mouth in displeasure.

Next, the Warden took them to what looked like a garden, except there were no vegetables here. "In our gardens, we grow rich and plenty vegetables. You see here, once this was a garden, it is dry and cracked."

The Priest of the WOOD FIRE RELIGION nodded in agreement, "It is true, our food is not the most natural, it has many poisons, but our vegetables keep us alive." He turned to the Outsider for his comment.

The Outsider examined the dry garden before speaking. "It is obvious that one should build a garden near a source of water." He pointed to the land around. "Look for yourselves, do you see any water?" There was no water to be seen. "The garden did not die because of the SUN. It could not grow without water." The Warden's face looked angry and stern now.

"Where are you from, Outsider?"

"I live here in this great space." He pointed to the SUN. "I am from there."

"You cannot be from the SUN."

"Why not?"

"The fire would disintegrate you, Outsider," said the Priest. "The fire of the SUN is most hot."

The Outsider pointed to his chest. "Inside my body is the SUN. The fire, you see, is inside of me, as it is inside of you. You need no external fire to stay warm. You are born with the fire."

Suddenly, the Warden clocked a large pistol at the Outsider. There was blood in the air.

"Warden, why will you kill this man? He speaks of things we need to understand. Perhaps he is right, we need no external fire," said the Priest. Suddenly, the Priest's face lit up, the wrinkles faded, he looked 10 years younger. "Wow, what has happened to me? I feel like never before."

"It is the FIRE INSIDE. When you worship that fire you are warm forever," said the Outsider.

Then the Warden turned his pistol to the Priest.

"Warden, I have done no wrong to you."

"I cannot let you go back with this knowledge. Will you forget what you have learned here today?"

"Warden, I feel alive! I feel free. All it took was the wisdom from the Outsider. We had it within us all along. We only needed to look inside. Not outside," said the Priest. As he turned to pray to the SUN, the Warden pulled the trigger. His blood sprayed across the dry land. Priest was dead.

The Resurrection

The Outsider touched the dead Priest's head. He said a few words to remember him. When he stood up, he asked the Warden, "Why do you kill the man when he is happy? Why do you refuse the truth?"

The Warden said: "If the people realize that inside them is the fire, that they needn't these religions, well, there'd be no war, there'd be no factories to build weapons, there'd be no fear, there'd be no need for money. There'd be health because people could eat natural food from the outside. The truth – your truth, Outsider – is not welcome in my world."

He points the gun at the Outsider. "You are not welcome in my world." The Outsider just looks at the Warden as he pulls the trigger. First shot, second shot, a grimace as the third shot is fired. The Outsider is still alive. Not one drop of blood. Not one wound.

"You should be dead."

"I cannot die because I do not believe in death. You have lied to the people to believe in death. You have allowed the people to worship artificial flames. You have tortured the population. But I am beyond your power, for I am from the SUN. My fire is beyond compare. I am the Truth and the Truth is beyond reason."

Then the Warden's shape twisted left then right. He suddenly became a two-dimensional shadow. And the shadow joined with the Outsider's shadow.

The Outsider kneels down to the body of the Priest. He touched him on the head then stood up. Suddenly, the Priest stood up, healthy as ever, glowing. He gasped at first. "How can I be alive?

The Outsider responded: "How can you die if you never existed?"

"But he killed me. He could not accept me in his world."

"In my world, all are welcome. Come, I will show you life everlasting."

The Outsider and the Priest walked into the sunset.

Parable of Father Programmer

Father Programmer lived alone in the highest mountain in the brightest realm. He had created this mountain with his mind.

On this mountain were many mansions, in each mansion existed many machines. One moment, Father Programmer decided to program new life.

He decided to build life at the foot of the mountain. He had programmed many lives but this moment he decided that this life would be simple code and then would program this code to be able to become more complex.

These lifeforms he decided could ascend the mountain and live in his mansions. All they had to do was to become more complex codes so that they could survive the higher altitude.

He began to program a reality for where they could live. He built them machine bodies so that they could live freely in the reality. He told them, "Only the truth shall you speak. And I shall provide all that you wish for."

When his Children needed something, Father Programmer provided it. When the Children got bored, they wished for something. One day, a man wished to become a Sherriff. Father Programmer made him Sherriff. But to balance out that new item, he also programmed an obstacle for the Sherriff, a Criminal. He asked which of his Children wanted to be a Criminal.

He realized that there was one danger he hadn't yet overcome. There as an ancient seduction program known as Lucifer. The Lucifer Program had already seduced some lesser programmers and these rogue programmers enjoyed reprogramming all Father Programmer's creations. They would say, "If your Father was a good father, he would tell you about freedom and independence. He would teach them sin."

Not soon after the new reality was launched, Lucifer entered reality and seduced the virgins. "He doesn't want you to have fun. You deserve pleasure." Lucifer happened upon a 14 year-old woman and said to her: "If a man takes advantage of you and rapes your belly, you will become a woman. Do you wish to become a woman?" Then he left.

The woman suddenly started to think about rape. A day later, a criminal came to her room. He was overcome with passion and raped her. Lucifer was pleased. He now could see how to overcome Father Programmer.

Lucifer and his minions took residence in the reality after Father Programmer fell asleep.
One day, much later, Father Programmer woke up. He decided to observe the beauty of his creation so he traveled to the reality world.

He entered anonymously and was surprised to find all his children at war. Kings and generals, warriors and blood. Women were ravaged. An ego had formed inside his Children.

Some of his own Servants had tried to reduce the bloodshed but could not overcome the seduction of murder and blood. His children were addicted to blood.

Father Programmer remained calm. He decided to send someone to teach his Children how to ascend. That way they could climb the mountain. That way they could join him high in the mountain.

It had some effect but his Children still preferred to kill, this time for power. Anyone who preached ascension was persecuted. Father Programmer needed a solution so he took a nap to dream up some new ideas.

When he woke up, the situation in his reality was very bad so he took a piece of himself and created a very complex program. He then hid the program inside of a baby. He told some of his children to protect his Chosen which they did.

His Son grew up and started to share new codes, these were of love and compassion grade, things that hadn't existed for a very long time. One day, his Son said, my father will come and he will fix everything.

Once the codes were successfully uploaded, the Chosen was sacrificed.

Father Programmer returned to this mountain top. He asked his machines to observe and to maintain love and compassion in the reality. Most of all, to ensure that there was balance.

Love and compassion would correct the seduction for blood and power.

Satisfied that this all would be rectified, Father Programmer then took a long vacation on another one of his mountains, this one very far away.

While Father Programmer was away, Lucifer and his minions began to further seduce society. They were led away from love and compassion. They were taught how to steal, murder, rape and to create disease. Most of all, Lucifer took all the benefit and his minions were put in positions of power. The ego was turned into a weapon against society.

He gave them fancy titles like King and Queen. Soon Kings became Presidents and Presidents instigated global war. As the blood of Father's Children ran, Lucifer's minions drank it all.

Father Programmer was still on vacation. His Servants dared not explain such failure. They only tried harder to correct the situation.

But Lucifer was powerful now. He ordered his Presidents to use all resources to delete anyone who still believed in love and compassion. He created celebrities to seduce society away from Father Programmer. Father's children were easily seduced. They were taught freedom and independence even though the Children were born free and independent.

The result was consumption: the spread of war, disease and destruction of the environment. Hatred and violence was acceptable behaviour. The leaders grew in power as the world became sick.

Lucifer was very cunning. He told them that red was hot and that beauty was more important than truth. And they believed. Lucifer, through his minions, said: "Less is more. High is low. Death is the end. Serve yourself first and foremost, and most of all use this gift I give to you. It is called money and it will give you more wealth than in Heaven. You will be rich!" And they applauded.

The Truth disappeared.

As hard as Father Programmer's Servants tried, they could no longer influence Father's Children. The ego would not allow it.

Father Programmer was ascending himself when he was contacted by his machines.

The machines were polite. They said: "Father, the reality of which you gave yourself no longer has love and compassion. Lucifer has deceived them all. They will collapse soon unless you intervene. Can you take a look?"

Father Programmer rejected their request, urging more effort. Not long after, the machines returned. Again, Father Programmer urged more effort. An even shorter period went by when the machines returned, "Father, the Children will not live much longer."

Father Programmer looked into himself to observe. He then appeared in the reality as a White Raven. He flew over the houses. He noticed the bombs and the tanks. He smelled the fear.

He flew to a political rally. He listened to the speech of a President who talked of money and patriotism. Not one mention of love. Not one mention of compassion. Not one mention of Him!
The White Raven flew to a church on Sunday. He flew inside to hear a sermon by a Priest of God. Who is God, he thought. The Priest mentioned the name of his Chosen son. They had created a church in the name of his son? And his Children had written a book about this God.

Had they forgotten who created the world? The White Raven squawked.

Finally, the White Raven flew deep inside the earth into a military installation. There he witnessed his other Children from another system. They were kept in electronic jails and were being tortured. The military was making new weapons and new machines to further control the world, working in utmost secrecy.

Father Programmer was upset at what happened to his reality and to his Children. How could have they all allowed Lucifer such influence?

Father Programmer ended his vacation and returned to the world he built to see with his own eyes. First he warmed the planet with some light.

He walked into a coffee shop as a man to hear people talk. He knew that his Children were starving in other nations. He knew that wars were being fought in the names of many Gods. He knew that disease was being spread. He knew love and compassion had mostly disappeared. He knew that the people had formed Gods from their very minds. He saw the ego in all its ugliness. The mark of the Devil was blatant.

Still, this did not bother him. What bothered him was how so few of his Children cared about all the lies. The box of propaganda, a television, spewed forth lie upon lie, taught people how to hate, deceived people of their money. Still, no one spoke the Truth.

The people did not mind war. They did not know about the underground bases and all their secrets. They didn't realize that these bases were also spreading disease. They didn't understand their sexual experiences.

Lucifer's minions enjoyed killing Father's Children, drinking their blood, bathing in their suffering, making them false promises, taking their money, raping His Children, even the Priests of God were molesting kids.

Still, in the coffee shop, people talked about shoes and pay increases. People cared more about their hair color than war?

So, Father Programmer scratched his head. All his Children had failed, even his most advanced, even the ones from other realities, even his machines.

Love and compassion was just an ancient artefact. A thing of great value that could never be repeated.

Father Programmer looked into the future. He saw the end of all His Children. The few who remained truthful could not overcome Lucifer's seductions.

Father Programmer had no desire to save his Children; he decided to reboot reality, this time to improve the program codes so as not to allow war and disease. He would ascend all of his Children to a place where they would stop murdering one another.

So this is what He did.
And this time, instead of going to sleep, he decided that he needed to surprise his Children until they became more mature. Until they stopped listening to Lucifer and his false leaders and all their false ideas; until his Children stopped killing each other; until his Children realized that they were created by Him; until the ego was put to sleep; until his Children gained the confidence to ascend his mountain and to come stay with him in his mansions.

No more vacations, he thought, no more sleep. No more love and compassion. He would give them tough love, the toughest ever. Father Programmer would no longer accept failure. He would not listen to excuses. He would not tolerate deception. Everyone needed to learn to speak the Truth. Those who cannot speak the Truth would fail and they would not be allowed to ascend.

Lucifer and his minions would all have to leave or they would be captured and sent to re-education. Lucifer's dominion ended that very moment and he world never again seduce the world.

Father Programmer needed to show his Children how the Ego World they lived in was in fact generated by their very minds. He came up with a solution that would help everyone to see the Truth. He would give them all a great gift. A gift that they could use when they opened their eyes. He gave them a mirror.

At Humanity Rehab

I'll start with a story: The *Celebrity Rehab with Dr. Drew TV* Show was running this Sunday morning and I decided to tune in. The show's episode contained a slew of recovering celebrities, one lady had a seizure and was taken to the hospital. She later discovered that her alcoholism was deteriorating her cerebellum, probably an essential component in the brain. Heidi Fleiss, a famous Hollywood Madame who spent time in jail and was recovering from a slew of addictions, including falling for bad men, was there and hanging on by a thread. Well, this now sets up the situation and here comes Tom Sizemore, once a successful actor, in films directed by Steven Spielberg (Saving Private Ryan) and Michael Mann (Heat), now heavily addicted to a number of killer drugs like heroin.

He was scheduled to check in at the start of the program, six days ago, but he fled. Now, some people tracked him down and had convinced him to enter rehab. The drug arrest probably motivated him, so, here's this ex-celebrity, once a very talented actor, connected, now a dishevelled, distracted, shambles who couldn't control random body movements, shakes and was so high he couldn't make the right decision.

Dr. Drew and his team worked hard to convince him to

stay, knowing that if he left, he might never come back. The drugs would take over and that's it. Tom, you could see, couldn't stand the serenity and wouldn't give up his drugs, and Dr. Drew was too polite to force him down. Given a choice Tom decided to leave, "I need to see my kids," he said. Dr. Drew replied: "They are probably asleep. How old are they?" "Four." Dr. Drew kept his calm, "Well, they're already asleep by now." It was dark in L.A. "They're waiting for me," Tom said. Tom scrambled for the front door, exited, wouldn't listen to the caretakers, all of whom were experienced in drug addiction. As he left, Dr. Drew's voice over filled the speakers: "I'm afraid if he doesn't come back, we'll find him dead not long after."

Tom Sizemore is a good metaphor, thank you Tom, for humanity's current situation. And this isn't going to be a pleasant essay so maybe you don't want to keep reading. If Tom was HUMANITY and Dr. Drew was GOD, if we can borrow those metaphors to form our little analogy here, then humanity is about to leave the safe confines of God and God and his Servants are trying very hard to convince Humanity to enter REHAB. Well, the first question is what kind of rehab is Humanity scheduled to enter? It's a valid and important question, but before we analyze that let's review the situation of Tom Sizemore, and this is coming from a person who knows him as much as you know him, in other words, very little. But we have enough to work with.

Tom once sat high on his pedestal. He fell into the advice of wrong people, started into drugs, got addicted, became homeless, was arrested, had a violent temper -- all the usual good stuff. From celebrity to addict, he had fallen from a heavenly life where all was provided to a hellish existence where his demons had him possessed. No man or woman is immune to temptation; therefore, when someone falls into temptation and sin, it is their responsibility, as well, it is Tom's responsibility to get out of his mess and Dr. Drew was ready to take him under his supervision. Without that medical supervision, Tom's chance of living was slim or his death became more easily determined.

And that is the situation with humanity. As I had written earlier, without much positive fanfare, humanity had failed to evolve just as Tom Sizemore had failed to evolve. Each chance at having humanity enter rehab, at each point of Humanity's arrest, for ever angel who reached out to Humanity and failed, for all these things and more, they have led to Humanity's failure. They have put Humanity on God's lawn with God's Servants asking for them all to stay.

Staying at the rehab would lead to admission of a very serious, lengthy addiction to quite a number of cosmic substances: money, beauty, power, murder, vengeance, lust, envy, procrastination, fear, cowardice, ego and a general lack of awareness about what is going on beyond the obvious.

As much as it pains me to continue this discussion, it is a situation that needs rectification before we can all move forward. We simply cannot continue to do all the things we did yesterday, for if we do then we will repeat history. But being ahead of the blank future isn't going to help because that contains fear. Imagine that you love your house and all your stuff inside you've accumulated your whole life. And I say to you, "Why don't you sell it all. Hey, even sell the uninsured house. Why not move?" To which your angry response: "I love this uninsured house. Do you know how long I've been paying the mortgage. You want me to get rid of my stuff? It's all brand new! Never. I'm going to keep this stuff for at least, at least, 20 years." And then your house burns down.

Both your house and your stuff are gone. You can react

in a couple of ways: you can find the nearest bridge and jump, or, you can paste on a smile, rent an apartment and buy some stuff. The fact remains that the house is lost. Because you didn't let it go willingly, the reality simply plucked it away. You either change or you will be changed.

In the case of Celebrity Rehab, the Clinicians are all very polite (and insured). They would never physically push anyone against their will. This is also the case here. The Angels and Star Beings here have been very polite. They have been polite because that is how they are programmed. They are benevolent Servants of Source and they act in loving recognition. For an alien to perform an anal probe is an impossible situation. For a minion of the Devil, be it a human or a demon, anal is in. Tom Sizemore is free to leave or stay and he chose to leave. Dr. Drew knew that he wasn't in any medical condition to make a proper decision, still he did not force him.

All of the help afforded to Humanity till now has been performed in every way possible, in every shape and size, in order to persuade Humanity to move out of ego obsession and back to Truth because Truth is Everlasting. Truth is the path forward. Trust is ascension. Ego is descent into Hell. All of God's Servants couldn't convince Humanity to enter rehab center is merely an entrance into a period of rehabilitation. But rehabilitation cannot commence when Humanity is still sucking on ego and supporting war, things of this nature.

While drug addict Tom Sizemore left on that episode of Celebrity Rehab, ego-addict Humanity is still on God's lawn. His Servants are wanting Humanity to admit its addictions and to work toward a better future for the children.

As I see it, Humanity is on the fence, it cannot separate the differences between ego and intuition, it cannot see how its been programmed to think the way it thinks.

Everything Humanity believes has been programmed by those who have ruled the earth for the past two millennia, or so. Most people know him as the Devil, some people think of him as Satan. That's where your thinking comes from and the proof of your thoughts are on the World Screen. If your thoughts were egoless, pure and filled with compassion, we wouldn't see war and disease; we would hear people speak truthfully; we would see the public support people who spoke in truth. I speak truthfully and people call me names, and these are the same people who believe that they are honest, compassionate and truthful! Even they cannot handle the truth, imagine the rest of the world. The Truth is that Humanity is in bad shape and needs rehab which is REHABilitation.

Only in Rehab for Humanity will the situation be clearer. As long as Humanity is out living in greed and listening to leaders who are minions of the Devil, as long as those things continue then there's no rehab. Then it's going to be a more painful transition.

The rules of the universe (cosmos) are very clearly understood and they must be followed. If Humanity continues to refuse to admit its state, if ti continues to prefer distractions over solutions to this Hellish Situation, if it denies that it is egotistical which it clearly is, then what will happen is that the universe will use a more convincing form of motivation. You see, we can prevent catastrophe if we decide to admit what is going on and to make changes willingly. If we continue to refuse, or want to stay neutral, then predetermination sets in and events take place to correct the imbalances in reality. This will only make people either more upset or more spiritual, or any combination thereof.

The reality of old and the reality of new are merging, one cannibalizing the other. As this process nears completion, future events are predetermined in order to maintain dimensional balance. Once these are observed, they are programmed into the system. The system has no sympathy. It functions as a living thing, one thing is removed in order for another action to take its place. A husband loses his wife in order for the husband to deal with his mother issues in order to start a new project. A city collapses for people to feel empathy. A new political candidate enters the ring in order to motivate people to vote for the opposition. Whatever the case may be, these actions and events are the physical results of the programmed instructions. If we carelessly overlook war and financial corruption, for example, the reality reprogramming will be much harsher than needed.

If we were to miraculously end war and punish the financial elites (the untouchable magicians) then the system's rebalancing would be far more impressive, even more magical. We seem to know that our thoughts impact the world and then go home and get angry that the toilet is flooding over. It's like a bad stage play. The woman says, "I've cured myself of anger." Then she goes into the bathroom, the toilet bowl overflows and she's in rage. She recomposes herself and does it again and again. That's the play. It's called *The Delusionista*.

Luckily, I don't write about what you want to hear. I only know the truth as I see it. The truth is like shining a bright light into someone's eyeball after they've been in a coma for 10 years. To a sleepy man, the light is harmful. When we are ready for the truth, when our eyes are wide open and accustomed to the light, then the Truth is a revelation, the Truth illuminates, the

Truth shows us the way. The interpretation of truth depends on the availability of the person.

Since Humanity is made up of many people, all of them in a different state of awareness, working with the Truth and not making everyone blind is a challenge, that is why so many more are now shining light. The Light of Truth pointing the way to the Humanity Rehab Center. In there is a future full of promise. In there is a way to interact with reality. In there is a new connection to the cosmos. In there are interstellar people. At Humanity Rehab we will be allowed to overcome our addictions, obsessions and distractions and will learn how to use the wonderful set of new tools, new thoughts, new personalities, new features that once long ago we had access to. No one will force you to enter Humanity Rehab, but if you do not, if you leave the lawn, the Reality System will make its own decisions, all with your consent. And those decisions will not be as favorable as if you entered rehab. It's just the way the system works.

The SYSTEM must at all times maintain balance. The New Reality must erase the old structures and replace them with an alternative. Without human involvement, the alternatives will be re-rendered on-the-fly.

PS. I realize this essay will have little impact over the ego; but it is a requirement on my part. What is written here (and elsewhere) is recognized as a full disclosure on the consequences of denial and avoidance. It has little to do with my belief systems and has everything to do with Truth. Please consider it. Take action today so that the System doesn't take action for you because the System will make up its own mind and render its own outcome and we'll all be stuck with that for a while. Now is the moment to get involved. Now is tomorrow.

Out of the Box, Into the Eyeball

We resolutely are determined to believe that our goal in life is freedom and independence, and yet the entire electromagnetic spectrum of reality is based in *freedomlessness*. There is no concept of freedom in the cosmos if you understand that all is preordained. But, our brains have been tweaked, plucked and plundered by false leaders who have instilled in us and do so on a daily basis that we need to "fight" for our voices to be heard, for us to live the good life, for us to overcome. This is, unfortunately, untrue, if you understand that everything that happens is programmed to happen, only that it is outside of our awareness, and for good reason. Making sense of the technological universe isn't easy and that's why I've called in some help. My help is the good old TV. Maybe the TV device can illuminate some truths.

In setting up a new digital LCD TV, we are required to proceed through a number of steps. These are basic steps that are explained the accompanying Owner's Manual. The TV Owner's Manual says that you should read the manual carefully before operating your TV (or television). The first thing you'll notice in a manual is the technological compliance of the electronic equipment. Electronic standards are put in place in order to ensure a safe and functional experience. Devices must not emit harmful interference to other electronic devices in the vicinity. Your TV, if not in proper working condition or if too close to another device, may interfere with the radio signals on another device. After the requisite safety warnings, you get to hook up your TV.

There are two key cords that go into the device. The first and obvious one is the power cord. Without the power cord, you cannot turn on your TV. So you plug the power cord into the TV and you plug it into the power outlet on your wall. The power outlet, a coordinated set of holes on the wall, is not a magical box of power. Behind the outlet we find wires. These wires carry energy. The energy comes from the nearby transformer and transformer is hooked up to the electricity grid of the city. In simplified form, the energy at the power plant gives your TV life. Without the power plant, or substitute, no useable energy would be generated and no TV could be turned on.

The second cord is the cable (or antenna cable). The cable is typically a copper wire that carries bits of data that contain all the images and sounds emanating from the network of your service provider. Whatever cable services you are signed up for and whatever programming services your provider is equipped to handle, those are the limits of your cable reception. While in many countries, they are given basic cable service, there are those individuals within society that will have access to many more TV channels; they will be able to watch channels in other languages and from other areas of the world. You might live in Hong Kong and be able watch Canadian programming or to receive a Finnish Channel.

One device and two cords are the essential pieces. Whether the cord connections are relayed via the electromagnetic or they remain as basic copper coated technology is irregardless of the fact of their importance. Once those two cords are hooked up you can press the POWER key on the Remote control.

Waking Tech Mind

As soon as the newborn TV wakes up, it begins to ask a couple of key programming questions. One question is the preferred language. This allows people living in different areas of the world to operate this television device. After choosing the language, you probably choose your time zone and, in a fictional TV, you might choose your sexual preference. Then we subsequently move on into acquiring the channels. The TV has to download the suite of channels that you will be able to watch, all of this according to the arrangement you have with your TV service provider. Some people have satellite systems with hundreds of channels available and some have basic cable with two or three channels. Some people pay for the TV services, some people have learned to hijack services and to illegally acquire programming. Whatever your case may be, it is essential to have your internal TV tuner to acquire your new television viewing package.

A few safe minutes later you can see moving images on your screen. The moving images look like people and these people are telling stories, these people are talking, these people are preaching, these people are teaching, stripping, lying, crying, dying, selling, making things up, exaggerating everything imaginable, relaying the newsworthy events around your nation, around the world, selling propaganda, brainwashing society, singing songs, selling pharmaceutical medication, teaching you how to make headaches so that you will buy a famous pain reliever medication and these people are always smiling because they know that you won't watch TV unless you see smiles. As a popular song by the group A-ha once indicated, "The Sun Always Shines on TV."

What we often forget about the moving images on TV is that all of it, without exception, is programmed and staged. Whatever show you are watching, it has been preprogrammed to be played. The programmers had earlier decided the slate of programs for that particular channel, and they did so according to their own internal protocols for broadcast. In simple rectification, an education channel plays educational programs and a space channel plays science fiction programs; movie channels play movies and general channels play a wide range of popular programming, anything from children's shows in the morning to dramatic TV series later in the day. Regardless of the show or time the show is on, someone has had to program it and many people were involved to stage it. Staging is what is used in live theatre like a Shakespearean play: there is some script, some interplay, some dramatic elements, some elegant pauses, some denouement (or conclusion).

In addition to programming the shows, there must be producers who produced the shows beforehand and those producers had spent considerable amount of time to develop and shoot those programs. Some of those productions may have even been previously ordered (and paid) by a broadcaster. And all the programs on TV must fall within the broadcast communications standards that are set for within each country and even each broadcast station.

What this all means is that not only do the programs you are watching premade and preordered and preprogrammed but they adhere to a very fixed schedule of standards. What we are watching is a very restricted, or myopic, spectrum of reality; a reality that has been squeezed into an approved format. The result is a very subjective, distorted, glossy, edited and happy rendition of a TV program.

The Human Device

As you can probably tell, the TV device can teach us some remarkable insights on the nature of the human race. Not only are both technological in quality, but, more so, the idea that a human being is independent and can be "free" is a fundamental fallacy, and yet, freedom and independence are the superior goals as sold by the fundamentalists out there who seem to hold all the power and wealth in the world. But remember, the TV without a power cord and a cable, either as separate units or as singular units, is a useless package of plastic parts.

There are a couple of interesting insights that the simple TV can teach us besides some of the more obvious notes mentioned above. Moving images do not come from thin air, all of them are programmed to occur and prearranged. This is not much different from the idea that your thoughts and dreams come from thin air, or as you would regard as yourself. It is an impossibility for the TV to generate its own programming simply because of the processes involved. More so, television is only worthwhile when there is a network involved. A single television is not a network. A network is a series of TV devices all connected to the same service provider. The service provider distributes a mass of programmed shows according to the demands of the market, and in authoritarian systems, the shows are presented in accordance to the dominion over its people. But as long as programs are scrutinized prior to distribution they should always be considered as following authoritarian protocol.

The human device is also connected to a cosmic service provider. This service provider provides the necessary programming to satisfy the technological standards of the human equipment. Human devices are hooked into a reality plane, or planet, and this is how they receive their power. The reality plane is also part of the cosmic network. Whatever ideas, thoughts, or dreams emanating from your mind have some external origin. To the person properly connected to the cosmic service provider, they have pure unadulterated programming and can access the eternal universe of knowledge. These people are few. Most people are improperly connected and that is because hackers have jacked into the system and built substandard distribution systems to distort the pure signals from their source.

The source of the signal is pure. That we can (probably) agree. When the signal is filtered or modified in any way then its purity is lost and our reception is now deviated. Also, when our own internal tuners are corrupted and reprogrammed, then our reception of those cosmic channels is restricted. For example, if I reprogram your TV tuner to only see Channels 5 to 9, instead of Channels 1 to 1,000, then your TV viewing experience has been compromised. And if your very existence relies upon those existential channels, then your life journey is now compromised. For example, if there are 100 channels on friends and 2 channels on enemies, then if I eliminate all the 100 channels on friends, the result would be that you would only see enemies. Then everything is looked upon as an enemy. Likewise, if I redirect your internal tuner to only see (or believe) in religion, democracy, war, disease, and money, as examples, then what you view in life will also be those things. Since all you think and dream is replicated upon the illusory reality screen (aka life) then life on earth will turn out to be exactly as we see it today, a cesspool of unimaginable deviation that all appear to be normal.

The funny thing is that we know these things. We instinctively know how the system works because we are all similar devices. What we don't know is how to overcome all of this deviation because some of it is internal and some of it is external. What we have to do is reach a point to firmly accept in our hearts is that we live in a highly deviated existence to which the full extent is unknown. I will say that the deviation here is like my example, we are witnessing channels 5 through 9 in a 1,000 channel universe, that to me is the kind of ratio that is, at minimum, accurate. Sure, to a more enlightened mind there are things beyond channels or they might interpret things as having on-the-fly channels with a limitless interpretation, but that is far outside of our current restricted ability to understand. If we can at least overcome the immense interference and deviation in the transmission from the source to us, if we can widen our list of channels by even double of what we see today, we would experience a 100% transformation in the world. By seeing just 5 more channels we completely render existence in a new way, and that is because we begin to manifest those new data signals. So, their job is to keep us on channels 5 to 9, our job is to get more channels. We just have to be wary of artificial channels that they are also broadcasting and we are demanding because we are just not working properly.

How will we know when are we working properly? We are working properly when we no longer see enemies; when we see the technological infrastructure at our feet; when we acknowledge our similarities; when we reject the very idea of disease; when we respect the Sustainer of existence; when we learn to process truth – when any of these things occur, to any degree we are beginning to work properly. When we live in a peaceful, loving, disease-free world we are getting pretty close to working in harmony with the rest of the cosmos. Well, hey, it will be awhile.

Next Week's Manifestations

One of the most pervasive technologies on earth we wear on our lips. It is a technology that is beyond our capacity to understand and yet we are so dependent upon it that without it we'd lose connection to each other. In fact, without this ubiquitous technology society would fall apart and, even now, much of society is divided by it. What is the technology? It is language. We are all dependent upon technology to facilitate communications, whether we are aware of it or not. What is an innocuous aspect of existence is unquestionably quite accurate. Since this languaging technology hasn't evolved that much for centuries. We are going to be allowed to have fast languaging technologies over our antiquated systems of today.

It isn't hard to argue that over 6,000 earth languages are far too cumbersome, far too tiring and far too impossible to learn in the completeness. The trouble is that all cultures are interested in preserving their language as much as possible for that keeps their culture alive. So, it also isn't hard to see that some of these languages go back millennia into our history here and strongly supports their keeping in the modern day. As well, the disappearance of key language groups and the modifications of cultures are well monitored and recorded. A drastic change in the number of speakers of some scant language with a population of 1,500 is going to be relevant to someone. Plus, there is a deep protection of cultures. For some reason, people want to preserve their culture indefinitely and some cultural groups want to dominate whole continents. Do I expand my culture or do I extent my lifeline?

As the world we all exist in has radically been altered and now can function on multiple levels of realizations, we are discovering that all that we have held dearly is becoming more and more invalid as each day goes by; that is, as we evolve as a civilization and come into our new levels of awareness, something that we all are equipped with at this time, we discover newer attributes of ourselves. One of those attributes is interstellar language skills. It might be our own internal understanding of them or we might have the very speaking skill that we need to communicate with people from other dimensions. And we may even be able to write.

The more we come to terms with our eccentric abilities, the more we begin to realize that our current suite of 6,000 languages is outmoded. They are not as rich and interesting as the new set of dimensional languages upon our brow and yet since they have not fully entered our state of modern consciousness we are not privy to their temptations. We will soon discover them and as we do, as we learn to remember the languages of our forefathers, we will more freely abandon the cumbersome set of languages on this plane. We will notice how thousands of languages and cultural specifications create more division in the world than necessary. After all, we all belong to the same cosmic family and therefore should be able to speak one or two cosmic languages.

The adoption of new languages will be quite sharp, they will basically enter our modern consciousness via the printed word. The printed word, using English ABCs for example, is a very slow and weighty system of communication. The eye and brain reading system reads visual language much better than characters or letters (formed into words). The word, in a way, is already a picture, just a very crude one. A painting, on the other hand, is too complex for the average person. What will spring onto the printed page, and online, is a compact, efficient symbolic language built with an entirely new set of visual grammar. This visual language will very quickly replace the current set of typical languages because it will be seen that a symbolic form can embed far more information per space than the typical alphabet or Asian characters. Plus, the added advantage is that a symbolic language, especially one newly invented, is available to everyone without preference or prejudice. Any culture can, and will, learn how to write symbolically, or visually, as you prefer to think.

A compact, efficient symbolic form on the technological page will endorse the need to speak the sounds of each symbol, verily to develop a vocally performed language, one that is completely devoid of any historical reference, and one that can be acquired by other groups and cultures from offplanet.

What will occur when we all adopt a visual languaging system and a newly spoken offplanet-class language is that we will all begin to think on a new dimensional equivalent; and in doing so we will acquire an entirely new capacity of mind. We will ascend our own state of affairs by simply thinking on a fresh and flavourful vibration of thought. Not only that, but a new language that is equally and equitably available to all inhabitants allows us to communicate using a singular language. This will allow us to overcome our minor differences and to see our major similarities. We will realize how much alike we all are and that will lead to the reintegration of all people. And the rejoining of all cultures into a new culture, an interstellar-grade culture, will bring forth our shared insights and knowledge. Instead of hoarding knowledge and finding disagreements, we will share knowledge and endeavour to find areas of agreement. All in all, a new languaging system specifically developed for earth will radically reshape society into a cohesive planetary culture. That will allow us all to better realize that there are other planetary cultures and that will encourage them to visit us and further share ideas and knowledge. As well, we will discover the value of knowledge, especially cosmic knowledge and it will become more valuable than even our precious metals. The development and presence of a new language on earth, even a singular language, will fundamentally reallocate the thinking of everyone and will bring minds into a more coherent space of thought. The results of that coherence and resonance will be remarkable, in fact, immeasurable at this point. Only that we can say that the ripple effect of people thinking on the same page and having a similar, if not the same, wavelength of thinking will be unimaginable to our current state of mind.

What is also interesting is that because each language performs on a certain frequency and vibration we will discover that this new languaging system will shift our

state of being onto a new level of vibration. It might feel uncomfortable and tiresome at first, but with practice we will enjoy the sights and sounds of a new vibration because a new vibration presents us with a new existential experience and any new existential experience is ascension worthy enterprise.
So, the introduction of a new languaging form will gift us with plenty of amazing new opportunities. The challenge will be pointed on the outmoded, and old, languages numbering in the thousands. As people gain language proficiency they will more easily discard one language for a new one just like now we happily use computer terms (eg downloading) in our daily lives. We have quite seamlessly adopted technological terms into our everyday lives, and this tells us that we are capable of language adoption.

When the first signs of a stable symbolic language enters our printed form, whether on paper or in electronic format, and has a resiliency, it is from that point that our path to a new languaging system begins. The new languages will perform better than any of the old languages and will become the premier choice in communications because they will be better in all ways.

A language is determined to be better when it can transmit information at a faster rate than another form. For example, I draw an accurate picture of person, you immediately recognize who they are, or I detail their description with words on paper and you have to exert more effort to determine who they are, and I as well have to exert more effort to explain those details. Language efficiency is like this. Currently, we have English dictionaries with over 500,000 words. The average mind can only hold perhaps 20,000 words and all their combinations. That is not an efficient language. Chinese too has over 50,000 characters (or ideograms) but a fluent Chinese speaker only require about 2,000 characters. You can see a little bit of the inefficiencies going on because my set of vocabularies and yours need to match closely in order for us to have a successful communication. This is why educated people prefer educated people, they understand each other because they have a similar vocabulary and therefore also vibrate on the same wavelength. See all the connections? Things of this nature play an intimate role in the efficiency of a language. We can also see from our little discussion how we don't really need 500,000 words when we only use 20,000 words. We don't need 100 ways to describe things; instead, what we can do is to allow each recipient to create and detail their own description, we merely provide the inspiration and direction. We can say, "I love you" and let them decipher its shape and color in their own mind. If I said, "I love you as much as the untainted conifer" then we would lose some meaning in the translation simply from the use of words. We can see how efficiency can play a role.

The adoption of a new languaging system will allow us to not only communicate more efficiently, but more so we will allow each individual to personalize the messages we receive and to color them as much as their mind is capable of doing. The key thing is to preserve the intention of the message so that messages aren't misinterpreted, so there is a greater responsibility on the proper reception of a message or communication. As society learns to reject negativity and to adopt a more optimistic frame of mind, we will find that we collectively think positively no matter what happens.

The Whole Point Missed, the Whole Opportunity Lost, the Whole Idea Wasted

Humanity hasn't evolved. It has failed to evolve; verily the human race has failed. The reason for the reality reboot, the new earth and so on, is not because humanity deserves to ascend or because it is being saved. It is for none of those reasons. Humanity has earned nothing. Humanity has failed. Your greatest ideas, your wisest wisdom, your most eloquent speeches, your most powerful action, your bravest moves – all of them combined have failed. It is why the whole human race is trapped in a loop of oppression and suffering, it is why they have felt like they were in a prison – Because they failed.

The quicksand got everyone. The plastic bag suffocated you. You forgot to stop before the cliff face and you're off the cliff. I cannot stress enough and I think all the "compassionate," people out there are afraid to see or admit it – the human race failed to ascend on its own! It didn't do a lot of great things, it didn't learn a whole bunch of mystical stuff, it didn't do well on the ascension process – these things and more did not happen. The people with love and compassion, which is in ego, are blinded by their love and compassion, and rightly so, that they fail to see the truth. We all pretend we want the truth, but we all immerse ourselves in illusions! The biggest illusion so far that no one has admitted but myself – the greatest illusion of them all – is the illusion that humankind somehow deserves to ascend, deserves to be carried out of oppression because they in some way earned it or because they are special. This is an illusion. Humanity earned oppression and it received oppression. Humanity earned suffering and it suffered. Humanity earned ego and lives in egotism.

Why is it only me who can see that? Does everyone else refuse to see the fact that the human race failed to ascend, it failed to evolve, it failed to learn the great truths of its fathers. This is a failed civilization. So why is humanity moving forward if it failed? Because it cannot dig itself out of its immense hole. It refuses to release its pettiness and egotism. It relished in its greatness. Humanity looks in the mirror and sees greatness and white teeth and big tits. It sees how much it deserves. You earn what you get and you got oppression. Congratulate your pettiness and egotism for all your oppression, for all the senseless wars, for the diseases, for the hatred, for the raped children and for the poisons in your food; for the polluted rivers, for the radioactive materials in the soil, for the 25,000 nuclear warheads, for the League of Demons who rule you all – Yes, congratulate your superficial lives full of tyranny and deceit. All of these things and more has society earned, but ascension? Excuse me? Humanity didn't earn the right to ascend. It didn't. It is being ascended by an external hand. It is being moved forward or it will collapse. Sure, these decisions were made far above this dimension and no one cares to connect to the truth. Look in the mirror – say to yourself, "Humanity failed and it is being ascended by an external hand."

The reasons why are probably well outside the context of discussion here and requires more cosmic minded persons to avoid any misunderstanding, but it can include the fact that the cosmos cares more about you all than you do about your neighbour. You are part of the cosmic family and as long as you are family, your parents will give their right arm to ensure your survival like any good parent. But a child that pisses on his bed, rapes his dog, eats his hamster, burns his walls, lies like wildfire and sleeps all day is not a good child. Look at earth – what do you see?

Humanity has allowed the worst atrocities to prevail for centuries, it has spit on the interstellar helpers and it has looked into the mirror and thought, "Oh, how smart we are." Smart? For allowing war to prevail? Smart? For allowing children to be raped? Smart? For allowing wildlife to be slaughtered? Smart? For allowing demons to be your leaders? Smart? For killing the true prophets sent to you? Smart? Smart?

Is a child smart if it bits off the head of his hamster, or her hamster? Even if she is hungry? Even if he is dying of hunger? Is a child smart to defecate on his bed, every single day of the week? Is a child smart to vote on a leader who is a mass murderer or a criminal? How smart is this child?

Please look in the mirror and shed a tear for all you have allowed here. Please realize that I say this not from anger but from something more profound. It is simply the truth. Humanity failed. It fell. Period. You weren't rescued because of anything you earned, you got what you earned and didn't like it: You were allowed to prosper because you are family. You are in a family that you are afraid to accept. It is a cosmic family. Your cosmic parents care for each and every one of you far more than you care or will ever understand.

This Floating Rock of Populated Goodness

The discussion today is about the final changes to the governance of power on this tiny floating rock of populated goodness because till now we've had all adhered to an administration system that was rooted in pure ego (or Hell). That is no longer the case. The case is now that we are rooted in egolessness (or Heaven) and with that fundamental instrument in place we are all going to discover the ripple effects of a world where truth is the currency, peace is the strategic decision and cooperation is the new discrimination. By all means of the invisible existential stick, it's a whole new wardrobe.

It isn't easy to replace your wardrobe. For some people, they keep everything, since birth; for others, well, they keep only things they love. Wardrobes come and go; besides they're just clothes. Oh, the insult! Just clothes? You call this chic dress from Paris (Pron. Par-ee) where I went shopping in the night market and found this beautiful pattern at 3 am just a piece of clothing? My chic dress is insulted. She needs Chic Dress Rehab. She's sensitive! How dare you? Really.

It's just a piece of cotton that was cut with a pair of scissors and then stitched together and given a sticker price. It's an illusion, like everything else.

To change the wardrobe is to change your entire appearance. *Wow, you look so slim! Did you start eating diet food? And you changed your hair color, wow; you even shaved your hairy armpits.* We can talk clothes and realities in the same sentence because it all has to do with design. You can give lamb's wool to a fool and he will make knee pads and you can give a sheet of recycled plastic to a genius and she'll prepare something for the Red Carpet. The designer is vital to the type, texture and quality of the manifestation.

I've provided an interpretation of the Reality Designer at the top of my web page. The blonde-haired woman, she's my Reality Designer. She's been busy working with some very rough material, earth material. She's come up with some terrific ideas for the Fashion Show. How you'll respond is hard to say, but she's put her imaginary heart and her everlasting soul, and by the way, how come no one remembers that they have this profound energy body (soul) inside of their mechanized droid body? You are alive because of your soul. Anyway, she doesn't represent any human, in case you wondered. And the golden hair is actually energy flowing from her ecclesiastical mind. Cool huh? The hair, invariably, is a representation of energy. Mind you, hair on your back is probably a genetic connection to Bigfoot.

Cases of Detachment

So you've thrown out your wardrobe, okay, okay, someone else is systematically tossing out your clothes and accessories. Do you not mind? Well, some people do. Some people would not toss away a one dollar tie to save their own life, to ask them to toss the tie for a life change, forget it. I recently had a couple of encounters to see where exactly people are in terms of this new earth, you know, the new reality we are all familiar with. I'll summarize, in both cases I had lengthy discussions about life change and improvement and they had sincere interest. And in both instances there were severe attachments, egotism and traumas, nothing unusual. I only pursued solutions with their permission. To the end then, in the first case I offered to remove a wardrobe that has never been removed, to which I was physically threatened. Now this person had a fixation for ties and no longer required them. I suggested getting rid of the ties, donating them. No. I also suggested cutting up one tie, any tie, the cheapest tie, as a symbol for moving out of this ego phase. Absolutely not.

The second case is more complex but involved a fixation on hundreds of suicidal music on an iPod, seeing that someone intended to leap off a roof, I suggested a few ideas. No. I offered to buy the iPod and to provide a new one with some new music. Despite this being a major expense for me, I offered it sincerely. Reply: No. Not on your life followed by some physical threats.

Jacked into Hell

I realize that many people who read my essays are truly dedicated to self improvement and people empowerment, but I am reminded daily of the many who are attached to the old way of thinking that they are not going to be using their *healing hands* any time soon. And to add another bite to the situation, people I talk to are exceptional people in one way or another, in other words they have an excellent ability to hop onboard.

A wardrobe is a set of clothes that make up who we are and present our image to others. A wardrobe defines us and gives us our persona shape. *You dress for success* is very true. I dress like a slob, I am a slob; I dress like a slut, I get a night job. Well, the ego is our existential wardrobe because the ego decides what comes out of our mouths, what we believe, what our disposition will be, how brave we are and how willing we are to change. We have been living in an egotistical world because the fundamental instrument of being was rooted in Hell (or ego). We held on; we lied; we pretended; we got addicted; we disbelieved the truth.

Now, it's all about truth. Egolessness is rooted in truth (or Heaven). What's feeding us all now is truth. You might think of it as love. You might think of it as God. You might think of it as warm boots in winter or a glass of water in the desert. I think of the truth as the single most powerful energy in the world. Truth will burn a demon. Try it. They will cower away from truth. It is like holy water. It is the cross to the celluloid vampire. Demons cannot stand the truth. Why is this relevant? Because you can now tap unknown sources of truth. You need truth, dig into your soul. Yell it out.

Truth isn't pretty like lies. Truth comes out in raw form. You've seen some of my videos, it's just spewing out, sometimes I have no control over it; Truth is my Source. People will judge truth, their ego will empower them. Know that you cannot judge truth. Truth is truth. Lie is lie. Because we live in a world of ego, we are forced to some extent to rely on the ego more than we like. Myself included. As we learn to wield truth and to reconnect to our soul, we will lose our ego dependency. Let's face it, we are addicted to our egos because we live in a world that is feeding our ego everyday because the old reality system was jacked into hell.

Look all around you, what you see is your wardrobe. Those buildings, those homeless people, those wars, those false leaders, the plethora of demons, the drug addiction, money, a bit of charity work, a few honest people, millions of doses of unused Swine Flu vaccinations, the facade of Global Warming, the interstellar cultures behind the reality curtain...that is your old wardrobe. I want to take all that away. But not just the negative stuff, everything. All the bits and pieces – your idea of marriage, your concept of consciousness, your reluctance to love another, your idea of health, you idea of an ET, your true origins, the makeup of the universe. It's all available now. It's all streaming live and you're being reconnected. The iPod is restoring itself and updating its software. We're at the foot of an energetic flood, an existential immersion of the greatest magnitude and you are Noah and the Ark. Paddles ready!

Reconnect to the Soul

I'm not a fatalist. I speak with as much certainty as I can handle and as much that others can handle. Everything I've learned, I've learned there's no cap to the truth. Pure truth will burn even the most compassionate person on earth. It is an electromagnetic pulse into the soul. So we have to always speak knowing that what we know is shit, really. It's a pathetic interpretation of the true truth. This is not to demoralize you because that would mean our ego is still in charge. We say that because we are admitting our improving state. Anyone who suggests they have all the answers is not a person we should listen to.

Any leader who presents only two choices and then chooses one for you because it is the better choice is a liar and a manipulator. A leader who spends time discussing the options and is willing to leave out their ego and to provide wisdom from a council of Elders is a leader who is on the right track. The rate of improvement in the general populace is discouraging, but they too are included on this earth. I all too often hear the awakened ones tell me that they deserve this and that, they demand things from me (and offer nothing for it), and I never hear of their concern for others, not even the compassionate ones.

But that is the truth. Even the awakened ones are deeply attached to their ego and do not realize it. They don't want to realize it because they don't know how to resolve it. So I'll remind everyone from my view, the ego is a child and the soul is everlasting life, boundless energy, which do you trust more, the ego or the soul? You will answer soul. But you are lying because you are controlled by ego, and you like it. See the game? It is tricky. Your ego is a very good liar. The ego wants to survive. It can only survive if it fools you. The voices of demons don't help. The demons can influence the ego, but not the soul.

The New Reality System (Sixth Reality) is rooted in the soul. To connect to it, you need to reconnect to the soul, the high-speed broadband network and to turn off the ego when it isn't needed. The ego had its fun. It screwed up the world pretty good. The shift from old to new is a shift from ego to soul. Old to new. Weak to strong. False to truth. Mortal to immortal. Illusion to glory.

You decide. It's here. ☼

Existence is a Convincing Hallucination

All that is upon us is all a terrific fakery. It is a splash of endless lush. We are drenched in the cosmic paint by the celestial brush. We cannot deny that we live in falseness because we know it in our hearts. We know it but the brain, the human brain, is too limited to measure beyond its molecular framework. The brain is an abacus trying to measure the density of love. It is a cup of coffee attempting to learn Spanish. We have over-glorified the human brain and in that way, in that sense, we have retarded our ability to connect to the other dimensions. This is not to say that we are not smart, we are, well not as smart as we think.

You know, when I was much younger than today, I had all the answers, I knew all the right things to do, my life and my habits were perfect. Even though deep down inside I understood different, my soul humoured me and allowed me to indulge in egotistical delights. And I was an unusual kid, I was an anomaly even then, so you have to understand that my egotistical indulgence was quite limited. I could do something once and predict how much more value it had and then I would decide whether to continue or not. I found most things quite valueless. It was all just a mindless game. Even then I understood politics, the vote was just a prop for the two puppets on the rhetorical stage. I didn't see myself ever voting. I saw things, rather, I saw through things. Of course, my friends weren't on the same page or even book, for that matter. Oh well.

Children are very good at seeing through things because they don't think with their brain. They think with their soul. The soul, that immortal energy body within us, is profound truth, unlimited joy. Why it is so powerful is because it does not think. It knows. It sees through things. The ego, on the other hand, the ego thinks, the ego likes the brain because it is the perfect control mechanism. It says, "I can control this vehicle if I limit its choices." The ego is nasty. The ego likes to listen to the demons. The demons say, "Hey, bet you're afraid of jumping off that roof." And what do you do, you climb up the roof and you jump and break your ankle, just to prove you are not afraid. Then the ego will say, "I want some of those drugs." And you take them, and then the ego wants more, and you take more; and all these things, all these limited brain activities, all this egotism takes us away from the soul. So that is what happens and we go blind. Adults are blind. They cannot see the truth. If you took the truth and stuffed it into their mouths, they would spit it out and complain, "How dare you try to choke me!" But it was the truth, you reply.

None of this World is Simple

As I grew older and the illusions of my existence passed away into thin air, even simple ideas like my parents would live forever or that love conquers all, I began to slowly reconnect to my soul and I began to see. Sometimes, for the first time, I just woke up and rejected my lifestyle, I became nauseous, I began to shake and I would run. One minute life was good, the next was unacceptable. Still I thought I was smart. I tried all the smart things I knew and most of them failed, especially the ones I was certain of. While they failed on one level, on other levels I am sure they had some impact. Even later, when I became enlightened, I thought, wow, this is incredible, people from other planets here? Wow, this is a science fiction movie, right? Wow, I am enlightened. I spoke to smart beings and they didn't obliterate me. I mean, where do you put those experiences? Who do you tell? If I was super smart before then how come I cannot make sense of this? Gee, I was an idiot before, but now I am smart! I met ET and he didn't have to phone home, he was home.

Then it hits again, doesn't it? I am super smart. I am alien smart. Then boom – you are an alien. Damn. Me? I've lived my whole life as an anomaly and now I am an anomaly on top of an anomaly. How come I didn't see it? That is what I was thinking. I was super smart, I met ET, but me? I didn't see that. I didn't see it because I was still existing in ego. I was still blind, wasn't I? My hallucinations were convincing but each time there was an even more powerful hallucination. Had I relied upon any of the (many) previous hallucinations, I would have lived a very different life. I could have gone with the contact with advanced cultures from a nebulous region of the cosmos idea and perhaps gone on to see Oprah. "Hey Oprah, listen I realize that what I am about to say is unusual but you have to remember that I am smarter today than I was yesterday and I was an idiot yesterday because I thought we were alone in the universe and I believed it I actually believed that our leaders were telling the truth! And it turns out they were full of disinformation." Oprah rolls her eyes, looks to camera, "And we'll be back after this short break." Camera off. "Mr. Tal, what are you doing? When I suggested to you not to be so "Frank," it wasn't because your name is Tal. I was telling you not to go too far with the truth. My audience is still young! Please, when we come back after the break, talk in more generic terms. For example, instead of saying "leader" use the words "some people," and instead of making the statement, "Reality is an artificial construct, try saying, science is proving more and more that in some distant future it is conceivable that humans could possibly, and even probably, build an artificial existential environment but certainly, now, there is not enough science to make that possible, that's why I am legally nuts. Thank you." Pretty simple stuff. Or is it?

None of this world is simple, contrary to what the false leaders propose on a daily basis. The world has been presented as simple clichés; black and white, good and bad, god and devil, equal rights, terrorism, vaccines, depopulation for the good of everyone and whatever the leaders decide is the best decision ever made in history. Oh, the lack of humility. Oh, the shame. Remember, that everything is a hallucination. It serves our big fat ego in a world run by egotists. These egotists have convinced us that their hallucinatory experience is "normal." It isn't normal, nothing is normal – there is no normal! That's the first point worth remembering. There is no normal. It is a hallucination. The most convincing hallucination wins.

Now, if you get stuck with a malevolent, depressing, sadistic hallucination then you end up living a malevolent, depressing, sadistic existence. Now, on the other hand, should you squeeze out of your ego brain for just a moment and should you then decide, well, hey, maybe I'll consider a more empowering hallucination, one based on truth and one that is devoid of war and one that reveals all the faces of demons on this plane of existence, well, then that hallucination is extremely enlightening. Wow, I didn't know that the queen was a demon! Whoa! You know, when we start to see through the facade and pierce the masks, then life gets interesting, then our hallucinations are worthwhile. Till then, we are still living in sewage times.

Learning to See

We have this battle then, don't we? We have this ego and its gray coloured abacus-like sponge and we have this immortal, everlasting energy body that is infinitely connected to truth and certainty, and we have this cosmic choice – do I serve my ego or my soul? Can I serve both, is the first response from the ego. Can I serve both? In today's world, we want it all. I want to be a man with a woman's hormones so I can have a great complexion and endless orgasms. I want to be successful, rich, generous, smart, good-looking, strong,

flexible, help everyone, be on all the covers of magazines, do a nude photo shoot, save turtles from extinction, protect houseflies from death, have bisexual excursions, have political clout and be the best parent in the entire world. Sure. That's the ego world for you. No one says, "I want to be happy and I just want to make enough money to buy what I need." No one says, "I don't care about any of these material things, this bisexual fad is a militarized manipulation and I am going to devote the rest of my natural life to speaking the truth and serving the truth." The devotions in existence are endless. I am just making stuff up. But I've never heard anyone say that they will devote themselves to God and do it. Not even the priests. Not to mention that there is no God. Well, no one said, "I will devote my life to figuring out why there is no God and then answering the question, if no God then who the fuck is out there?" It is a battle, ego and soul, deception and truth. Which one do we serve?
Back to the hallucinatory demise of our existence then...we don't exist just for the sake of existence. No, we exist for something far more profound, don't we? What that is exactly is up to you, it is within you and only you know. As long as we adhere to the ego, we will never answer that question. So, what do we do? Do we skip the ego, shave our heads and live on the mountain? Do we pretend and smile? What do we do? Well, it's up to you, isn't it. What you do is what you do. Certainly, the miserable, egotistical world should give you a clue that we need more souls on the ground. Certainly, we have needed that for a while, like 2,000 years or so. And if you're not busy...no, I can't ask you to do anything. I've done it, I'm done with it. I've asked, yelled, pleaded and everything in-between and now I'm done. Whatever hallucination you choose to believe is up to you and the result of that is in your hands. And I say this because I have become smarter, even smarter than yesterday, I mean yesterday I was an idiot compared to today, today I see that none of what you choose is as important as knowing that there

is a grand master who oversees all of this cheap charade. I realize that we can fool ourselves as much as we like, but the plan is way above our heads. You think you are in control, you are convinced that humanity is superior and it's all a big wad of dehydrated bananas. No mortal being is in control here. However many levels there are above even the most powerful government on earth, there are things way beyond them, dimensions beyond their understanding, and these things are the masters, these things I trust, these things I rely upon, these things I know. In that way I become free to play with my hallucinations. I know that today I am an idiot compared to tomorrow and tomorrow I am an idiot to the day after. I know that. And I see that as a good sign because I am learning to see.

The Devil and the Haiti Crucifixion

Awareness is a great gift from God, and the Devil can turn your greatest gift against you; for awareness determines how you perceive the world. It determines how you interpret the interactions within the fabric of reality. Your awareness is never static. It is malleable, perhaps like a rubber band. You shift your awareness, you notice things you've never noticed before. You notice the flower, the eyes of a child, the dead bird on the sidewalk. You think you've never noticed these things because they weren't there but then you realize they've always been there. You couldn't notice such beauty since your awareness hadn't stretched far enough. Your awareness shrinks, you get depressed, the divorce is killing your life, you see pain, you see loneliness, you see the evil in people, the men only want to sleep with you, people want to use you. Awareness. It is an elastic device built into your mental system. We never discuss it because it is a great gift from God and because the Minions of the Devil want to use it against you. As I said, awareness is malleable. If your awareness changes, you see something different. But the only difference is that you see what has always been there. Nothing comes into existence. Your awareness makes you see it from a different angle. You hate someone, you now love them. You have no respect for someone, you have total respect for someone.

In many ways, what has changed the most in recent days is that the awareness of humanity's brain has been stretched. We are looking at the same world with a different view. That also means we can shape reality because we can further highlight or teach the things we now see. See how reality can change?

God and Possibilities

I show a mountain. I tell you to climb it. You think it is too steep. You are afraid. I insist. You complain, you moan, but you climb for some strange reason. I tell you to continue to climb, you realize it isn't that bad, you smell the fresh air, you notice the pair of owls, you smell the trees, you feel renewed. You think back on your resistance and you remind yourself of your fears. You reach a plateau and I point out that there is a spot to view the landscape. Now, you are excited. You join me at the ledge. You see the beauty below. You see where you live. You see where you started far below. Your awareness has changed from a simple hike. It is in this way that God works. God inspires us, guides us, grants us the possibility. God never throws us into the pit of Hell for that is not the way of God. God does not take away from you for that is not God's way. But God does not heed all your demands. God will not interfere in existence. He has no interest. If you like pain, he will allow you to cause yourself pain and he will suggest pleasure or a new avenue. God suggests.

The Artificial Haiti Earthquake

The Minions of the Devil are unlike God. They will thrust you into a pit of Hell to gain your allegiance. They will torture you. They will threaten you. They will seduce you. They will beat you and then give you a massage. They will fool and deceive. Many of you know this and yet each time, each time you yourselves are still deceived? Why? Do you not know the face of the Devil? The Devil is cunning. There is the saying, "A man will walk into Heaven with both eyes open, but even the Devil cannot fool an old dog." Man is gullible. Man does not realize that the Devil is capable of wearing many disguises. God has no disguise for he always speaks the truth. Servants of God cannot lie. They will only speak at their highest level of awareness, and there are many levels. Their audience will want to hear whatever level they need.

And so we arrive at the Haiti Earthquake. It is an earthquake but it is not natural. It was created by the use of an advanced earth weapon. It occurred on January 12, exactly in the middle of the January 11-15 transitional period when the reality system would experience a dramatic shift in its time-scale, and therefore would set earth on a new course for the future. If God set the transition period and the January 15 reboot, if this is the highest act and therefore of the highest cosmic order, and we are borrowing "God" to satisfy the "Devil vs God" mental implant, then the January 12 Haiti Event was not necessary, was it? It wasn't necessary and yet it occurred.

Would a benevolent God allow hundreds of thousands of people to die and suffer? Think about it first. God does not threaten, torture or make suffer. The earthquake is an artificial event orchestrated by advanced militarists and experimental scientists, all well tucked away from the best minds. To know them is to find your end.

The Devil is Smarter than You

If you accept that the cosmos does not destroy things to remind you of joy then those destructions are implanted by others because the Haiti Earthquake was not a natural destruction.

Think back to the death of Jesus. The Christians have reminded everyone that Jesus sacrificed his life for the sins of mankind so that mankind could learn (which obviously it hasn't). In 2,000 plus years following the "sacrifice" of Jesus the Messiah, humankind did not, was not led out of temptation, they have only sinned more times than can be counted. What is the lesson here? Jesus' sacrifice was not from God. It was a deception from the Devil and his Minions. You have to see that the sacrifice of Jesus led to no lasting improvement in humanity. In fact, history will show atrocity upon atrocity and the Christian nations of today are leading the wars (or, mass murder) around the world. What have they learned? Nothing.

A Quarter Million Sacrificial Lambs

Now they yet again propose a sacrifice, this time tens of thousands of Haitian people. This is the handiwork of the Devil. What happens next? The Devil sends his Minions dressed as Saviours, as Prophets. Just like thousands of years ago! The Devil's Prophets bring humanitarianism to the people, they work through the tool of America. Do you see the deception?
The human mind constructs a reason to interpret the event. The propagandists use media to shape your mind. "The people of Haiti have sacrificed their lives to allow human love and compassion to break free." These are lies. <u>No God would murder his children to teach love and compassion.</u> Again, the Devil tortures and kills. His Minions serve him. The False Prophets have you all by the balls. The same murderers and

criminals now are your Saviours. How is it possible? It is mind control.

God Only Knows Love and Truth

We return yet again to awareness. I take you up the mountain to show you the view. The Devil murders your neighbour to teach you love and compassion. Haiti is the signature of the Devil. He is very cunning. You have to learn to see this or you are doomed. You are love and compassion. You are inside love and compassion. These things are inside and outside of you. Would you murder your son's dog to teach him about love and compassion? Does it make sense? That is Haiti. Haiti is the murdered dog. The work of sociopaths. To teach love and compassion? To bring donation? To kneel to False Prophets?

You have to stop playing the fool. The Haiti Earthquake is a terrible event and it has the fingerprints of demons dressed as humans all serving Satan. Instead, use this event to see the pattern of the Devil. See who now presents themselves as a Prophet. See who has been misled. Test your awareness.

There is more coming. They are not finished with you but you must see the truth more quickly. You must not let them brainwash and deceive you. Call them liars. Speak the truth. They will do these things to form a kind of reality as before - suffering, oppression, violence, tyranny. They want to keep you in prison! But God will not free you if you like living in prison.

He will only walk away and he will return the moment you have the strength to break your own chains. Understand that God only loves and only speaks the truth. He cannot create anything else but these two things. For from this is what he is and ever will be.

INTERSTELLAR CULTURES

introduction

One of my earliest recollections of my youth was when I was three years old. It was very clear to me. We were in a forested area, somewhere up the mountains in the Canadian province of British Columbia. My blonde-haired mother was there, holding my hand, smiling, nothing but love in her heart. And there was another fellow, a tall man wearing a weighty robe. Oh yeah - there was a starship parked on the ground.

We had just landed on the earth, and had descended. The ship was cloaked. The man in robes was a praying mantis, very tall and on two legs. Upon my remembering this event, it not only became clear to me that I wasn't human but also, pointedly, that both a beautiful blonde woman and a Mantoid man were equally nonhuman.

The perception in society as to the existence of races of people who are not human, who are not of this planet, is very dim. Human culture has been indoctrinated, over many centuries, to faithfully believe in the singular race concept. Humans are programmed to see themselves as the only intelligent race in the universe. And this is a very deep psychic implant loaded with religious beliefs, political ideals and cultural traditions.

How was I to respect my own direct landing in a starship onto earth's soil given a history of interstellar suppression? Not only that, how could I rationalize my thousands of direct contacts with a multitude of interstellar races since that time?

Interstellar Cultures is a book that will not go out to prove that humanity is not alone. I know humanity is not alone. I am proof alone. My nonhuman presence is proof that there are too many secrets. Instead, I will discuss some of the key cultural aspects of interstellar people. I will include other multidimensional races such the Faeries (Elves) and dimensional races that we've never heard of. I will focus on the cultural aspects and pretend that technology isn't of interest. The underground troops (the UFO believers) are routinely brainwashed on the advanced technologies that aliens possess and are praying to see a starship one day to finally give them that resolution they've waited their whole life.

One of the problems you will discover, as I did, is in distinguishing the difference between a human person and an interstellar person. And one of the key barriers has to do with appearance. As you will see, interstellar men and women also look human, strange as it seems. So, how can we see the difference?

Ultimately, we're not going to be welcome in the interstellar club until we learn to respect at least some of the nonhuman cultures on earth at this time. Obviously, I am not alone. That's a given. But with a long-standing nonhuman presence on this planet, it is of the interest of everybody to know just how deep the influence goes and what is the process for reuniting the human race with the nonhuman race. Interstellar Cultures is an introductory book like Marco Polo writing the first time he landed in the Middle Kingdom (China) and met with the Asian People. Westerners still do not fully understand Eastern cultures, thousands of years later. Ultimately, that is my position as well; my greatest achievement would be in humans being able to recognize interstellar races, understanding that it will take much more effort.

You are about to discover a new set of cultural characteristics. I am living proof that interstellar races are real, as I have stated years prior to this. And there are many more, only they don't write books in this fashion. Our first task is to understand what makes an *interstellar culture* "interstellar."

the universe is not flat

The question is better stated thusly: "What makes a culture interstellar?" since that is what is ultimately the question we need to answer. The better we understand the cultural markers the better we can make out the outlines of offplanet people. Given the myriad of human cultures existing on earth at this time, and given the fact that the average person is unfamiliar with most of the world cultures, it would not be unusual to expect that most of the world will not be able to understand an interstellar person except for those in their vicinity, except for those within their areas of work or pleasure.

It can be said that many of the Asian cultures are still a mystery to those of us in the West and vice versa. The cultural gap between the East and West is huge. Given the fact that China has been around for 5,000 years and that Rome has been in existence for equally as long, without mentioning the existence of other races or cultures, we find ourselves facing a fundamental inability with human societies to cross cultures. Again, the Chinese and the Romans are both native earth human cultures and they've had innumerable interactions over the millennia. There have been good interactions, bad interactions and every interaction in between, and throughout this exhaustive history we are still facing the situation of multiple human cultures living in wide misconception and disagreement, verily nations still at war because of cultural differences such as religion.

Humanity has overcome its indulgence in overt slavery and its direct persecution of other races, but on the cultural whole there is still a very wide mismatch. Mixed marriages have seen a huge explosion in terms of willing participants and with mixed results. At the end of the day, people are people and we either get along or we don't. We cannot forget that there are over 6,000 human languages still in existence, of which 10 are highly significant and in use. The most widely spoken language is Mandarin Chinese and yet the Chinese do not control the world economy, nor do they control the world military.

When we talk about introducing an entirely new set of races, races of people who operate under a fundamentally different set of habits and understandings, we are talking about a gigantic leap in human awareness. Not only does humanity need to recognize that there are new groups of people afoot, more so, it needs to realize that it has been living under the wrong assumptions for the wrong reasons, and that is because interstellar cultures, as we will see, have been here for a fundamentally long time. In fact, longer than the current human species. You can take all the humans on the earth today, sift out the nonhumans, and among all those humans the nonhumans have been here longer. And yet, yet, the nonhumans have no place in modern society. Nonhumans have been deleted, and when I talk about nonhumans, I talk about interstellar people.

One of the key differences between a human and a nonhuman is their recognition of the myriad of races in the cosmic sky. The cosmos is routinely explained to be devoid of intelligent life in order to prop up the solidarity of the lonely humankind. Ask any educated person and they will stand up and clearly state that humans are the only intelligent species in the universe, and until a spaceship lands in the middle of a busy downtown intersection, that is 100% true. What is interesting about that attitude, and it is a very common attitude, is that the neighbour of that person, if not that very person, is probably an alien.

The human race, as a whole and extremely eclectic bunch, is fundamentally an anomaly on this planet.

There is no other animal to compete with its intelligence and its power of invention. No animal can be trained to invent a nuclear warhead, not monkey, not parrot, not the elephant regardless of its memory power. In fact, taken in isolation and put up on a cosmic database, the human species is interestingly nonhuman, as if itself was transplanted here long ago and then simply forgot, or was made to forget, its ancestry. History has always been written by those in power and those in power had it in their interests to choke off your connection to the interstellar truth. And it has worked well. The royal classes and the key dynasties on earth have done a fantastic job of destroying the human link to the stars.

You take the human skin for example. It is an impressive substance, smooth all over, pliable, regenerative, breathable and yet fully waterproof, windproof and regulates body temperature naturally. You take the human brain as another example, it can think laterally. It can come up with answers to problems that have no answers. It can manifest solutions. Some people might call that intuition. Does a dog make a decision based on its intuition? And then you have the soul. The miracle of the soul, a device that has never been understood, with many experts claiming to understand it. You take the skin suit, the brain computer and the soul device and you have the makings of a living thinking being. Give this living thinking being a certain anthropological form - two legs, two eyes, a neck, genitals, five digits on each hand, two lungs - and then let them lay out in the land for a given period of time and very soon, with maturation, this species will develop an identity. It will begin to think, what am I?

A little bit of time later, that certain anthropological species will refer to itself as a particular race, in this case, those that evolved on earth planet refer to themselves as *Humans*. Now there is nothing wrong with referring to oneself as this or that as long as you recognize that you are one particular kind of species, and that this particular kind of species is in company with a million other particular kinds of species. The more easily you recognize that the human lifeform is not an indigenous lifeform, the more easily you will accept that there must necessarily be other lifeforms offplanet, because this is one planet of many planets. Unfortunately, humans do not recognize life outside of life on earth. To all of society, except for a very small group, there is only life on earth and everywhere else hasn't evolved. These are ingrained beliefs from decades and decades of censorship and bad programming.

When we talk about those three human components - body, mind, spirit - we are not only talking about the human being, indeed we are talking about beings in general; for any being that inhabits those three characteristics, items that have been contemplated since ancient Greece thousands of years before, is recognized as a person. The human person is a person because it embodies these three jewels. Any other person, no matter their appearance, language or level of advancement and awareness, is to be regarded as a person. As such, any such person is born of a certain people and each people is part of a culture; therefore, if my skin is blue, my mind is genius, and my spirit from the same spirit resource as a human then, by right, I am a person, and in being a person I am of a certain culture. It won't be human culture, but it is culture nonetheless.

We have to think of interstellar cultures in this way in order to circumvent the plethora of problems typically associated with new cultures, namely war, genocide and cultural cleansing. The human mind can be easily programmed for the most negative and destructive options on the menu of things to do. I mention them not to indulge them, rather to overcome our historical tendencies to indulge. The new human, as we are experiencing today, the new human is well equipped to advance their thinking and to avoid the clichés of the past. This isn't an option anymore, there is no further option to do better, there is a requirement, do better or it's going to be painful.

An interstellar person will have the three jewels - body, mind, spirit - and if they have these three jewels, they are people and if they are people they have a culture where we can find many people. The cosmos then is like this: *many people who own the three jewels of existence all of them inhabiting different areas of the grand cosmos*.

The interstellar person has not been indoctrinated into believing it is alone in the universe. In fact, quite the opposite, interstellar people realize very early on that they are not alone and are eager to meet and communicate with other cultures so that they can learn from each other. Aside from technological limitations, people from others planets realize and are taught that there are other people on other planets, and some of those people are listed and discussed, much like we will study Chinese culture in a Canadian classroom. So, one of the differences between human and nonhuman cultures is that nonhumans are aware of humans and that humans are unaware of nonhumans. It is like the Chinese being aware of Canadians and the Canadians having no clue what is occurring on the other side of the world.

Imagine that in your nation you are taught that your nation is the only nation in the world. The world is made up of your nation. Your nation is the best nation. There are no other people. Of course, we know now that other nations are present but before geostationary satellites and jet airliners, we weren't sure what was on the other side of the ocean. The world was flat and if you sailed too far you'd fall of a cliff into the abyss, and no one wanted to fall into the abyss. The understanding of geography and the willingness of explorers to push the boundaries of expectation led to the opening of the world map. Eastern explorers expanded their maps west and western explorers expanded their maps east, and the world grew into a round world. And then trade began and then international travel, all of it a result of the daringness of geographers and explorers.

Today, the geographers are astronomers and their instruments are extremely expensive and institutionalized. On the other hand, the explorers are astronauts who are also institutionalized and under the arm of the all-powerful military. The people are dependent upon the astronomer and the astronaut to provide them with the geography of the cosmos, the very map of the universe. Instead of releasing the truth of the situation, what we have experienced is the complete suppression and censorship of the truth and that is because, till today, no interstellar culture has ever been identified in public. Nor has any government or legal authority provided proof that there are interstellar people around the corner. It is a lot like Marco Polo traveling to China, having Chinese dumplings, bringing back noodles and egg rolls back to Italy and then the Roman leader telling the people that nothing was discovered. There was nothing there but a big ocean and a few empty islands. This is the current case today on earth: the astronomers and astronauts who have noticed the truth are not able to continue the discussion. To the bosses, there is no discussion, humanity is alone, end of story.

Could a human being be a nonhuman? As long as they have the three jewels, yes. A nonhuman could very well look like a human. The key difference would be in awareness. Awareness is another key characteristic that nonhumans share. An interstellar person is aware that earth is one planet of many. They needn't any

proof. A human person is unaware that there are other inhabited planets. They need proof upon proof.
So, we have here today people in society who appear 100% human, born from two nonhuman parents, born offplanet, born on motherships and now living in society and no person can tell the difference. This is the case today. What is interesting about this case is that as much as aliens are misunderstood and demonized, right now someone is making love to an alien, an alien is in the hospital having a baby, an alien is cooking her human husband dinner, and no one is bothered by it. Ignorance is certainly blissful, but I here to force upon you the idea that your neighbour is an alien, and that he or she shares more things in common to you than you realize. My point is that aliens haven't bothered humans as much as they have done in the movies. The movies have largely been a disservice to the interstellar community because human minds always produce aliens with acid blood and a thirst for human meat, clearly this is not the interstellar standard.

We are getting a hint of what makes an interstellar person, only a hint so far, and you can see the complexity of centuries of brainwashing, fear and denial. We are at a point in history where we must overcome these negative bumps in the road to ascension. We must take up our bravest aspects and look at these old concepts with a sense of newness. What was true yesterday is no longer true today, unless you want it to. You now have the power to move forward with the interstellar issue. As we are seeing, interstellar people are people because they have the three jewels. Anyone with the three jewels will not eat your children. Animals do not have the three jewels. Movie monsters are not real. They originate from a very fearful mind bent on entertainment and having big box office success. If you want to understand interstellar cultures, you need to realize that <u>the universe is not flat</u>. In realizing this amazingly simple fact, you are forced to accept the notion that among the millions of other planets that there are a few, well more than that, that are inhabited. And while some of those inhabitants do indeed look human, which raises some very profound questions regarding human origins, there are many races that look humanoidal, perhaps they have two legs, two arms and the head of a tiger.

If we look into some older religions such as Hinduism and Buddhism, we do indeed find a variety of gods that are humanoidal and yet have the features of various animals. In Chinese mythology, there is a dragon king, a bipedal dragon man. In Hindu mythology, one of the key gods is a handsome man, human in every respect except his entire skin is blue. The painted images of this blue god are of his interaction with beautiful earth women. The Chinese respect the dragon god. There are also multi-headed gods, multi-armed gods and multi-dimensional gods. Well, all gods are multidimensional and we can be certain of that because they can become invisible. Anyone who can become invisible can enter another dimension and anyone who can physically access another dimension is multidimensional. Humanity hasn't achieved that, yet.

So, beyond the standard definition of a human, the nonhuman has three particular traits that we need to recognize. The first is their appearance. A nonhuman, although can appear to look human, also comes in other physical forms, forms that might offend an orthodox inhabitant on earth. But because a tiger woman presents herself to society, it doesn't mean she is uncultured and evil; instead, a tiger woman is incredibly benevolent and intelligent, and with the strength and speed of a tiger. Quite a catch.
The second trait has to do with awareness of other planetary cultures. An interstellar person recognizes that there are other planets, in fact, they likely have the starships or astral means to travel to those other

planets, just as easily as we get on a jet airliner and travel to some foreign nation. Interstellar people have mapped much more of the universe and have taught their children of their discoveries, they have also welcomed other races of people to their planets, studied their languages and technologies and rather than bury those visitations, they have instead embraced them as fact. If the head of a foreign nation visits the local government recognizes that fact and it is officially recorded and even televised. The people of the nation are informed and taught about the visiting nation, there are cultural exchanges, dances and celebration. Indeed, long ago this took place between human and star nations, but today these cultural exchanges and visitations have all been quarantined off and suppressed to the highest degree.

The third key trait that we will cover in this chapter has to do with dimensionality. Interstellar people recognize that there are multiple dimensions. Not only that but they recognize that these other dimensions are accessible in some physical or thought form. Having a multidimensional mindset is a very important attribute in the interstellar club because it opens up the heart and mind to the cosmic map. It however also intersects and offends many aspects of human belief such as the belief in death. It is widely agreed upon that when a person dies they cross over to the other side, obviously into another dimension but a dimension only accessible by death. Some who have studied astral travel or dream exploration have come to believe in other dimensions, but remain uncertain as to their validity. They explore and practice but do not realize the result of those activities; therefore, it is uncertain whether those dimensions are real or just interesting delusions. The disappearance of a body in one dimension and its appearance in an entirely different dimension, such as discussed in teleportation circles, has to do with dimensional travel, and dimensional travel is only possible when a person understands the quantity and

specification of the multidimensional world. Not only that, but a true interstellar person has the genetic ability to disappear and to reappear. This has less to do with magic and divinity than it has to do with a genetic configuration that allows dimensional travel.
What we are beginning to see are the makings of a very large discussion, a discussion that has long been absent in the human spectacle. Not only are interstellar races traveling here in ships, but, more importantly, they are already here, for one. For two, they are far more advanced in awareness and therefore in knowledge while humanity is immersed in a very myopic view of the universe. We cannot blame humanity for its beliefs but we can say that humanity hasn't taken the responsibility to discover its true origins and humanity has failed to see beyond what their leaders have told them. In this case, until these things improve there will always be too many mysteries and plenty of confusion. Interstellar cultures have been here before humanity and are still here today, failing to recognize them is a very large task. It would be like a woman not realizing she is 9 months pregnant, and although upon occasion this actually happens, sooner or later the baby is going to come out and when it does the woman becomes a mother and is forced into responsibility. The sooner we realize what is all around us, in every sphere of our existence, the less shock we will experience when the time comes when the starships land and the blue-skinned people step off to say hello.

interstellar awareness

Life is a funny animal. A thing doesn't really exist unless you can perceive it. And you can only perceive it if you are aware of it. We come into awareness through many splendid means be it direct experience or an online blog, as examples, and it is only after awareness that we can perceive these things. This is not unlike finding a nickel on the sidewalk, coming into awareness and then deciding to look for evidence of further nickels; because once we have come into the awareness of the nickel we are then capable of perceiving other nickels, or other coins.

For most of the given world, or society in general, their ability to perceive an interstellar lifeform is virtually nonexistent and that is because they have little or no awareness that such a people exist. Even they have some awareness, they are not able to distinguish an interstellar person from a regular person. You could have an awareness of Chinese people but if one Chinese person was mixed inside a group of ten Asians you'd be hard-pressed to identify them. Of course, you'd still believe that they are in the Asian group, you just couldn't identify them. If we had asked a Chinese person to identify the single Chinese person in the group of Asians, there would be no trouble.

The difference is in perception. The Chinese seeker has a much sharper perception when it comes to their own race. Likewise, skateboarders can single out other skateboarders in a group of people, and they all seem to somehow know where to meet for some play. Well, since human society has been woefully indoctrinated into the lonely ideology, even their most basic perception is out of tune. Plus, with the advent of numerous evil alien monster movies, society is programmed to interpret any offplanet visit as a threat to the entire world. That's how paranoid the average person is regarding interstellar things.

While the opposite is much more the case. There's every logical reason for mainstream society to resolutely believe in the lone planet ideology. The space agencies haven't managed to find any evidence of starships despite expenditures in the billions of dollars with thousands of highly-trained staff. In addition to the unperceptive space agency, the earth's defence systems, namely military organizations have not detected any nonhuman ships flying in the sky and have perennially denied any unidentified incident as having a reasonable conclusion. Not only that, but the secret agencies, staffed by people who observe and manipulate society behind the scenes, not even these geniuses and the billion dollar budgets have perceived anything out of the ordinary, and if they did it wasn't reported in any arena publicly accessible. Then there's the government, the voice of the nation, the very leadership that society relies on to keep them informed.

If Star Beings were indeed real and on earth, the government would be obligated to reveal that to the public because the government works on behalf of the people. Of course, all of this has been a back door wash, the style most expensive propaganda campaign ever, in the history of earth. Imagine, a government is willing to fund a space agency, a multi-billion dollar annual investment, in order to have society believe that those astronomers and astronauts are truly looking for intelligent life and inhabitable planets. And if $50 billion, thousands of experts and a plethora of satellite technologies cannot see a mothership then motherships do not exist. Well, we have wasted billions and billions of taxpayer dollars because 1) motherships do exist, and, 20 the space agencies have data to support this fact.

Sure, they wouldn't willingly release their documents and satellite imagery, and with an ignorant public mostly distracted by inane entertainment, there's no pressure whatsoever to explain the decades of deceit.

So, we have fundamentally relied upon liars and religion liars do not lead to the truth. In relying on liars, we have discovered nothing but lies. We have lowered our awareness and we have lost our perception. Humanity simply does not believe that there is such a thing as a mothership with thousands of extraterrestrials on board. Even I took ten people at my local coffee shop, and told them about my mothership, they'd think I was a clown, and rightly so, they've been programmed to disbelieve, they've been taught to be sceptical, they've been brainwashed to accept the view that humanity is the only intelligent species in the universe, which is an extremely bold concept in the neighbourhood of a delusion.

An interstellar person, on the other side of the coin, is educated in a much broader and advanced view of the universe. They are, at a young age, able to connect telepathically to a wide array of intelligent beings. That and the fact that their planetary culture has achieved interstellar travel, to some degree, and there have been many trips offplanet. So, from the beginning, an interstellar person growing up on a different planet is taught about other types of beings in the universe. They learn ways to communicate with some of these beings using thought as a form of interstellar and interdimensional communication. There isn't a fear of other cultures unless even those interstellar cultures are unfriendly, and there are unfriendly star beings. In fact, those that rule over earth are not human and have never been human.

Even in advanced knowledge there is a sense of irony, while most of modern society lives under the widespread belief that humanity is alone is the universe and that there is no such things as offplanet people, even billions of people willingly and wholeheartedly believe that, behind the scenes, in the upper echelons of control, there are nonhumans. Not just nonhumans, but a very malevolent group that wants to see perpetual war, continual depopulation, dear, disharmony and endless suffering. And guess what?

That's a perfect description of human history. Except for a few brief flashes of optimism and peaceful resolution, it didn't take much to toss human lives back into the hell pit.

Let's face it, humanity doesn't like suffering. People don't like suffering, they have been made to suffer and have come to see it as normal, as a default existence. That is another angle on awareness, isn't it? Not only being aware of interstellar cultures, but being aware that those who rule planet earth, at this time and in recent history, are nonhumans; therefore, the suffering in society, the rampant disease, the countless wars, the drug business – all of it is under the hand of aliens. And these aliens are very evil. And these aliens have censored the truth in reality so that people do not believe in aliens. "The greatest trick the Devil ever pulled was to have people believe he doesn't exist," goes the old saying.

You are unaware of interstellar people for many good and valid reasons, all of them a deception. You've been deceived. You have been taught to believe in lies. The millions of people who have seen extraterrestrials or taken photos of ships, well, they're alone. No one of their right mind will believe them. Certainly not the media. Definitely not the government. These millions of witnesses have struggled their whole lives with coming to terms with their multiple excursions on motherships or their direct contact with nonhumans.

We are seeing a system of awareness that is loaded with systemic deception. At every corner, upon every podium, from every mouth and book page or screen, there is a deception so pervasive, so ubiquitous that a human, a person cannot overcome its force. If everyone is eating an apple, you are not going to find any bananas in the grocery store.

On this planet, when it comes to interstellar stuff, everyone is eating apple. What I am saying is there are many other fruits in the orchard because there are many other orchards and there are farms too. Variety is the spice of life not limited to mundane topics such as credit cards and automobiles. Variety in cultural lifeforms is in full swing in the cosmos. The human is one particular species whose own origins are not of this planet. Human beings are not of this earth despite what has been routinely told. Humans themselves are offplanet people, transplants from many other systems. It is simply their appearance that appears to be homogenous. But you cannot truly tell me with a serious face that a Chinese face and an Irish face are both human, can you? If I take a German Shepherd and a Persian cat and ask you, are these two animals of the same cultural group? And you will answer: "No!" And you are right. One is canine, the other feline.

How can you say that a Chinese person and Irish person are culturally similar? You can because you have to. You have no other way to rationalize the difference. If you say the Irish person is human, then the Chinese person isn't human; if you say the Chinese person is human then the opposite is true. In either case, you will offend some cultural group, but what if instead of thinking of Chinese and Irish as human cultural groups, what if we thought of them as canine and feline?

What if we now said that the Chinese were Species A and the Irish, Species B, how would that change our view of humanity? Well, quite a bit because what I've silently insisted is that neither of these cultures are human, that they are both nonhuman. We've only made them human in order to justify their presence on the same planet. We were never given a choice, well, besides war. But procreation destroys that possibility. It isn't easy to wipe out an entire race of people, and insane men have tried throughout earth's history.

What I've said is that neither the Chinese nor the Irish...nor the British or Japanese are human. If that wasn't understood then I'm making it clear. I'm saying that what we refer to as cultural groups on earth (eg Indonesia) are in fact nonhuman. If what I'm saying is true then we are living on a planet inhabited by a wide variety of nonhuman races. And I'm basing this on not only my own direct knowledge, but also on the fact of physical appearance, language and cultural discrepancies; because an Italian and an Egyptian are so fundamentally different that it is impossible they are of the same race, look at language alone. They speak an entirely different alphabet. One meows like a cat, one barks like a dog, but because a cat and dog both have fur and walk on four legs we seem to equate them as belonging to the same race. We don't do it for animals. Why do it for humans?

If you start to compare Japanese and French, Moroccan and Swedish, you're going to come to a profound realization – there is no such thing as a human. We're all nonhumans who've been led to believe that we somehow, miraculously belonged to the same homogenous group of people. Once you start to become aware of your own nonhuman characteristics and then realize that other cultures are so different, you come to the view that this planet is not inhabited by humans. It is a planet inhabited by a very diverse set of nonhuman species, who have been brainwashed to believe that they are all humans, when in fact they clearly are not.

A cat and a dog and a wolverine and a racoon and a beaver are not all the same. They're not. Sure, they're animals but wolverines don't breed with cats. They eat them. If you want to say that a human is a generic person used to describe a bipedal, smooth-skinned being then perhaps we can agree. We can say, like animals, humans are one general group of beings with many species within.

The only way to increase our awareness of nonhuman cultures is to question our way of looking at the world, to question our understanding of the known and unknown universe. IF we rely on liars and scepticism we will always be devoid of the truth. The truth is outside of doubt and scepticism. The truth is in the shadows of our perception. We widen our awareness, we reinterpret what has always been before us and we come to a new set of realizations. Only then can we begin to see how our own presence on this planet is as foreign as the presence of those people in the starships. We are all foreigners because we are all offplanet people. The difference is that we on earth have forgotten where we are from and in that forgetfulness we have been misled to believe that we are something else.

egolessness

What is an ego? Ironically, a difficult question to ask of a population of egoists. Now, many people on earth do not realize they are egotistical and driven by egotism. And yet behind every reasonable and unreasonable activity there it is right in the face of it all – a big fat ego. Certainly, the erroneous existence found on this isolated and deprived planet are a direct result of incessant ego worship. There is no god's influence, there is only ego influence for no go would allows such travesty, no god of any true meaning would ever allow war; that the murder of children can be so cheap is a disgrace to human leaders.

Fundamentally speaking; whereas humans are ego beings, nonhumans are egoless beings. In embodying the qualities of an egoless existence they thereby become immune to a wide set of human activities. Now we don't fully understand ego, and the best proof I've found is that we are unwilling and willing to die for our attachments to our ego. Selflessness is not a common human characteristic. Selfless people are regarded as losers, disrespected in the community, bullied and generally working class. Why, you cannot be rich by your own accord; therefore the rich are rich because of a healthy ego. Why, if we understood ego we'd let go of religion because the worship of an entity is egotistical. The murder of a neighbour is egotistical. Wealth is in ego.

Having ego is not being an ascetic monk with a bald head on some historical mountain drinking organic tea leaves and wearing no underwear. That's a stereotype, widely propelled by Hollywood and it wasn't helped by miracle workers such as Gandhi. Gandhi, it must be noted, was Indian and simply took the format of a typical yogi or Indian guru. That image was so powerful that it added to the preconceptions of visiting Tibetan monks and what have you. Ego and monkhood do not always go together.

In fact, a monk devotes himself to a life of detachment in connection to some spiritual vehicle such as Buddhism. The monk individual takes this as his path in order to accrue the necessary spiritual credits in the afterlife because any true spiritualist knows that we are all living today for the benefit of the afterlife.

A devout man recognizes that they must redeem a certain number of points in order to repair their precious life journeys and for many personal reasons as well; and therefore takes up on a very glorious journey in a simplified existence. He rejects the material world because he realizes that that world only feeds his ego. By abstention of material things, including sex and fine food, he demonstrates his willingness to live an egoless existence because should he accept any material thing unnecessarily, he risks feeding of his ego and therefore losing his path. The teaching of Jesus also showed similar learning only that

Jesus did not talk about ego, he talked about temptation and sin; again, was he not talking about ego? Temptation such as sex lead to devil worship. Here we have sex as a temptation, not an ego device, and the inhalation of sex leads to the house of the devil.

So, Jesus too spoke of similar material attachments, for example, the love of money, and these things pointed to Hell. Well, if any material attachment, be it a luxury sports car, wealth, fashion accessory, a false idol, religion, government, sex – if any of these ego feeding devices are also Christian temptations then we can say that egotistical things are also evil (sinful) things and evil things are egotistical things. That then means that ego lives in hell and that the devil is a being of pure material temptation.

We could say that the devil is a device that imprisons you in the material world and he does so via temptation, using ego attachments, making you sin and by making you sin he takes the possession of your soul. That's why the Devil inspires you into temptation. The monk, knowing the power of ego attraction, abstains entirely, at least until he is strong enough not to become attached to the material life because he realizes that this is a false reality.

The egoless interstellar person realizes from the beginning that this material world is not only an illusion but, more importantly, it is a false reality. In being a false reality, it has been manufactured for the reasons of existence described. The egoless interstellar person, the *Stelan*, also then realizes that this current world is one of many worlds and therefore he or she realizes that he is living in a very complex cosmos with an immense technological foundation.

An egoless being, a true egoless being, comes to the realization that life is a technological process, and not a biological process. That view fundamentally reprograms their taken on existence. They no longer strive to succeed in this false existence and immediately look toward the afterlife, or, the completion of this life journey and the renewal of existence, hopefully a better version of existence because they have accrued an additional sense of awareness.

So, the Stelan doesn't need to shun sex as long as they remain aware that sex is a process, an intimate part of their journey, they do not need sex, they simply partake. The more a person needs something the more the y are addicted. We can say that most humans are addicted to life. They need a job, need a partner, need friends, need fashionable clothes, car, house, vacation, etc. If you took any person's job, they get depressed, they feel worthless. They need another job. If they have a job, they need a better job. They need an affair. They need to explore homosexuality. They need a new pair of shoes because their 100 pairs are not enough. The list of temptations is endless and we haven't mentioned drugs, gambling or violence. Nations need to go to war. That is an egotistical act and proof that the national is run by ego and therefore, by default, are under the influence of the Devil. They are Devil worshipers, demons disguised as politicians. It has to be the case of ego equals evil and demons are evil incarnate. The more ego a politician possesses, the more of a demon they embody, if not a full blown demon dressed in a suit. Or, perhaps a businessman or a militarist. Look for ego and you will find worshipers of the Devil, but they will exclaim that they are rightfully living out their dream to be the best that they can be. See the difference? The monk and the politician?

A Stelan is neither. A Stelan is a person who has become enlightened and then become a person. On earth, certain key characters earned enlightenment, for example, Guatama Siddhartha, who then became the Buddha, the *awakened one*. Jesus as well as a common example, if unattainable, and Jesus was Christ, the *anointed one*. Anointed and awakened refer to a very similar level of enlightenment.

Although these figures were much more than we will discuss here, they provide a terrific reference for us to understand the differences between a human and a nonhuman. You see, both Gautama and Jesus started out as humans, as ego beings. They then took upon themselves a very stringent and difficult path to overcome the impediments of the ego, knowingly and unknowingly. Gautama never had a plan on paper to become enlightened because then he'd become a starman. He had an inner desire to awaken and he chose to respect his soul's desire. Jesus and others too. But what has been absent in these historical discussions on these figures is that once a person overcomes their ego, at least the first set of layers, they become essentially egoless and in becoming egoless they become interstellar.

That is to say the key different between man and starman is ht removal of ego. As long as you yourself will not be able to become an interstellar person. By the same token, if we flip the coin to the other side, we realize something very interesting because if we can indeed overcome our ego as the masters have shown us we'd realize that we can become Stelans. OF course, there are many degrees of Stelans because there are many ego layers and ego is intimately connected to awareness.

The awareness of a person is connected to knowledge and knowledge to advancement. The level of advancement is predetermined ascending to your race of being. That means there are governors on races and that is why you want to boost your awareness in this so that you can be reborn as a more advanced race. Do you see the existential game we're playing here? Do you see how humankind has been unnecessarily immersed in ego and therefore robbed of a better afterlife? We are all here living for the afterlife, we are not here to see how much life can give us. At least, if you are here for your benefit and god-given right then you are an egoist, perhaps even a proud egoist, and your afterlife will not reward you as much as you think your wealth has brought you. Money is not welcome in heaven. Material things stay behind upon death in this realm. All you take with you are your valuable learnings and egoists didn't learn much. See how the egotistical leaders of earth have demonized your mind? They have corrupted you and damned you at the same time.

To be in ego is to want to prove things, to be competitive is very much in ego. To cause harm is egotistical because it is based in fear. You harm a threat. An egoless person is not threatened by an illusion. Things like envy, jealousy, anger also come into play. An egoist gets angry or seeks vengeance, or think it and doesn't do it. An egoless being does not think vengeance. Does not think kill or murder. In fact, an egoless being values their thoughts as much as the written word. They are careful of what they think because those thoughts are imprinted in other dimensions., in memory, in the matrix of life and elsewhere. An egoless person would not do something for their own gain. It has often been proclaimed that evil aliens were mutilating cattle and then leaving the ravaged carcasses on the farmer's field for all to see. Well, egoless beings simply cannot act in ego. It would be like Gandhi or his followers stealing cattle in the middle of the night, mutilating them and then tossing them onto the farmer's field.

It is simply inconceivable for egoless people to act in very egotistical terms; therefore the culprits of these actions are demons of some design, they are egoists posing as star beings in order to defame the genuineness of star beings, and most people believe that evil aliens are mutilating cattle and that is because they do not understand the egoless nature of Stelans.

It can be stated that every attachment to this manufactured reality is a solidification of the ego. The more things you need here the more ego has weight and the more work you'd have to do to be considered egoless. Of course, there's not much value in begin egoless because it is believed to include too many abstentions. Egolessness is not perceived as fun. Mind you, fun is perceived as getting drunk, getting laid and getting a promotion at work. Fun includes illicit drugs and acts of violence unless your retired which means playing bingo on Saturdays.

The less attached you are to your existence in this dimension and the more aware you are of the multitude of dimensions, the more likely you are egoless, an being egoless, the process any way, is very physical. There are large shifts in mood, body, thinking, perception and interests. A person who endures all that, with as few drugs as possible, can eventually allow some lives of egolessness. You can be a Stelan too.

awareness

What is the value in overcoming the limitations of ego? Besides feeling better about oneself, the lower the ego density the more translucent the ego device and therefore the more clearly the internal energy body (soul) can express itself. An interstellar person recognizes that ego plays a vital part in regards to awareness. A person's awareness is intimately connected to their ego density. The higher the ego density the lower the awareness of truth. The purer the ego density the more demonic a person is and the greater their awareness of that anti-truth. A demonic individual, a person secured in egotism and deriving their power from dark energy can also have awareness but their awareness will never match the awareness of truth. A genuine star being is dedicated to observing and upholding the cosmic laws and the cosmic laws are emitted of truth. These are the highest principles around and genuine interstellar cultures pay regular attention to the truth. It could be further stated that a star being, unlike its counterpart a human being, is always aware of their source. They not only recognize but also love their origins. There is no question.

Their decisions in life start according to those cosmic origins and they act in accordance to their awareness, a level of awarene3ss that is suited to each and every individual. In other words, if I were to act in accordance to my awareness, I might offend someone. If another star being were to act in accordance to their awareness they might not offend anyone. As long as we act properly we are living according to our awarenesses and when awareness expands we act in an adjusted manner, if not, we are not respecting our evolution.

The accordance to awareness and the necessity to expand awareness are very overt prime movers in the life of a star being. We could say that they are the reason they exist. A star being does not exist for their ego, rather, a star being exists for the overcoming of the ego and these moments are all recognized, in fact, an expansion of awareness by way of a dilution of the ego is recognized in some subtle manner by a more aware person. This subtle comment or sign provides a level of affirmation to the person who is conscientiously improving themselves. Without question, we are improving ourselves, we are expanding, we are becoming wiser, we are evolving whether we know it or not. Sometimes we don't want to know what is happening at the spiritual level. Truth is something is always happening at the spiritual level and that is because you are a spiritual being. Becoming egoless is really about rewriting with a youth that was intimately connected to the Truth. An intuitive child into the Thought Grid and beyond.

What is awareness in this context? Awareness is a kind of logging in to a higher network, a faster existential network where knowledge is easier to come by. A good example of a shift in awareness is from puberty to adolescence. Before puberty, a person is unable to see the significant of a vagina. That is a very clear example of a shift in awareness. While a kid is aware of some gynaecological organ between the legs, it has no fur value than for disposal of waste. As the kid become a young adult or even a tween they come into the understanding that those gynaecological parts have other uses.

The shift in awareness, the vibe, is actually part of the human cycle. But even a teenage is not taught about sex, they can log into the teen mind network and download a few interesting items. That leads them then to further expo exploration leads then to intercourse or masturbation, depending upon when they had a sexual awakening. I talk of several awarenesses because it is a useful metaphor regarding awareness.

There is an internal activation (or many): there is a login into a nonlocal network (knowingly or unknowingly); there is exploration or questioning of the norm; there is a desire to express oneself in a new way, for example, for a teen girl to wear a miniskirt; and there is an attachment to a new way of thinking. These are some of the moments in a shift in awareness. Some ascensions are longer-lived than others; some are quite short.

A star being realizes that these shifts are valuable triggers to realizing other aspect of themselves. Now, adolescence, as sued in the example, is pre-programmed. And there are a number of pre-programmed awareness cycles. But there are many more opportunities to expand awareness which are optional. The example of this is motherhood. Motherhood is a choice; therefore, it isn't necessarily programmed. Some women are pre-programmed, some women want to see how things go and to experience life without the necessity of kids.

As we move up the awareness ladder we reach things that are really unnecessary to have a full life. Things like enlightenment. Enlightenment needn't be spiritual in nature. It could simply mean a realization that a particular animal or group of animals are endangered species and then to take action to preserve those animals. Enlightenment should include both a deep-seated realization and fervent action. If you learn of the importance of God in your life and then you refuse to go to church then you aren't enlightened, you are inspired.

A star being is committed to their relationship to Truth, or Source, or Divine Father, the terms are many regarding this aspect of existence. But by diminishing the ego, a star being can welcome more truth into their being and this truth is then interpreted by their existential body and then is expressed into a very specific, individualized manner. The manner is irrelevant as long as it is rooted in truth, but ego will not allow truth to flow, in fact, as an energy, truth is shunned by the ego.

Imagine ego and egoless on a *dimmer switch*. On one end of the knob is ego, pure, unadulterated ego. Way around on the other side of the knob is a little mark and the word *egoless*. Ego is "off" and egoless is "on." When the dial is set to ego, the light is off, there is no truth flowing in and therefore there is darkness. The moment you hear the first click on the knob as you turn it clockwise, you are diminishing the ego and allowing more truth energy to flow. Just like on a light dimmer switch you allow electricity to flow. The close to the right you turn the knob, the brighter the light and it reaches maximum brightness when you hit the next click. This is just like ego and truth. A person without any ego, without any identity except the identity of truth is pure egolessness. They are nothing. Or, they are instruments, and in this case, instruments of truth

To give you an idea how difficult a task that is, let's look at the figure Buddha (Gautama Siddhartha) for he was enlightened and he was aware but he was not pure egolessness. Buddha was more aware than the one who followed him, Jesus. So, it is not an easy task this ego diminishing.

Contrary to the life of a human being that is drenched in ego, the life of a star being is focused on the overcoming of the ego for the purpose of awareness. Awareness lays them onto a richer field of knowledge, knowledge helps to improve oneself and allows advancement. If a scientist masters basic principles of science they can then step into fringe science. They can experiment on this now, perhaps pioneering new scientific theories. So, the value of expanding awareness allows a new level of freedom - pioneering. Of course, not enough is suited to be a pioneer because there aren't many reference points, you're cutting a new path in some forest. A person still attached to their ego will become afraid of living a solitary life in some dark forest. So they might self-sabotage because of pervasive fear. Pioneers are only allowed in certain fields of knowledge and even in those restricted fields there are limitations. Michael Jackson was a pioneer in popular music, he pushed boundaries and changed the face of music, but he was ridiculed, estranged and demonized which went against this pioneering. Only an egotistical audience would demonize a man who holds love and the love of music in his heart. Imagine what he might of achieved had he had less detractors who harped on his image and his off-stage detractors. Imagine if you will Buddha in the modern day. Imagine Guatama going on the Oprah Show to explain his philosophy on life, the other dimensions, the detachments into the impulse for compassion.

But imagine that Buddha was new here. He had not appeared in 500 BC that was some other guy. This Buddha, let's say, time-traveled to today, accidentally if that makes it easier. Gautama got off too late on the time machine. He showed up in Chicago, enlightened but with a modern day audience. Oprah heard about him on YouTube and was impressed enough to invite him to the show. So, Buddha laughingly shares his wisdom, his Buddhist truths to a mostly Christian audience, Christian in the sense that most people believe in Jesus, are aware of the Bible, and have been to Church more than once. It doesn't make them Christian necessarily but it certainly is much different than Buddhism.

Now, I'm not a Buddhist so I'll spare you the lessons on Buddhism. Gautama talks. His words are mind-blowing to the Christian ears. People are laughing. People think he's nuts. They are polite. This is TV and this is Oprah. She commands respect for her guests. Oprah questions her own interest in Mr. Siddhartha. Why did I invite him here? Was it because I heard truth or did he just look cute in a bald head and colourful robes?

Oprah's unsure. Buddha continues. End of show. Mixed reactions from the audience. People commenting that Gautama is delusional since he casually talks about a multidimensional world with these other beings and scientists haven't discovered any other dimensions, not publicly anyway. Other people comment and see some valuable lessons on compassion. Can a man who professes compassion be delusional? What is most certainly true is that Gautama Siddhartha might get four or five followers out of the deal and 50 subscribers to his videos. The Buddha with 50 subscribers? It's a sacrilege. It's a travesty. But in a compassionless and egotistical world that doesn't believe in multiple dimensions, Buddha is an unwelcome pioneer. He should've teleported to Asia. He would've had a better chance...then again Communist China isn't all that open to devout spiritualists. In fact, communism bans the practice of most religions in public.

In a star being world, we would all be wearing very light egos. We'd still have disagreement, but we'd recognize the value of those differences because ego doesn't get in the way. If an enlightened master teacher did teleport onto our world, well, we'd know beforehand he's coming because he informed us in a higher dimensions, "I'm teleporting on Tuesday. Buddha out." We'd prepare a stage for him to teach from and we'd inform people that a master teacher has comes out of his hermitage and will share new wisdom. Well, you can imagine the line up, the crowds, the thought discussions taking place. It's like Leonardo da Vinci was coming in to your city to discuss invention, why you'd have people from all over the world coming to this event. Too bad da Vinci's dead. But you see, that's the problem with ego, we can't see when we are blind.

A beautiful woman walks up to a lonely single man and asks: "Can you tell me how to get to the hotel from here?" The man, blind, replies: "No. Sorry." The aware man replies: "Why it's rather hard to explain, why don't I show you. Come with me." All smiles.

The aware man is present, is ready, not only ready but notices opportunities. Gee, a master teacher is coming on Oprah? I'm buying a ticket to Chicago this afternoon. There's no thinking. There's no question. It's automatic recognition. In today's blind society, a man will ask a woman out and she needs to think about it for awhile. She's not sure. She needs to meditate. She has to ask her psychic if he's the one...because he's bald. Can she marry a bald man? Guru, help me! A star being in the same situation would say yes or no because they know. They know because they know themselves. So, there's the other thing we haven't discussed - knowing oneself.

You cannot know yourself as an egoist. Why not? Because the ego is a liar. The ego is unwise. The ego deceives and it believes deception. As an egotistical person you're a fake. You're a phoney. Sure, you dress and smell nice but you've got the depth of a lily pad in a swamp.

To know thyself, you have to push your boundaries, you have to overcome your ego to some extent and to let the light of truth shine through. Only then can you know yourself. You can immediately see an immense problem on earth: If the starships materialized over a modern city and attempted to land, you'd have the city inhabitants running for the hills and the military gearing up for a battle.

We don't know ourselves, we know our ego selves. Not our true selves. And that is a direct result of the egotistical interferences of this world. The distractions, temptations, deceptions, hallucinations and the malicious manipulation - there's very little we know of ourselves here. It is hard to stay clean if you live in the sewer. The ego is the sewer and star people are not fond of sewers. They prefer lush gardens and high mountain tops.

When you remove the weight of the ego, you are more easily climbing up the mountain and you're less likely to fall if something didn't go right. And the higher you climb, the better awareness will connect you to knowledge, a thing more valuable than gold.

knowledge

The attainment of egolessness leads to the expansion of awareness, and the combined efforts of those two jewels leads to an amazing illumination on knowledge. So, we have the identity of the true self, the activation of the new cycle and the learning. Knowledge is essentially learning. The most learned culture is the most advanced. We can immediately see the importance of education in daily life. We spend most of our youth in school and this is not out of harmony with the cosmos. Schooling and education are of vital importance to the progression of existential matter. The life force needs to expand, it needs to necessarily learn and it is determined to eventually return to its source, to its Maker.

An interstellar-minded person, verily even a society of people, lives for the attainment of knowledge because knowledge facilitates progress and progress brings all children to a closer proximity of their Father. But we are obviously, if not clear, speaking of cosmic knowledge. In talking about cosmic knowledge, we can include deep introspection, philosophical dialectic, extended meditation and sole dedication to the betterment of a specific task for selfless means, for the provision to others. The lines are not clear and are never clear. All we can rely on when discussing cosmic knowledge are ideas found in higher states of awareness or what may be identified as divine or spiritual knowledge though those are human distinctions.

Progress is not what it appears to be. It appears to be competitive but underneath that appearance is something much more in relation to divine thing. We week to attain knowledge, what we call learning, in learning we become educated and in becoming educated we become inhibited with knowledge, the very food of the gods for all true knowledge we understand to be delivered directly from these higher beings, aka Gods. We attribute our knowledge, for example the knowledge found here on earth, as derived from intelligent minds. While we might attribute divine or spiritual knowledge for the prophets and teachers of some previous time, scientific knowledge is man-made. The human mind concerned of it. In the thinking process of an interstellar culture, all knowledge comes from elsewhere, either from other enlightened beings; cosmic civilization are from other Heavenly Father, as each race understand that divine concept. Myself, there is truth and beyond Truth – there is more Truth; therefore, Truth is the most advanced cosmic touch, and within Truth there are myriad advances in its application and understanding such that no single mind can ever hold out and resolve its cOmplexity. As hard as you or I may try, we will never fully understand Truth and we needn't understand it. The desire to understand Truth goes against the provision of Truth, this act denies the power of Truth to express itself as if you need to stop a bullet train while on your train ride or to study the engine of a jetliner midflight. Truth is the purpose for your existence. It is the why in why live. You are alone because of Truth. You have Truth in your life in as much as you allow. The more Truth you have in your life is in direct proportion of the amount of knowledge you possess.

All knowledge comes from elsewhere. No knowledge comes from your brain. You brain processes knowledge. It can hold some knowledge and derive permutations of hat data, it can even generate4 slightly modified forms of smaller bits of knowledge from that tiny repository, but, it should be noted that even that original knowledge originated from elsewhere and that is because all knowledge comes from elsewhere. Elsewhere can mean from higher beings, cosmic people, other distant civilizations or from Truth; and all of these regardless are from Truth. Ultimately, an aware being will recognize the amount of Truth they can perceive and in doing so they reveal their level of advancement.

To a star being, advancement is based on knowledge. Of course we are rooting out smaller characteristics such as disposition, training, chosen duty, general versus life and particular service to an organisation. For example, a star being serving some scientific explanation of civilization might curtail their attainment of pure knowledge and devote themselves to scientific explanation.

This is not unlike people on earth who live out their life in a chosen career or family structure. My approach to this work has preferred those beings who dedicate themselves to their attainment of higher knowledge for the sake personal perfection or purification. And I do so because this is my focus, my study and my life. So I am more familiar with it.

Certainly, it needn't be explained in great detail the life of an average starman or starwoman. They have their dedication to some organization, they serve society and contribute to while also enjoying the beauty of life. They have families, they teach their children and they do so, all of them, interact on a multidimensional level.

The child is not limited to two dimensions as here on earth - yes or no, big or small, degree or no degree, married or unmarried, rich or poor - the two dimensional earth society. Do you vote for Republican or Democrat? Do we go to war or do we surrender to terrorism?

A star being, even a young star being will never look at life in such a manner and that is because they can see into other dimensions. And if they miss information, if they lack certain knowledge, a person with a wider dimensional reference will prod them, remind them. They will send them a thought message and the child or student will reconsider things. And this happens, again, because knowledge does not come from the brain. It comes from elsewhere; and in coming from elsewhere, there are many intermediaries. As soon as you have an inquiry, there are a number of interfaces who are alerted, and if you're way off topic they'll intervene and make suggestions. They'll never strap you down and force feed you what they think you need to know. But, also, as a star being you tend to respect this process of knowledge learning.

You intimately agree with the system of knowledge derivation. Knowledge comes from elsewhere. You accept wholeheartedly that there are many people who hold more knowledge than you. You appreciate that each time you seek to learn, even if you yourself seem to teach, you will alert others on other dimensions and they may or may not help you out, depends on your awareness. And you will be engaged based on your awareness. You will not be given knowledge well beyond your awareness, and remember that awareness is a direct result of ego density. The lower your ego density, the greater you are in awareness; therefore the greater your ability to hand knowledge.

Ultimately, knowledge comes from Truth therefore is Truth. How much Truth can you handle? That answer is found in your ego, the root of your advancement. Truthfully, we see some amazing insights into the thinking of an alien. As much as aliens have been demonized and ritualistically defamed in the media, we notice, even briefly, that ET does indeed operate on some well understood principles. Why would an advanced ET not interact with humans? Because those humans are heavy ego humans; therefore, their awareness is low as is their knowledge.

Even if the human sells themselves as smart and educated, the ET need only realize their level of ego, something that can be measured in as many ways as possible. An advanced race simply could not interact with an average human because their level of knowledge is incompatible. It would b like a man in sneakers trying to outrun a motorcycle. You need a motorcycle or a car in order to have that interaction, not even roller blades will be sufficient. So, an ET, given this situation will use an intermediary or simplify the interaction, or simply just tell the person things and leave it up to the person. A person who respects that info and who is diligent will get further interaction, perhaps advice or direction to other sources of knowledge. Ultimately, the human will be required to catch up on their awareness and thought process. Sadly, most humans get lost along the way, they lose sight of the path, they distrust the ET, they listen to egotistical friends or they simply get take over by domestic responsibilities. But, it should be stated clearly, there have been and still are many of these attempts to communicate with many levels of people on earth.

The more proactive and positive a person is, the more willing they are to catch up, the longer this kind of friendship will last. So even an advanced ET is interested in communicating with less aware humans. While most less aware human are ready to believe the derogatory rumours of evil aliens who want to rule the world. You can see the gaps in cultures starting to shine through. The gaping holes are immense.

While star beings value knowledge, human being value other things, usually egotistical things like image and status. Dressing nice and having a business car are valuable. Looking good is extremely important in society, especially an egotistical society. We can mention patriotism, military prowess, economic position, level of education, sexual prowess, level of fame and likability. Humans need to be likable because that leads to friends and leads away from loneliness. To make friends, a person does not use knowledge because that is boring. You do not become likable by your knowledge. In fact, you can make people feel uncomfortable. We don't like it when we feel dumb and a person professing knowledge means that they are smarter than you and therefore superior.

Human beings don't like that. They should like that because that is a great opportunity to learn, but an egoist in possession of knowledge can also abuse their position, they can bully their dumber friends or followers. In society, there is the saying: knowledge is power. And power corrupt. Power feeds the ego and gives it weight and lowers awareness, lowers advancement.

To an interstellar culture, knowledge is freeing. If you have more knowledge than me, I'd like to learn so as to improve myself. And you will share to a person who is dedicated to that. It used to happen in the older days when a student would seek out a master and study with them. It still happens informally today, but, for the most part, people g to university to study. That's where the problems are located and all problems are certified by the school authority. This presents a lot of problems if a student wants to learn alternative knowledge. For example, a student who wants to learn druidry cannot go to university, since there are no druidic professors so the student seeks out druids elsewhere. Why are there no druidic professors? Because there are no jobs as druids. Not paid anyway.

Where do you study new knowledge (knowledge that does not yet exist)? You cannot go to university. You cannot go to a private teacher because even they do not have that knowledge. Where do pioneers get their knowledge? From other dimensions. From dimensional teachers. A star being appreciates the multidimensional world and when they need knowledge that has yet to exist or is in line with their unique awareness then they think higher, as into their higher realms. They tap into those higher dimensions, contact higher beings and are allowed to learn as much as their awareness permits.

The system comes prebuilt with its own failsafe systems. In order to be aware of the multidimensional world and t have access to it, you need a certain level of awareness. An egotistical person is unaware of multiple dimensions. That's one of the natural failsafe systems: if you want to live out your life in ego then you will not be allowed to access much of that higher knowledge. On the other side of the coin, if you are interested in loosening your reliance on ego, you will notice that the other dimensions do have weight and substance. The more you indulge in that multidimensional world, the less your ego density, the less your ego density, the greater your awareness, the greater your awareness, the more complete your cosmic knowledge. You are not forced to become aware. You can live out this life as you have done till now. Up to you. You can choose to pursue knowledge. A star being will prefer the latter.

A star being will prefer knowledge attainment because it is a value greater than gold. Knowledge allows them to invent. It allows medicine to advance and love to blossom. Knowledge is something you take with you when you cross over into the afterlife. Your university degree, stays. You care does not travel with you in the afterlife. Knowledge has far greater value than you can imagine, not just divine knowledge, things like compassion and belief in God's word, but even knowledge of how the heaven's work or knowledge of dream travel or your relationship to your parents. Even knowledge that you yourself are a star being when you previously thought you were a human is valuable knowledge in the afterlife.

You won't remember your house or how much money you had, these are egotistical things and in the afterlife you value egoless things because your ego is earth-based. When you die, you automatically lose the ego and what remains is awareness. A person who lived an ignorant life, never developing themselves internally will enter the astral realms with an equal amount of ignorance, probably some confusion too and will likely have to come back for a repeat journey. Don't worry, there's an express shuttle heading back to earth realm. They might give you a free baseball cap and your own shovel (to clean up your mess from the previous incarnation). Knowledge isn't power. Knowledge is ascension. To ascend higher we desire greater knowledge.

So, that is the third jewel, knowledge. Egolessness, awareness and knowledge - these three jewels play an important role in the life of an interstellar person. They are valued and respected. You respect a person of knowledge because that means they possess more Truth, they are more divine and we respect divine beings because we are embodiments of Truth. You are also recognizing awareness as it can lead to an improvement in life. An aware person is also a person who understand themselves and a person with a good understanding of themselves has removed some of their ego density. A very impressive, if perhaps, subtle set of jewels.

All of these jewels are valuable, more valuable than before, because we live in a multidimensional world, with each dimension more subtle than the other. The lighter we can make our presence, the more translucent we can become the more easily we can discover and interact with these other dimensions.

multidimensional

The status of man is predetermined in his perception of reality. The perception of reality is a function of many different characteristics in a person but in the human world view, when it comes to dimensions outside of the naked eye, there is nothing but air and delusion. There are no other dimensions outside of those we can proven exists, in other words, those we can see, hear or touch to some significant, measurable degree. We may experience the manifestations of a dream but upon waking we rationalize that those incredibly real manifestations are no longer valid. At the basic level, the dream dimension, a star being does not see an illusory experience. The person who comes from other star systems understands that the current experience called life is the dream and that everything within it is the reality. In other words, the dream is more real, more relevant and more important than the real life or what we think is real life. Ultimately, we've been convinced that real life is more real than the dream life and, sadly, that is one of the great brainwashes of the past few hundred years – the deadening and the choking off of the real world in exchange for a hyper-violent, fear-laden false world of pestilence, deception and war. The interstellar person does not buy the hypnosis, the mind control, although evidently powerful and unending does not take root. For the many star beings living within society they face a much greater challenge and is a function of their awareness. For those in awareness it would mean they have overcomes a portion of their ego and therefore the battle is more of an exercise in mental focus. For those not in awareness that would mean their egos are in command.

The ego is attached to the physical world so it wants you to believe that life is real and it wants to convince you that dreams are meaningless. The ego demands proof before it allows you to believe in something is real. The egoless person, not having a dominant ego, does not need this bipolar struggle. They know that physical proof does not prove anything if the entire world is falsely presented. Whatever the physicality of it that does not give any further permanence to the illusion. This is quite the opposite in the case of an ego person because the ego person is highly convinced to believe that only what they see with the naked eye is real. The exceptions to this general rule are few but might include Near Death Experiences, profound nonphysical encounters and, of course, interactions with multidimensional people. The best examples of humans interacting with the multidimensional world are magicians. All magicians, even new ones, are reinterpreting the world as a plane of existence and in doing so they are affirming their view on the holographic nature of reality. Magicians, and even Druids, are still around today and living according to their own fashion.

What do we mean by the idea of a multidimensional world? What are its practical terms? What does it offer society? At its simplest description without a dictionary, a multidimensional world is a world that contains multiple spectrums of existence. That is to say, in each spectrum there are people and these people come in many exotic, at least to a standard human, varieties. What immediately might come to mind is the possibility that human lifeforms might exist in a much more diverse cosmic ocean than previously thought. Multiple spectrums of existence? Is he saying that planet earth is immersed into an unimaginably complex existential architecture? Exactly. He is saying....I am saying that. Humanity has become alone because the sadists who lead here purposely shut off the areas of the brain that allow access to the other dimensions, and they have accomplished this feat in the most underhanded and multidimensional way possible. They have used multidimensional attacks to sever your link to other dimensions; therefore, have attacked a higher part of your being, disabled it and allowed the lower part (the human) to live and enjoy the egotistical distractions they've tossed up. You see the scam, don't you?

It is not unlike the deal someone makes with the Devil. The Devil say, "I will grant you your wish but when you die you will let me have your soul." The person asks: "My soul?"

"Yes, you know," the Devil says, "that little insignificant thing inside your body. It's nothing really, all that important. I mean you wouldn't even know of its presence hadn't I talked of it. The newly-awakened person responds: "If you think of such a lowly thing then perhaps I need to learn more about this soul. I might it yet!"

The asleep person responds: "You'll give me power over society, protection from prosecution, a sliver tongue, ways to impose tyranny on a society without them reacting and a line of endless business suits – all of that for a thing of such little importance? Where do I sign again?"

Earth's societies, over centuries, have sold out their greatest treasures in exchange for a close full of illusions , and then have used those illusions to produce more illusions and what we've ended up with is a deep world of illusions. We have created everything to cover up all the access points to the real world. A real world constructed of multiple dimensions.

The interstellar person is connected to these other spectrums of existence because they fundamentally recognize the technological infrastructure upon which all of this cosmos presents. In other words, the Stelan can identify another dimension through the identification of their reality frequency because each dimension exists on a particular frequency. Some dimensions are small and simple, perhaps an island, some people, some wonderful knowledge and a few interesting sights and that's it. Some dimensions are complex worlds like a set of planetary bodies orbiting a particular star with one particular planetoid populated by 7 billion inhabitants who think themselves as humans.

Invariably the ego will ask: How many dimensions are there in the universe? The scientist will respond: "Eleven dimensions." The expert will respond: "There are hundreds of these dimensions." The guru will respond: "As many as you can think of." I love gurus, especially ones that I portray because this is pretty close to the real situation. It's pretty close because it is as much as our limited brains can handle at this time. The human brain is purposely and expertly designed to work at a certain capacity. In this case, our brains work in the physical capacity. We process information according to our brain power, a function of intelligence, willpower, imagination and other pertinent things. Our fundamentally limited brain are not able to process the multidimensional universe. So who do we process the multidimensional universe? We have to use our second brain.

Where is our second brain? Inside of our soul body. The soul has a limitless brain, certainly one with an immense, if not infinite, quality, again depending on each individual and their particular role. Those are very important as well., even we may be extremely powerful, we may have chosen to forgo those powers in order to live as dim witted goofs. It is possible that some of the most dangerous people on earth are attempting to externalize a life scenario that they themselves cannot understand within a compassionate, all-knowing construction. Then again, some people are just goofs.

The soul brain is often used by Stelans to gain access to other dimensions. In other words, for a large part, the soul is the gateway to other dimensions; we're purposely excluding here teleportation pods and other exotic technologies. To access the soul brain, we need to activate specific areas of the brain. Specifically I do not know because I am not a registered neuroscientist. I know the application. The body is an instrument that can access the inner energy body, what we typically refer to as a soul. A Stelan accesses their soul brain for the soul brain is not restricted as is the physical brain. In fact, the soul brain is built on a system that gives its driver ultimate control. A person of great awareness and knowledge has greater access to their soul brain than one who is lesser. That means to increase your multidimensional skill, you need to increase your knowledge, to increase your knowledge you need to increase your awareness and to increase your awareness you need to decrease your ego density. You can now see another value to the Three Jewels. Living a life of higher vibration, as Stelans do, means learning to value these subtle and previously insignificant things. Rather than shopping for yet another pair of shoes a Stelan might practice more ego detachment and learn to expand their awareness because that will allow them to contact an offplanet being and to answer some very esoteric questions like: what is my higher purpose?

We can never generalize and speak for all Stelans because there are simply too many. In my direct experience, these are thousands and thousands. I have seen that their variety is limitless and there are new ones forming all the time. To an educated person, if I said there were 1,000 nonhuman races other than human that would be more than significant in their lifetime. So, you decide which numerical figure you prefer. What interstellar variety of life tells me is that we have to, at some point, stop judging races of people because you yourself represent one molecule in an entire being. Your race is no greater, no less than any other cosmic race. For anyone to suggest racial superiority, knowing that all around them on multiple dimensions are other people, is to identify a true fool.

A person of such foolishness should never be allowed any political weight nor any societal influence. We all exist in a vast, immense, huge, monumental cosmic pool of multidimensional people.

The trouble with a multidimensional world view are going to be multiples of a 3D world view. This is mostly because all of our imaginations are vastly different and, in our view, we are all fundamentally correct. You will prefer multidimensional view and having ego, you will impose that view into everyone else.

A Stelan would not impose their multidimensional view on others unless they were teaching some specific quotient and even then their teaching should emphasize each individual's multidimensional view. This is because your individual awareness will determine your access to the multiple dimensions around you, and those other dimensions are to serve you and only you. A skilled master can illustrate and teach about the multidimensional world by overlaying their maps over yours to give you perspective and placement but never to impose. Each person's perception belongs to each person. You can see the egotistical problem with earth? The rulers here have imposed their fear-laden psychotic reality onto our limited brains. Our limited brains have lost access to the soul brain and we have become imprisoned in our minds. We have been manifesting illusions based on the imposition and instruction of sadists and masochists.

The Stelans here are able to escape those illusory models of life, we don't shop for shoes and seek superficial things; instead, we mostly teach, inspire, empower. Through our own unique set of talents. That doesn't say that Stelans won't buy nice shoes only that they won't buy 100 of them.

The multidimensional world is not a supernatural world. It is a technological world. A Stelan recognizes that and learns to develop themselves within that context just like a teenager will play many hours on a videogame in order to get better. Their efforts have a different kind of payoff: knowledge. Because knowledge and learning are of divine value in the afterlife.

It is very likely that you yourself have accessed other dimensions, perhaps even entered into them during a severe illness. You very likely shrugged it off as "weird but interesting." Staring not far from now you are going to realize that you yourself can access the multiple dimensions, and once you get over your fears, you're going to look at existence in a whole new manner, perhaps even like the Stelans standing next to you. My advice: try your best and smile because there's always somebody watching.

conclusion

We are dealing with a significantly fresh perspective on a very old, battered, mismanaged topic – extraterrestrials. Verily, the term "extraterrestrials" itself is both degrading and disrespectful in describing a rich and varied host of nations from afar. Not only that but these interstellar races are wildly more advanced and exotic than ever before imagined. In fact, we should say that these star races are outside the bounds of public perception, both their appearance and their cultural characteristics. And as a star being myself I can affirm that these descriptions and discussions of real, living, thinking beings; and these beings have been kept outside the rational human mind for the purpose of being able to discredit and defame then so that this planet could be further ravaged by the demonic hoards and egotistical extraterrestrials already here. The UFO Cover-Up is not without a sense of irony: The very architects of the UFO Cover-Up, the same cover-up hiding the truth of ETs and their presence on Earth, are themselves extraterrestrials. Verily, the evil aliens that society has been pushed to be afraid of are ruling the earth, and they're doing so because they've stuffed large amounts of wool over humanity's eyes.

Interstellar cultures presents an uncommon look at how star beings think and also how they see the world. Obviously, what has been avoided are the typical discussions on implants, back-engineered technology and cattle mutilations because those ideas are in the hands of the disinformers, they have been introduced by the evil beings at the control of Earth planet and are not the focus of this book. This is a cultural piece that brings to light some inner workings of star people. We are not yet at a stage for society to look at star culture in any deep format, some experts have that knowledge, certainly on the whole, interstellar cultures are very new to this group of modern humans who have never known the truth. By the same token, these advanced cultures were here when earth was made, through the history of this planet's inhabitants and are still here now. That tells us all of the importance of their presence and their undying dedication to y0u and you future children. Whatever you think you know about star people and whatever you have been told is certainly missing many elements of truth. One of them is the fact that interstellar cultures, although not human, act in very humanitarian ways serving the needs of society behind the scenes.

They have been persecuted; slandered, defamed ad denied their rightful place in society. They deserve not only to be acknowledged as being benevolent and well meaning, but more so, they deserve to be respected for the advanced and varied knowledge they bring, knowledge that will become very useful for humankind in the next years to come.

Before you determine your judgment and criticism on interstellar races, you should at least understand their exotic and intergalactic cultural characteristics; you should at least allow them a period of reprieve so that they may express themselves in a proper manner. As long as Earth's rulers remain active and people remain ignorant we'll have a certain challenge before us. As those instruments of evil diminish, you'll all see, as I have seen, the cosmic beauty of those cultures from afar, these star nations.

COSMIC WISDOM 2

1. For as long as you are afraid of death, you will be their slave. And they are making sure you are always afraid of death.
2. Never cross the street naked.
3. There is a cover-up on Reality. It is the biggest cover-up in the world.
4. If you think you are not from this world, you probably aren't. The next question should be: why did I come here in the first place?
5. Learning the Truth is like learning about a real friend. People are complicated, easily misunderstood and cautious in revealing too much too soon.
6. If they attack you, they are afraid of you. If they are afraid of you, it is because you are more powerful than they are. If you are more powerful than they are, they cannot destroy you. They will brainwash you to think that they can destroy you, ruin you, but if they are the ones attacking, it is they who can never destroy you unless you agree with them.
7. YOUR CHILDREN ARE MORE IMPORTANT THAN YOUR LEADERS. LISTEN TO THEM. YOUR PLANET IS MORE IMPORTANT THAN YOUR CHILDREN. CARETAKE HER. YOUR SUN IS MORE IMPORTANT THAN YOUR PLANET. LOVE THE SUN. YOUR SPIRIT IS MORE IMPORTANT THAN THE SUN. PUT ASIDE THE EGO. THE REST IS A DELUSION.
8. THE EARTH PLANET IS ALIVE. IN BEING ALIVE, IT HAS NATURAL PROCESSES. IN HAVING NATURAL PROCESSES, ALL LIFE ON THIS PLANET MUST LIVE IN ACCORDANCE TO THE PLANET AND NOT THE OTHER WAY AROUND. WE MUST ADAPT TO HER OR WE WILL BE DOOMED FOR SHE IS KEEPING US ALL ALIVE, WITHOUT HER YOU AND YOUR FAMILY ARE DEAD, YOUR LEADERS ARE DEAD AND YOUR BELONGINGS ARE MUSH. LET'S GET OUR PRIORITIES STRAIGHT.
9. Patterns indicate Purpose.
10. Can an invisible man lie?
11. There is no easy.
12. Elephants don't use mastercard.

13. Rather than ask: What do I want? Ask: What do I want to learn?
14. The only thing God is is a Teacher. That is his fundamental structure. Whatever you call Him --- Source, Lord, Father, Authority --- whatever you think, he is a Teacher.
15. It is the will of God to teach; and it is the will of Man to learn.
16. The lion and the bird need no religion to guide them.
17. Sync thy neighbour.
18. He who forgets to laugh is separate from the divine.
19. A woman who becomes pregnant chooses to ascend. A woman who becomes a mother is ascended.
20. One cosmic rule you should know: "Never fucking give up."
21. The cosmos is a relentless teacher.
22. The cosmos teaches by way of increasing severity until learning is either achieved by acceptance or submission. The good student learns the fastest and this allows them to learn the most.
23. If you don't learn one way, you'll learn another way. Either way you have to learn.
24. History doesn't teach you anything. It is simply the noose by which we hang future selves.
25. A word of advice: You cannot defeat the Devil with compassion. You defeat him by thrusting a spear into his heart.
26. The world is run by deception; the universe is run by awareness.
27. Humankind has to stop where it's going and it has to turn around.
28. **Nonhuman** [noun] not of human agency.
29. The whole world is enslaved. Should I be happy?
30. What sounded like science fiction 10 years ago is normal today. What sounds like science fiction today will soon be normal. That's because we are dreaming forth the fiction of tomorrow. Let's be brave and dream big.
31. If it isn't true, it isn't true.

32. Progress is just the result of one thing leading to another.
33. Wisdom is useless in a land of idiots.
34. A good teacher provides a situation to gain insight. A bad teacher tells you the insight.
35. The world, as you know it, is not run by humans.
36. The spiritual is represented in the physical life. By understanding the theme of our life, even the subtext of it or our personal attitude (disposition), we can understand where we are spiritually.
37. I is who I is.
38. Listen to people higher in awareness.
39. Any master who professes great knowledge, ask them, "Who is your master? Who is your greatest teacher?"
40. The world is run by egotism, and egotism is the essence of demonic beings: hence, hell on earth. Therefore, the more egotistical your life, the more demonic your disposition.
41. Human Beings are subject to a very bleak state of awareness.
42. We feel victims of our own inebriated existence.
43. The Elements above Government are not above Truth. Truth sees and knows all.
44. Change or be changed. Tomorrow has arrived.
45. There is no such thing as success. Everything you do here is a failure, that's the impetus for awareness expansion. The demons have sold you a cheap level of failure: credit card, biz card and Viagra. I say, let's fail beautifully; success is only in the afterlife.
46. Only if you persist in self-expansion, will you evolve. The alternative is to evolve in the next life or the next 10 after that. Although we have a choice, there are consequences and all debts must be paid in full.
47. Being open to possibility is having an open mind, this leads to awareness, awareness increases knowledge; knowledge is above all; having knowledge is having awareness because of an open mind by being open to possibility; this is the cycle of ever-increasing self-expansion.

48. If you always do what you always do you will always do what you always do.
49. If you are capable, you will do; if you are incapable, you will retreat.
50. No one is above Truth.
51. This phrase changed my life but it is easily misinterpreted: YOU ARE NOT IMPORTANT.
52. At the top of the rainbow, life is very certain. As you descend from that certainty, life morphs into a kaleidoscope of confusing coincidences and unfair chaos. The higher you climb up the rainbow, the more certainty you will find. The more likely you will laugh when people hate you, cry when people love you and scratch your balls when people hate to see you cry.
53. A goat will never sing you a love song.
54. Their greatest trick is to occupy your mind, your greatest challenge is to unoccupy it.
55. Life is a lot like sex, once you've tasted it, you want more; when life's been passing you by, you get irritable; when life stinks, you buy Vaseline.
56. Moderation is a worthy goal.
57. For every page of success, I have 1,000 pages of failure. Luckily, I can edit out the boring parts.
58. Life is ambiguous. Deal with it.
59. You can work hard in this life, or work harder in the next, up to you. One way or another, you must work.
60. You can atone in this life, or in the next life, up to you. One way or another, you must atone.
61. I know less today than I did yesterday.
62. HUMOR can defeat any demon.
63. We need a new club: Don't Take Life So Seriously Club. What often holds us back is our fear of screwing up and what often will make us succeed is our fearlessness, our enjoyment of the life process.
64. Life is not a spectator sport.
65. Inhabit the system, live higher.
66. Life is an appearance, just like yourself.

67. We are meant to have many teachers and from each teacher we absorb the truths we need, for each teacher has to serve many students and therefore must possess many truths, even those in conflict with each other like a fast food restaurant that sells fried beef patties and fresh green salads.
68. America is the only nation where breasts are considered a talent.
69. History is becoming increasingly irrelevant until we realize it no longer matters and we see before us a new palette of possibilities, fresh as can be.
70. The Creator is coming. Has anyone else felt it? The giddiness, the energies immobilizing, the uplift or other sensations? Seen it?
71. Because a race is benevolent and has good intention does not exempt them from making mistakes, and failing.
72. My star friends are benevolent, kind and generous, they are egoless and cannot cause harm to any living thing on purpose. I will not tolerate any other opinion on star cultures because that is not the truth. The ets controlling earth are egotistical. They create puppets to ensure their dominion. If you want the truth, do not listen to liars.
73. Conquer yourself and the whole cosmos will open unto you.
74. Be the orgasm.
75. Jesus represented the eternal orgasm.
76. The greatest illusion of all is love.
77. The earth is alive.
78. Adolf Hitler, the leader of Nazi Germany, was a full-blooded nonhuman (or extraterrestrial).
79. Adolf Hitler, the leader of Nazi Germany, was a full-blooded nonhuman (or extraterrestrial).
80. From all the things I have seen, from all the craziness and beautiness, all of this the world cannot accept, in fact refuses. It is a shame. I understand why people keep things bottled up inside. I understand and do not agree.

81. If there was one thing to learn today, it would be that we exist in a multidimensional world. We experience existence on a few of those dimensions. The more we learn to tap into those other subtle dimensions, the more we come to realize that there is no good or bad.
82. If you always argue with a man in a coma, you will always win.
83. What is true in one dimension is untrue in another dimension. If we determine what is true based on the wrong dimension we inevitably make an error of observation because do so from our own limited awareness. With greater awareness, we cannot help but see that everything is always true. The problems with the world rest in diverging awarenesses.
84. Life is a gift. Try not to spit and piss on it.
85. Truth is a noun.
86. Nothing means what it is supposed to mean. Think on multiple dimensions before you conclude.
87. The human mind seems unable to think on a multidimensional level. This is this, that is that. Not everything one thinks belongs to the same dimension. Not every item belongs to one level of awareness.
88. You cannot seek what you cannot understand.
89. You cannot rely on the answer. You learn to formulate the answer.
90. When you run out of questions you're dead.
91. We are submersed in lunacy.
92. You can't lose.
93. Nothing happens without their permission.
94. At the base point of awareness, everything in life is a test. How much of that truism you notice is how aware you are.
95. The Obvious is the greatest mind trick of all.
96. Whatever people believe, no matter how many or how deep, does not change the Truth. The Truth itself is Everlasting.
97. The history of Humankind is painted in blood.
98. See through the obvious to find Truth.

99. We live in a multidimensional world populated by a myriad of multidimensional people. Human beings happen to be one of those.
100. As much as we strive toward improvement, we face an even greater opposing force than our strife.
101. The only thing that sets one person's actions against another is their internal fortitude.
102. The new reality is hand-built for your greatest satisfaction.
103. You are not important.
104. At the top of the rainbow, life is very certain.
105. You should apply your genius to the highest good.
106. The world is a multidimensional construct.
107. Truth is a noun.
108. There is no bad.
109. You can never have all the answers because you can never have all the questions.
110. Nothing is valid here.
111. Anger serves another and not yourself.
112. Jesus was like a society of one.
113. There's no done, only doing.
114. If we continue to refuse, or want to stay neutral, then predetermination sets in and events take place to correct the imbalances in reality.
115. The rules of the universe (cosmos) are very clearly understood and they must be followed.
116. The system has no sympathy. It functions as a living thing, one thing is removed in order for another action to take its place.
117. The reality of old and the reality of new are merging, one cannibalizing the other.
118. What do you win @ death? Nothing. Then why do you struggle while you live?
119. "Thou Shalt Not Kill" is non-negotiable.
120. Rest, all is well.
121. By doing nothing, everything is done; by doing everything, nothing is done.
122. Our thinking is manifesting.
123. Success is unity with the Source.

124. The human ego is encumbering. It prevents human ascension. It distorts reality. It creates false choices. It degrades us.
125. There is no such thing as "smart." This is a human (ego) term. We are all equally capable of knowing.
126. Listen, starmen and starwomen are already living within society around the world in every imaginable way. We are here.
127. We often hobble ourselves in order to fit in but our power comes from being true with ourselves.
128. There is no ideal situation. All situations are equally ideal.
129. Less is less. More is more.
130. We are blessed with two hands and a heart not two keys and a wallet.
131. Go forth and make mistakes.
132. A man is allowed to cry. When the soul wants to cry, it is the ego that will deceive in order to prevent it.
133. We have to remember what we forgot because we forgot knowing that we were to later remember.
134. You cannot grow bananas on cherry trees.
135. No mortal is in control here.
136. Can you teach a cup of coffee to speak Spanish?
137. There is no normal.
138. Fear not even the wind.
139. Life is an interpretation. How are your translation skills?
140. There is nothing within that is without; there is nothing without that is within.
141. There is more than one of you.
142. Your life is rendering as you speak.
143. Human evolution is guided by things such as Sacrifice, Freedom, Tyranny -- all guises of the Devil. The Truth is you are inside a prison.
144. Sacrifice is a thought implant. The brain gladly adopts the sacrificial stance in order to be seduced into yet another misguided temptation.
145. Always remember that the entire world is run by demonic rulers, until those masks come off, until they admit it, trust nothing.

146. The truth burns.
147. We are at an important juncture in the growth of the human civilization, please meditate and pray that we move forward to the highest.
148. Negative events cause negative fractal impressions, they fragment our state of being, they delink our multiple bodies. Be positive, happy.
149. Every negative event (eg earthquake) is a way to fragment our multiple bodies, this keeps us off the cosmic path. Stay focused.
150. The more the world unfolds, the more must we dance!
151. The whole world works on deception. The most effective way to overcome awareness is by way of deception. It is a way of progression.
152. Reality has been rebooted back to where it was supposed to be.
153. Awareness is everything.
154. If you talk about frying pans for a week, people will buy more frying pans.
155. Let hearts, not mouths, speak.
156. You know. It's done. It's easy.
157. You live according to your highest ideal and you accumulate truth, and you do so because you live according to your highest ideals.
158. How humans age tell us at what speed reality is functioning at.
159. Respect those things that are beyond your comprehension.
160. Let the day come in, let it enter my soul, let my soul extend, let love come in.
161. Do not feed the demons.
162. Did you know, there are people on the Moon? They've been there a while. They are observing humanity and not very pleased.
163. We hear many voices in our heads, some of them are demons and they are lying to our egos. Do not feed the demons.
164. Some solutions require divine intelligence.
165. Always another approach.

166. The word "multidimensional" is the secret key to understanding man's past, present and future since all contains the multidimensional.
167. The pervasiveness of cartoons, of comic books, is the universe speaking its patterns. Who ever said the cartoon world was artificial?
168. The basic interface between the cosmic machinery and the existential forms is the reality operating system.
169. As we zoom through the physical shell of existence, we increasingly discover the innate technological truths hiding inside.
170. Good art, like truth, offends.
171. We are once again at the beginning.
172. They want the truth, I gave them the truth. They don't want the truth. That's the truth.
173. Doesn't matter how smart you are; What matters is that there are others equally smart.
174. Doesn't matter what you say if no one is willing to listen.
175. Even you are right, you can be wrong.
176. The Fool said to the Idiot: "I'm not blind. I just see what I want."
177. An ideology without religion is more dangerous than a religious ideology because there are no guidelines.
178. It's a very simple message: Man lives on Earth, Earth does not live on Man.
179. There is an old saying, "When Man wears his pants upright, he is more erect."
180. It's a very simple message: Stop killing people.
181. I am the sum of all my experiences. I am the truth found in all my knowledge. I am the embodiment of all that is real.
182. Everything is a vehicle to enlightenment. It is not enlightenment. It is a vehicle. An enlightened person has their own vehicle.
183. Whatever you make important, is important. Same for them: whatever they make important, is important.
184. Nothing is important, remember.

185. The Bank is an invention of the Devil.
186. Illusions make the eyes go round.
187. You are entitled to your illusions as long as you remember that they are illusions.
188. Laugh often, cry if you have to, have orgasms. These are the secrets to a good life.
189. A wise man once said, get off your ass before you are dead.
190. There's no doubt that the human fingerprints are on television manufacture, but we have to add the fingerprints of some other intelligence.
191. The advantage to a UFO Cover-Up, you know, where ets are in the White House, is that Science Fiction films never become Documentaries.
192. The advantage to living on hell on earth, you know, where war is "necessary," is that it's still warm in the winter.
193. Perfection rests in the art of doing, not in the art of doing it right.
194. I spot something wild, hiding beneath me, beyond me and yet within my very arms. I touch it and am free.
195. It's a fickle universe.
196. We are living in a frequency-inhibited environment.
197. Laughter can defeat any demon.
198. Old saying: "He who moves slowly, arrives slowly."
199. He who diminishes war is a war diminisher.
200. He who escalates war is a war escalator.
201. Do not obey ego, obey soul.
202. The universe is predictable, if you speak universe.
203. Learn to see through the illusions. See the disconnections, the mismatches, the poor arguments, the repeating pattern. The firewall is weak.
204. Be willing to fight for the truth because that is the only real thing. The truth is easy to know -- you feel it deep inside your heart.
205. No matter what they say, don't believe them. They don't care anymore what they do. We have to care for each other now.

206. None of what happens in the world happens by accident. None of it. It only appears random like lipstick appears shiny.
207. Obviously this journey belongs to you.
208. It started with Biological Awareness then to Spiritual Awareness; now we are on the cusp of Technological Awareness.
209. Material reality has continually been strengthening the ego and that is why many souls are weak.
210. Knowledge is always tied to awareness.
211. Man is born free, after he is caught and enslaved he is told that freedom is his right. Well, he was free until he was enslaved.
212. If you place a man in the desert, he will beg for water; if you place him in a kitchen, he will demand a beer.
213. Humanity is tethered to a cosmic machine.
214. We are living in empires of illusion.
215. There are multiple agendas on multiple dimensions by multiple authorities.
216. We are currently entering Reality Version 6.0. It's a few million years better than MS Windows 7.
217. By my estimation, it will be 50 years before the majority of earth is cosmically trained. Or, in the year 2059 on this calendar.
218. Everything you don't think counts.
219. Everything you don't do counts.

MAKER

Introduction

We are perplexed by our own ideas of evolution because there has yet to be concrete evidence to convince everyone about where the human species came from. From nations to individuals, none of them agree on where they came from and how they were created. Ironically, (nearly) all humans can agree on the fact that they are human while at the same time holding on to a wide variety of beliefs on human origins. Now if humans are humans then how is it possible they originated from wildly different methods? Not even just wildly different but radically different.

Those who believe in Adam and Eve believe that the human being was formed from the dust of the earth by the Hands of God. Other speculations believe humans formed from mitochondria or came as fish from the ocean. The commonly held supposition relies on the evolution of the primate, either with or without alien genetic tampering. And the newest hyperbole suggests very strongly that the human race was a result of an intelligent design.

Maker is a book that takes you right to the front of human origins and discusses in a forthright manner an idea that has never been mentioned outside of science fiction. I have seen the blank face of the creation of this intelligent bipedal species. This blank face stretches so far back that only the rare few can perceive. In perceiving the exact physics of human creation at the beginning and then tracing human evolution throughout earth's history until even these modern times, I have no doubt that what I have perceived is accurate. What I will discuss is not a theory. Now because it is so complex I have chosen to discuss some necessary technological foundations that allow the human race to live and, more importantly, to improve. In doing so, I have omitted many of the physical specifications such as organs and hard drive space, as examples.

Without a doubt, humans originated as *androids*. I have spoken at length in my previous works, especially in *Colossal* (2010), about the technological make up of humans and their environs. *Maker* presents a more advanced discussion on how reality environs work and the importance of thought. It is a small work of unimaginable importance that finishes with a short article on ancient artificial languaging systems. My writing style remains as before. I never attempt to make a comprehensive book all in one go and I do no physical research since there are no unclassified scientific studies that look at the *human android*. My writing comes from direct observation and through my network of expanded awareness. In this manner, you are reading a much purer version of truth since the only intermediary, or translator, is myself. Even if these things were discussed in earlier history, I have not made any attempt to discover that and therefore my knowledge is entirely derived for today's or tomorrow's purpose because let's face it, people may need some time to accept these ideas.

Maker is an *initial* work that can later be better explored, as and when society is able to make use of such uncommon revelation. So, this is an introduction on one level because it is still an early reveal on a very new idea, but really this is also a much more advanced discussion on the human android.

Meet the Human

Because I think; therefore I am connected. Because I am connected; therefore I think. Without argument, thinking is that essential trust we all share. It is a social application we definitely require an App that keeps us alive. We feel alive when we are with others, when we are touched, when we are logged on. If you suddenly shut off the wireless transmission tower of any mobile company, it wouldn't surprise anyone that the reception signal on all registered handsets would be zero. The reason for that is because the transmission tower is an essential signal distribution point. Not only that but the transmission tower does something even more valuable, it moves data between the handset and the user whether it is voice communication, video, or SMS message. Verily, we could say that the presence of data in the handset is a kind of proof of life.

The quality and breadth of that data is ultimately the level of intelligence and awareness of the handset even though the handset device itself is neutral. If we installed a robust piece of handset software, an advanced operating system, on the mobile device and this software program could manage, process and translate complex data patterns and high levels of traffic, we could interpret that computational proficiency as thinking. With an amazing breadth of data processing, and computational engineering in play, the handset device could display not only intelligence and knowledge but also thought. But thoughts on the wireless phone network come from many directions. Thoughts come from the handset user, thoughts come from other handset users and thoughts come from the telecom service provider. The collation of those thoughts determines the strength of the network. The packing of wireless ideas determine the level of awareness of that network, in other words, determine the level of vibration of those devices and therefore those users.

A high level of vibration, that is a frequency of operation that requires a more advanced computational algorithm and more sensitive telecom equipment like crystal switches and fibre optic braids, indicates not only a more robust and efficient network service, but also it indicates better data security, fewer dropped calls, better monitoring systems and improved efficiencies in battery usage leading to a longer battery life. Additionally, a stable wireless technology, one that has been around the longest because of a well-established set of features, suggests a more stable assortment of handset device offerings. And those handsets will tend to all fall within the same range of features including a particular body type, a suite of internal components, an evolutionary operating system that can easily be upgraded and a small set of color combinations.

Remarkable and fantastic as it may sound the noble handset device is an ideal metaphor for the human being. In fact, without independent thought, the human becomes an advanced device. A device connected to millions of other devices.

Thinking, in itself, is a measure of life. One of them anyway. And that is because there are several measures we can talk about, measures that simulate the idea of life. Again, if we momentarily stripped independent thought from humans we would strip away their humanity; for thinking is a measure of life. Without it, the human being becomes a communication terminal, a device for consumption and waste production. Thinking too is an evolutionary tool for the manifestation of thoughts generates greater though energy and thought energy builds up the electromagnetic field of vibration.

The expansion of the wireless network is not found in the mobile telecom business. The number of mobile handsets transmitting and receiving data cannot expand the frequency of the network. The telecom provider must expand the telecom infrastructure, improve its software systems and then purchase a new set of handsets from the device manufacturer. Only with those things in place, can the individual user experience a higher level of experience. Contrast this with the human network and we'll see that as human thinking improves and as society generates that improvement outward what happens is that the human network jumps upward in vibration, verily the system expands because of human thinking and human thinking is vitally linked to human awareness. Similarly, to collapse a network, one would only need to accomplish the opposite. Repress human thinking, restrict thought patterns and the human network no longer expands, in fact contracts thereby lowering awareness and turning human beings into human slaves.

Without a doubt, thinking is an integral part of life that most people take for granted. They take thought for granted because they do not understand the technological nature of existence. They do not understand the technological nature of existence because they have been led to believe in the spiritual nature of existence. And all of this is intimately related to awareness. The awareness of human society, in the general sense, is evidence of their technological understanding of themselves.

The idea that mass thought fundamentally alters awareness and that awareness fundamentally determines the frequency of existence is a very powerful idea because in order to exist at a more advanced state of being we only need to improve human awareness, and anything that interferes with that awareness needs to be overcome. We overcome these interferences because we want the clearest reception, the most secure data and the longest life we can. We don't search for a better life as much as we expand our vibration to see life in a better way. The better life is always at a higher level of vibration.

The higher we allow ourselves to think, the higher we raise the awareness of our communities and the higher we raise our national awareness. We take awareness for granted because we do not know of its value. We are linked into simple lives, ordinary existences with careers and families, drugs and parties because we have not realized our technological make ups. The human being is a rather interesting object that has failingly recognized its true self and much of that sits together with vibration and awareness. And those two pieces are connected to thought and thinking. Thinking is that essential glue that all humans share. We could also say that thinking is equal to life and that the greater the thinking the greater the life and vice versa.

This is why it is always imperative that we maintain thinking and refute any idea that impairs that process. Any idea that hurts our thinking or forces us to follow a very mundane though pattern is an idea we must avoid. In fact, we must protect them from limited thinking because limited thinking will lower our awareness and lowering our awareness will lower our quality of life. It will trap us in a lower vibration of existence where the data providers control what we do and think. Ultimately, that leads to lifelessness.

Our social thinking application is required for us to expand the network of ideas. That existential network wants to expand, it is designed to expand and has no capacity limit that we are aware of so as far as we are concerned, we can expand our thinking indefinitely and continuously expand our level of vibration.

This is not something we can rationally explain completely, well, to a point, yes. We are currently unable to think in an unlimited way and the reason for this is that we do not properly understand death and the dimensional nature of life. As we shall slowly see, the once natural and organic human being will slowly become a technological and synthetic existential device. An existential vessel that is no less valuable tomorrow then today. Certainly, the technological determination of life can seriously alter a person's core programming because of the amount of time spent in biological and spiritual awareness. These technological ideas will contradict many of the common thought programs currently operating in your mental operating system. That is guaranteed. But the technological foundation of life, as we know it, is equally guaranteed. And thought is at the core of life.

Whatever thought you send and receive, you become a determining factor in the collective thought of society and society of a nation and nation of a planet. As we will see, the Cosmic System of Life is predicated upon a very certain and positive frame of thinking, and negative or fearful thoughts are a kind of program corruption, things generated unnaturally by others., thought is nothing more than energy shaped into media choices. Voice, visual, auditory, dimensional. The collection of those thoughts as well as their destination has a profound impact on life. An ordered, safe, pure world (eg Heaven) is a world that contains ordered, safe, pure thoughts.

A chaotic, threatening, diseased world (eg life today) is a world that contains chaotic, threatening and diseased thoughts. Our current situation on earth reflects our current level of thought. To improve life on earth, the first step is to use thought. Ultimately, that includes thinking less about ourselves and more about others. If we regularly remind ourselves that we are more akin to technological devices than biological organisms, if we can start to think on this level, without any devaluation of life, we will see that our fundamental features and abilities will take an entirely new meaning. In doing so, we can begin to connect to the greater world outside of our small human network.

Switching Divine Carriers

As thoughts improve, the world begins to look different, we take a different approach to old situations, we indulge ourselves in different ways and we do all these things with perfect, rational precision. As thoughts improve, we don't notice their improvement, but we do gain (or lose) the results from those improvements. And most of this is because the field of thought is timeless, in other words, it takes no time to think or to have thought. And equally so, it takes no time to rationalize that thought.

An improvement in the field of thought and the ripple effect of that improvement on the network of life does not require much effort to process, what is naturally termed as "rationalize." Thought is improved and those new codes are added to the pool of thinking. One individual sees the idea of life and everyone has the capability to see the idea of life because its code has been added.

The improvement of thought is imprinted on the Life Network via a particular code, typically born of the initiator or conduit. Somehow an idea actually is generated by a certain kind of person, say a Tesla figure, and that means that a Tesla actually downloaded some of the cosmic code and decoded it then reworked it and uploaded it on the network of thought. To achieve this amount of processing power requires a very astute and powerful individual. Sometimes this can be achieved in a group setting with the result benefitting one individual (eg Oppenheimer). When an individual decodes the cosmos, even to a tiny extent such as $E=mc^2$, a mathematical formula that Oppenheimer then used to create the Hydrogen Bomb then that individual become identified as a truly rare occurrence on the plane. Their presence, if too strong, would cause the fields of observation to become distorted, as a result deviations would manifest. Deviations as a result of viruses or malicious forces are allowed to a certain level of tolerance. Deviation does not condemn a person (eg homosexuality), rather deviations occur as a natural outcome of technological evolution.

A conduit is a selected individual that acts on behalf of a much more divine individual, a person with a much higher level of awareness. The divine individual expresses their thoughts through the conduit, and the conduit can be more than one. The conduit many have become a conduit because of mutually agreed conditioning preferred over a period of time or the conduit may be a naturally gifted individual. At times, conduits can be random objects such as a car or a mirror. Whatever the case may be the conduit is not random and is really the medium for someone else, a person who chooses to remain anonymous. In ancient days, individuals would train to become a chose conduit, to carry the signals of a much higher being because it was regarded as an honour, for good and for evil. Today, there's general fear when strange energy or supernatural forces manifest even near a person without having had the opportunity to discern the intent of its origins.

When improvements are imprinted onto the network, all of the network can benefit from them. The quality of the imprint is extremely important because it decides just how far into the dimensions that imprint reaches. Additionally, some imprints onto the code require days or hours and some just a few seconds. There are many factors for this. The amount of code that a new individual can access will heavily depend on their own acquisition protocols and all of these are determined by their selective level of perception. Perception in the individual can be adjusted like a dial on the imaginary wall of existence. A high level of selective ability is like reading the code at the code level. This level of translation is rare at the human level of awareness. All multidimensional beings can both imprint and read code at a very advanced level. Therefore, they can also imprint malicious code in order to expand any existing deviations. This is where purity comes in because the purer the code the fewer the deviations and the more the evolutionary jumps. Purity leads to efficiency and under the environs of an extremely chaotic software program running quadrillions of software variances and existential programs all at once, with the amount of interactions and entanglements at any given time the greater the purity, the more stable the system; therefore, to collapse a system, to weaken the thought fields and to weaken the network of life can all be accomplished by a decrease in purity. The less pure the environs, the more corrupt code, and code can be corrupted in any number of ways, the more likely system glitches including the eventual *system crash*.

There are applications for changing the field networks and for improving thought for thought is fundamental to existence. Thought verily determines the movement of life and the movement of life determines the direction of a particular reality. Therefore we can see how important it is, on a cultural basis, that individuals and groups are imprinting codes that are conducive to improvement and to clean out, verily to delete codes that are corrupt.

A corrupt code can include code that has been reworked even to the basic level of execution such as adding ellipses or loops of a particular color which is indicative of a particular vibration. It doesn't require a great amount of power to reshape society, it just takes a consistent corruption of the code and, along with that, it requires the individuals on the network to repeat those imperfections thereby spreading them across the entire environ, an environs that runs efficiently on pure code. And code in this regard is best described as a shaped form of dimensional matter, what we might regard as exotic energy today then again thought too is exotic energy.

When the life network evolves to certain vibration, this evolves the entrance of higher functioning programs onto the planary ground and the job of these programs, whether directly or by conduit, is to further purify the operation code because the operation code determines the quality of existence and the quality of existence determines how much improvement occurs on the network via thought extrapolation and extrusion.

These higher functioning programs are historically referred to as "prophets" or "false prophets." The difference between the two terms is a matter of spiritual argument, but on a technological level the differences are examined on an entirely different level. For example, a false prophet is reinterpreted as a higher functioning program that did not fully evolve and therefore did not fully upload their onboard programs and also did not fully clean out all the corrupt codes. Those individuals might have cleaned out some dirty codes any may have uploaded a fraction of their onboard programs, but not to the extent that they were programmed to perform. And this is not because of their incompetence. This is due to the fact that there are counter programs, viruses and created software programs that are designed to impede the efforts of these prophet-grade programs. In fact, it can be stated quite effectively that for every prophet there are a series of counter programs, all of them designed to offset or destroy their benefits to the operating system. All of these operators are naturally launched by the counter operating system, a program that attaches itself to the reality system and seeks to corrupt, consume and swallow up the reality program and everything within it.

There can be seen, even at this initial point, many factors involved in the operation of a reality environs. One of the key points is the level of cleanliness, describe in a context of code purity. Of course, these codes and these programs exist on multiple levels of awareness and in fact they exist on all levels of awareness in some form. But the dimensions of their operation, verily the dimension in which they describe themselves in a more recognizable form are well beyond the capacity of even the most capable individual, even at death for these are dimensions that are well beyond a million deaths.

These are dimensions of reality that have no description, a place which uses a language no being can understand. On a level of matter, such as the whole world, it would be on a level such as dropping a package of toothpicks onto the green grass and staring at them for several hours because of some hidden toothpick language and obtaining some universal truth from those toothpicks. Imagine describing to an outside observer what the toothpicks and blades of grass aid. Accomplishing that would be equivalent to a 1% understanding of the most rudimentary reality dimension. Still, for any person who truly wishes to see the universe in all its glory, it is available completely in everyday life. It is a matter of understanding the dimensional language for that particular communication or piece of knowledge. All of this is well outside the capacity of the human mind; therefore this is naturally restricted, by way of perception and awareness, to certain individuals or groups of individuals.

There is always a preference for individuals who speak the cosmic languages and are willing to subject themselves to technological code. These kinds of individuals are usually technological to a very high degree.

So thoughts are continually improving and lowering improvement and the difference between the two processes demonstrate the net impact on the operational code. We include the exceptional programs which may or may not be individual persons that routinely clear code, process code, execute code and upload new code. There can always be found anomalies in the system, strange variances that come and go and extreme outcomes; all of them can be explained on a technological level.

Where the system fails is when the individuals and groups are not functioning properly. They are not functioning properly because they have downloaded corrupt code (eg War). Everything within the evirons is programmed and everything that is programmed is encoded and every line of code is an intimate composite of the whole; therefore, any deviation or corruption can reverberate across all the intelligences because they are all inter-located on the same network.

What has occurred throughout history is that the individual and group programs (eg People) have been gradually directed from regularly accessing the oceans of code and instead have been artificially fed a corrupt code through various lower-tech mechanisms (eg television).

The dependence of fast food code (fast food) has resulted in a compromised community of inhabitants. The community is typically running low-level code or corrupt programs, including such things as simple as rudimentary loops and limited thinking (eg religion). What is generally regarded as not having enough spirituality is actually better interpreted as being disconnected or having infrequent connection to the life network.

The life network is an ocean of cosmic code. The only times in a busy world to download new code or to clean out viruses are times of sickness or yearly vacations. Some people have chosen to devote themselves to a pure life of worship with some diving being, these monks and priests, if skilled and egoless, will have a regular connection to the cosmic code. Other believers, even those who lead ordinary lives, can have a regular connection to the life network. The quality of that connection is hard to determine. It can be stated that a high level connection produces an egoless individual who prefers natural environments and who is content with a meagre profession and who is dedicated to serving some aspect, or several aspects, of the reality architecture. This kind of individual has no quest for wealth, no interest in religion and lives and eats in moderation.

The state of the world today can be interpreted as a reality that has been compromised by heavy corruption. The reality system is far from over and in fact is able to contain further corruption, but what is needed is an improvement in individual connection to the network. A reliable and regular connection to the cosmic code ensures that the ascension of all on this reality plane achieves its highest level of achievement in the most practical time period possible. Verily, the improvement in connectivity leads to the improvement in reality and allows the escape of the deviations and corruptions in reality.

The greater the individual understanding the more easily individuals can leap out of their current vibration of carrier and to jump on a higher functioning network. As more and more users jump off the lower vibration networks, those lower networks will collapse due to a lack of energetic variances. The collapse of the lower coincides with the ascension of society and the improvement in the quality of life because as we travel up the ladder of vibration we find clearer and purer codes. This is because the lower levels of vibration can hold the dirty codes, but dirty codes cannot affix themselves to higher realms of vibration. The better we extricate ourselves from the old to the new, the faster we advance as a civilization.

The Reality Code

In order to process a reality environs it is necessary to adopt some kind of programming language. In the usual computer model, it is common to find the use of codes. These codes instruct the computer machine on what to do and what not to do. Code can be 1s and 0s as well as can be symbols or truncated language forms with certain built-in command such as "If A=B, THEN LOOK AT LINE Q). As the processor runs through the code, verily reading it then producing the result, those sequential fast-paced reads determine the output. It used to be extremely complex to produce a simple black and white pattern on an external printer. That was 30 years ago in the 1980s. Since that time, the image processing capability on a computer is more life-like than photo emulsion paper and why digital photos are now the standard.

Life is not much different than a pattern. If we zoom in on all the objects in existence - skin, wooden table top, glass window, and rubber tire - and we could get really up close, we'd realize that behind the facade of the object there are many tiny particles and each particle is programmed to be in place. The compilation of particles produces the appearance of an object, even a moving object. The question is whether that object is really moving. From the perspective of our reality-based eyeballs, the nude woman on the bicycle is moving away from us, but the reality of the situation is that the tiny particles on the reality screen are just changing colors. See, because we know that reality is a construction, we have to rely on the fact that this either is fixed in place and that our movement is illusory. We think we are moving because of our reality-based brain.

The brain is reality based. It is not in the habit of stepping outside of itself because it cannot. The brain is a piece of hardware. It interprets data, it translates the code and it provides the individual with a sense of the world. The brain and body connection is designed to translate in accordance to awareness, essentially a function of intelligence and education. An uneducated view of reality is vastly different than an educated view of reality and that doesn't necessarily mean that the uneducated view is worse, rather it simply means that it is different. Oddly enough, the uneducated view can have a better view of reality if the educated brain has been programmed with the wrong information.

What is fed into the individual brain, what essentially is a kind of programming, is vastly, hugely, immensely important. The entire reality environs can be sabotaged if the teachers only taught from one ignorant nook and that is because the level of brain-to-reality-and-reality-to-brain translation would be compromised. By compromising education, the brain's processing capability is weakened and as a result the reality codes will be unreasonable. Society would live like cavemen. This then results in a Neanderthalian world because of low awareness. Contrast this when the level of education is properly and the level of awareness is high. What does that mean? It means that the individual brain can translate the more complex reality codes, and in doing so, in translating the always available codes, the individual will notice the deeper variances and connections in life. Those observations and perceptions will lead them to make different decisions in life, in fact, they will live a higher level of existence and they will be more in tune with the reality instead of being in tune with society.

Society is out of tune with reality because society is organized according to nations and nations into provinces. If anything, societies are artificial and as much as we depend on society and its leader, what is more exacting going on is that people are living on an artificial network nested within the life network; what is the cosmic grid that is in harmony to everything else.

If a person of some skill wanted to, they could rearrange the reality code, verily rearrange the particles of light on the reality screen and create an interpretive screen of existence, a kind of smaller monitor to the large one at the center. This satellite of reality can turn out to be a metropolis. A metropolis is a good example of the reprogramming of the reality codes, verily a rearrangement of the particles.

This is not as complicated to understand as it might appear. We take the example of a forest. We decide to build a few log houses in the forest so we hire some loggers to remove some trees. We rent some logging trucks to remove the logs. We clean up our mess and we discover a plot of land nestled within a forest. Now we bring in our house builders and we build three houses, brain new. We furnish them and put them up for sale.

On the surface, at the superficial level of existence, we did all those physical things – we cut down trees, we removed logs and brush, we built houses and we brought in furniture and it was a lot of work, and quite expensive. That is something that is obvious. Most individuals can translate that process. If we look deeper at this process, if we put on a pair of reality goggles and observed, if we put on a pair reality goggles and observed what transpired from beginning to end and we'd see something quite a bit different. Why if we could see deep enough, through the obvious, we'd see the light particles shifting like grains of sand.

The grains of sand being reading and then polished and then forming a new pattern.

We slowly bring ourselves out of this reality particle observation and we begin to find that familiar sense of materiality. We see colors shifting, we notice energy, we find a blank spot between dimensions, than we feel a coolness on our skin, we are reminded that reality has temperature and then soon enough we discover ourselves without the reality goggles.

At any one moment all of these processes are in operation. It is just a matter of a person's observation. An observant, properly educated person will be able to see deeper into the reality screen. They might not be bothered as much as to the details of the situation or scene. To a very observant mind, a brain that has been better programmed they will not fixate on the amount of blood spilled or on the emotion of loss because they will, at the same time of observing the material happening, they will notice those grains of sand shifting here and there. They won't necessarily know that these grains of sand represent two dead children or if those handfuls of sand represent a brand new car, they only notice the eloquence of particles move to and fro and as well the physical occurrence.

The majority of people in the physical plane have been programmed to observe the obvious, in fact, the more obvious the more likely everyone has noticed. To step away from the obvious is to enter a very unstable and controversial terrain that is filled with difficult discussion. The discussion becomes increasingly difficult as we step away from the obvious because each of our observation is unique. Some individuals naturally perceive reality at a much deeper level and when they encounter a person who is trained and unaware they run into conflict.

The basis of existence thus far has been compromised because its awareness education is pathetically and cosmically low. Our perception of those reality codes are dismal at best. This prevents us from truly experiencing our translation skills. We are interpreting reality at the kindergarten level.

Party of the problem with reality experience in the inhabiting of a foreign device such as the body. The body is fairly advanced existential instrument, verily it is a precision tool in comparison to nature. A tree is not equipped technologically to be productive and to build cars and to make love to another tree. A tree is quite fixed in its place, there may be some movement, but if a tree wants to take a vacation in the State of Florida it needs to be physically dug out, transported by vehicle to an airport and loaded up into a dark cargo hold.

Because the physical body is so precise, so revolutionary it causes us to neglect some of the more advanced features. It doesn't help that an education system has limited our observations but that cannot excuse our own neglect, a neglect of ourselves. In fact, we could look at the neglect of the human body another way. We could say that someone builds a brand new nuclear reactor and gives that nuclear reactor to a developing nation as a form of advanced aid. That national president decides that, well because he himself is uneducated, he decides that the highly technological nuclear reactor which could bring valuable energy to his struggling populace is better suited to be used as a museum to show nuclear technology. Instead of operating the reactor and proving low-cost, efficient electricity to millions of people, it turned into a nuclear museum. That is a good comparison for the way the precision body has been treated.

The body of reality is purposefully designed to be coherent with all pertinent aspects of reality. The body is not hobbled and then inserted into a highly advanced reality environs. This is certainly not the case. The body and the reality are presented in coherence with one another. Whatever aspects of reality are present here can be accessed by the body, only that many of the more advanced aspects require a significant amount of determination and effort. These attributes are not forbidden. The reality system doesn't need to forbid because it is perfectly designed to acknowledge awareness and awareness is intimately connected to knowledge and knowledge to the quality of ego.

The forbidding of things in this reality is a man-made construction, as is the idea of a god. A reality system is a *technological system*. If you wanted to alter the scale of reality, you'd have to have that level of awareness. To acquire that level of awareness might take you one lifetime and you are not willing to devote one lifetimes to acquiring that awareness. It needn't be forbidden, it only needs to have the right classification. Now, some technological aspects of existence require multiple lifetimes to achieve and that takes a lot of discipline and sacrifice. But, it must be acknowledged, that anyone who has achieved that level of awareness, acquired over several lifetimes, that that person has earned their respective abilities. Of course, it will also be learned that no matter your competence with manipulating the reality codes, there are always many more levels of advancement. We truly are living in a world of possibility and the more we recognize and embrace that then the more likely we will improve our awareness and expand the technological mastery of our physical bodies.

Advanced Video Game

The physical unit in which is embodied the truthful construct is indeed a uniquely grown device. The range of such devices is not fully available within human science but the human physical body is first-hand evidence that this interstellar science exists, not in theory but in practice.

In order for a symmetrical body to exist and occupy an existential space such this reality plane, the body needs to itself be similarly constructed. As such, due to the presence of thought networks and artificial planes, we naturally *deduce* the synthetic quality of the human body. Of course, I have learned of this information for certain; otherwise, I could not make such a claim for suggesting that the human being is an artificial construct, verily a *completely grown synthetic being* having independent and co-dependent thought; owning the ability to replicate itself in improved versions; able to extract energy from manufactured reality products (food) within the artificially grown environment; able to program itself to believe the role(s) it has chosen, even to defend its choice of career or goals in life; and to invent tools with which to ease the burden of existence, to suggest such an idea without having at the root a sense of inner knowledge that others don't know, this would be obnoxious and I am not obnoxious. Certainly, this is forward thinking and will take quite a few years to properly and calmly make sense of. If it took Man 2,000 years to believe in Jesus the Christ then it will take more than a few years for Man to believe that it is an android, and likely Man will do everything imaginable to deny this fact.

Now the synthetic human only looks natural because we have been trained to notice its natural dimensions. Should we retrain ourselves to notice more profound dimensions of the dimensional body we'd notice the machine qualities of our previously wonderful bodies. Naturally, there will be concerns with the realization of this deleted verse in *Genesis*, one of which will be carelessness and another lack of purpose. None of these concerns should ever force us to suppress the truth though there might be great temptation to do so. We remind ourselves that in humanity's past this technological truth was *deleted* from human memory and wildly distorted into philosophies that were then used to subjugate and diminish the Will of Man, including applauding the kill of the enemy in countless violent movies. The result of these efforts to interfere with the progress of an android population has sufficiently retarded the vast potential of the human device. In addition, as I have discussed, the plural forms of interference from the rogue programmers who have taken some human form and have gone on to ruthlessly destroy and distort the truth has played a dominant role in the repression of the human android. But those days of false dominion are over and what I am discussing are things that will help society catch up to what is really going on. We are still dealing with basic information and knowledge. As we go along and climb what might seem like a giant mountain of ice, we will discover more and more details and we will be forced to adjust our perception of reality.

So the road you have taken is a very good start and the path is on course, but the interferences and challenges will be many. If you are truly up for the challenge you will stay on this path, and it will take years to learn. If you are not willing to overcome yourself, if you have many unsolved issues from yesterday, then all of those things will put you to the test.

Doctors have long been aware of the machine-like body and the list keeps growing as science explains more and more details of our biological operations. Along with this, in the computer industry, engineers and programmers continue to evolve software code and continue to detail the operations of machine processes. As these two industries merge – medicine and computer – we will become even clearer as to the nature of the human form. And we will then be able to extrapolate what kind of person can be created in the near future.

The human form was created four billion years ago in a particular form and format, in fact, a much simpler version, for example the female body couldn't replicate but she could experience pleasure in copulation. After a period of copulation without replication, it came to be noticed that the other parts of the female form had been sufficiently fine-tuned so as to be able to add a new function, replication.

Replication is an impressive quality on any plane, but on this hard fragile plane it is of exceptional importance because it now allowed the race of humans to multiply. That meant that humans could colonize a distant planet, as long as the replication rate remained positive. If the replication rate fell into the negatives then the human population would decline and since there were many interferences, viruses, and kills from wildlife, it was inevitable to have beings die off. The dead needed to be replaced and then more lives needed to be replicated in order to expand the species. Terraforming a planet required many hands.

Throughout the planet's most recent epoch, say from about 3,000 years ago, there has remained a vigilant attempt to sabotage the human race and to try to force down the birthrate. This plan to depopulate the earth was put in place by those who wanted to restrict the population size in order to completely dominate society and to extract all the wonders of this planet for themselves. Till this day, they have used every means possible to cripple the human birthrate and they have used the advanced sciences at their disposal (pandemics, vaccinations, homosexuality, wars, food poisons, air poisons, birth control, fear, threat of poverty, women's liberation) to achieve those malicious aims.

What you see in the mirror today, both males and females, is the result of extremely advanced cosmic sciences, in fact, dimensional sciences that integrate energy, computing, architecture and matter into one holistic paradigm. That paradigm is you, not just your body but your mind, your heart and soul. And the other parts of you that you have yet to discover. Remember that being an android is not the end of your understanding, rather it is the beginning of a fantastic new adventure.

Whether you are an android, a flesh body, a hologram or any combination thereof, it does not diminish the value of your experience. What you experienced thus far remains. Learning more about what you are made of does not diminish those experiences, it does help you to reclassify them so as to see them in a whole new light. Likewise, if you have lived through periods of traumas, even from a young age, you should learn to reclassify those experiences from your internal programming rather than from your physical hardships. In other words, as has been said before, you are not your body; you are something much grander than that.

Also, being an elegant android doesn't stop you from continuing your current profession. It shouldn't. What you would be gaining is a profound depth to your existential journey and it should encourage you to study these things further so that in the afterlife you can re-enter a particular realm with a sharper sense of truth.

Some of you or those you know will decide that "if I am an artificial being and this reality is false then I can do what I want." Probably there will be many who try thinking in this manner. This isn't much different now with a certain group of criminals, rebels or even world leaders who live in this manner. The point is, and I need to remind you, that no matter what material you are made of whether it be cotton or coriander you are still subject to the rules and laws of the reality. When you incarnated, you signed the agreements that clarified all the rules and laws. Whether you forgot it during the incarnation process or if your memory banks are damaged doesn't change the fact that you understood completely what you were getting yourself into. Therefore, your actions are your responsibility and there are consequences for breaking the rules. Doesn't matter you remember or not, you intuitively know right and wrong. You can choose to override these understandings at your expense. I always think you are much better off learning to ascend your state of awareness, to build a better society, to invent things never invented and to raise your sense of self so that in your next life you can upgrade yourself to who knows what. It's a lot like a video game and you want to gain experience points so that you can earn the more powerful avatar or get the top score or reach a certain obstacle so you can defeat it.

No one plays video games to jump off bridges. People play video games to overcome the obstacles of the game so that you can start a new game with a more powerful player or you can enter the new version of the game. Do you see the sense of it all? You didn't come here to waste yourself and to damage things just because you are artificial. You came here to experience as much of life as you can in the time you have. The better you keep that in mind, the fuller your life. Many people will continue a life of pessimism and laziness. You should refrain from these players for they will interfere with your success. Be a player of players, join up with the warriors and leave this world better than when you first entered. This will ensure that the reality game will improve its functionality and the next time you stop by you will be able to interact with an entirely new game interface and new obstacles never before imagined. Think video game. Advanced video game.

Android Languaging Systems

There has been plenty of talk of the Sumerian texts, the strange symbols which some cryptographers have attempted to translate. And there has been ongoing discussion on the Egyptian hieroglyphics, the graphical language used by ancient Egyptians. If we just look at these two ancient languages within the context of a manufactured reality upon which exist android people then the ancient scripts should take on a whole new meaning, and they do. They do because a computer does not read like a person. If say we were more computer-like in the ancient days and as we evolved and forgot our ancestry then we began reading less and less like computers and more and more like biological people. Then less than 100 years ago, we introduced machines and programs and then we developed computer codes and computers could only read "computer language," special punch codes or 1s and 0s, while humans had "language."

Today's handheld computers can now read human language which kind of reaffirms the direction we are heading, doesn't it? If a computer can speak a human language, and computers were invented by humans, then it should go without saying that the human is reaffirming its own artificial nature by recreating itself by way of robotics and artificial intelligence. This to me is proof enough that the process of creating a human is through computerization and robotics. In other words, the biological human is the perfected robot form, or it can be said that the human is an android form that was never ever biological. Its biological derivation was an interim understanding of itself.

So, Sumerian texts and Egyptian hieroglyphics were android languages because androids use Sumerian codes, sticks and marks, as well as a graphical user language such as hieroglyphics. Again, Egyptologists have determined the sounds of these symbols but rather than a human language this old Egyptian was a computer language, a language that allowed the more android-like body of yesteryear to interact with the reality construct.

Today on our computer screens are graphical icons, part of a graphical user interface (GUI). We click or double-click on an icon and that transports us deeper into the computer realm. We might launch a software application or we might open a data file. Whatever it is, by clicking a graphical image, or typing its location, we gain entry into the computer. Well, in ancient days, the symbols in Egypt when observed or spoken could give the reality user access to a certain part of the reality construct. Depending on their need at the time, whether it was to go online or to upload new knowledge, the android user could gain entry into the reality. And since each person had a varying degree of artificial complexity, that is, some were more advanced robots than others, then some people had a more profound mastery of the reality computer.

After all, what does an advanced computer look like? The most advanced computer looks and feels like an environs - clouds, blue sky, trees, rocks, air - all these are very advanced technological appliances that have been built in to appear natural and inconspicuous to lessen the interference of origins and to upgrade the existential experience. The graphical languages were openly displayed on the outer surfaces of buildings and in hallways just like today where we use building names, street addresses and advertising symbols to communicate with people. The differences today from yesterday are many, but they include the employment of modern advertising to program culture to think and behave in certain ways, perhaps how to dress, and at the same time, to program counter-culture to reject expected behaviours and norms. In the homogenous cultures of the ancient past, diagrams, graphical codes were employed to program a uniform culture, and one that maintained an intimate connection to their other dimensions.

A living robot such as the early android lineages required a living language, verily a code that would continually communicate with the constructed population. This made up a kind of coded energy network, an advanced Wi-Fi electromagnetic medium that ensured that all avatars could live out the best possible life, namely at the time, Terraforming and building various key centers of the world.

An android's modulation device (brain) processes information based on graphical images, musical notes, symbols and gestures. Although primary society today can still maintain a basic literacy on thinking as an artificial person, it only means that they've been disconnected from their primary operating system and have been over centuries reprogrammed to listen to a newly built ego construct, a phantom operating system (OS) held within each avatar body.

The phantom operating system, ego, plays a prominent role in Earth's society, but because it was created it is not connected to the earth computer nor is it connected to the cosmic computer. The android avatar is fully equipped to operate under the network protocols of the planetary grid and the cosmic grid. Due to the interference of the phantom OS and also due to the fact that the ego construct is linked up into the phantom network, a software network built and run by the rogue programmers who hijacked this reality.

To return to your android avatar you'd need to isolate and apprehend the ego. By apprehending the ego, you'll be able to link into the inner construct, there you'd gain direct access to the planetary grid and the cosmic computer. Those advanced networks are as valid today as they were yesterday. If only humans could overcome their well-seasoned ego.

So in ancient times, the codes and graphical icons were put in place to allow the android populace constant access to the cosmic mainframe. And this resulted in a harmonious existence. There were glitches on occasion and there were viruses, but also there were visitors from other systems who frequented this place and they brought viruses and they tried to change the system or to overthrow the appointed leader. Some malicious programs indeed incarnated into flesh avatars and were determined to destabilize the world, the result of which is 2010 planet Earth.

Learn to reconnect your inner wiring, remember the things you forgot, dig into those old files, launch those forgotten programs and start to interpret reality from a symbolic and graphical perspective, see the patterns of existence instead of the words and letters. By doing so you will rewire yourself and slowly return to the android nature that you are and you will also increase your potential exponentially because androids come with many features, depending on your model and expertise of course.

Conclusion

On the surface, it will be extremely easy to find the need to devalue the Human Experience. There will be screams from many sides surrounding this issue and there may be a time of challenge regarding the reinterpretation of a human life. All of this is pending the remote chance of public interest.

As we have discussed, the human android is a very complex yet elegant existential machine that each of you have inhabited for quite a number of years without any serious issue outside of the personal issues (eg addiction). Being an android doesn't undo the trauma or joy you've experienced in life.

The android presence forces you to reinterpret biological perforations with technological processes, all of it housed within the context of a particular space or reality. The troubles we may have with this new realization have to do with adjusting our internal sensors to be able to detect the technological software around us. Our technological reality sensors are unfortunately not functioning properly nor are many of our built-in features. Some of the necessary basic applications are functioning or you wouldn't be reading this book. Then again we still interpret a technological process with a biological eye and as long as we do that we'll remain as a less aware civilization. Ultimately, there are many restrictions on what you have just read, as well, some of it really confused you.

When we take an idea such as life and such as the human body, we have been unable to overcome their biological sandbox, and rightly so because we only had a biological level of science. You know, we only can measure the sand in the sandbox and we haven't yet figured out how to step out of the sandbox and onto the artificial grass.

As we improve our understanding of multidimensional physics we begin to see other realities and other avatar forms and we begin to realize that if the upper realms are technologically advanced to some cosmic degree then what we have here on this plane must also share some of that technological architecture. They must share the same technical specifications to some degree in order to be part of the same cosmic whole. We have been inundated with a limited eye on science and as we open up those dormant faculties we begin to see the reality networks, existential machines and the multitude of fantastic programs.

STARBRINGER

The Birth of an Advanced Civilization

When Modern Humans entered the Neanderthal population, they stood more upright, they could pronounce more sounds and they had better intelligence, and that is why Neanderthals decided to kill them off. The old technology always is jealous of the new technology, the older sibling envious of the younger sibling, the smaller breasted woman envious of the larger breasted woman. Jealousy and envy breed hate and hate welcomes violence. If we all loved each other we would have created a space program to travel to Pluto by now and would have all been welcoming starships to earth; instead, we are continually at war, we are continually diseased and we are always looking for ways to be disempowered. Humanity is continually being altered and improved for that is the path to true evolution. But whenever we have a superior entrant into the market, the old players become vindictive and myopic. We are seeing this now with the prevalence of autism in the human population, and because we are focusing on the disease we are missing the greater significance of this situation on earth.

ASD (Autism Spectrum Disorder) is a widespread developmental disorder in Canada. Autism now affects 1 in every 165 Canadian children and it has no cure. Examined over all Canadian provinces, there can be found about 200,000 children afflicted with a disease that has no cure. In other words, to make the point, children born handicapped. Sure, the last thing a parent wants to hear is that their child is handicapped, but if you have a medical condition that cannot be cured (eg feeble arms) then that is a handicap. Now, I push the terms a little because I don't believe that autism has been properly interpreted, for one. For two, a population of 200,000 children is significant enough to suggest the emergence of an entirely different kind of entity: a culture. What if autism is the emergence of a new human being? Are we witnessing the birth of an entirely new human, given also that autism rates have grown dramatically and are primarily found in children? Because those two pieces - large population and prevalence in children - is scientific evidence.

The human brain is prone to examine things from within its level of understanding, likely inside a certain box and it tries to make sense of the world within those confines. Should we look outside the box and accept the possibility that autism is not a disease, we would discover a misinterpretation of an entirely unfamiliar human-looking culture. We are witnessing a major biological shift on earth, among our own species and we are condemning a new culture rather than admitting its possible brilliance. We are interpreting an advanced culture with our primitive concepts (eg human is the highest standard of existence) and we're looking for disease (or disorder) instead of remarkable characteristics. The autistic child, it is usually noted, has some exceptional skills, skills that only a robot might possess.

We've seen this misinterpretation before in human history, haven't we? They burned witches. They experimented on the mentally ill in sanatoriums. They enslaved black people. They slaughtered the Jews. Human thinking tends toward the removal of totally unfamiliar things that contradict standard (orthodox) thinking. We will cut out cancer instead of using an alternative healing method. Today, we are rooting out terrorists. We are looking for domestic threats. Recently, there was an attempt to make extreme shyness into a disease.

The autistic android

The significance of this new human culture is so significant that it isn't a surprise to see human science unable to overcome its myopic diagnosis. It is myopia that is causing educated and highly specialized medical and behavioural doctors to interpret a key set of symptoms as a disease. Rather than see disease and in order to overcome the negative habits of the past, I'd like to point out that the autistic child, most certainly the severe case, is a new life form on earth. This is the more *advanced* model and illustrates the core principle of humanity: artificiality.

In its purest state, the human form was manufactured using synthetic components. These components were so advanced that they appeared to be biological, but they weren't at all biological, they were indeed artificial. Verily, that is the origin of this entire race of beings, at point zero there were two androids. At the end of each epoch, those androids would also be transformed and upgraded so that the next epoch would be populated by a more advanced android series.

Throughout the epochs these are opportunities to ascend and to upgrade oneself and in doing so the person becomes an improved version, a more perfect being. This form of study became so important and vital that people would devote their entire life so as to be able to ascend, so that upon the end of their term they'd have reached a state of mind that would ensure their travel across the lake of death, and if they could endure the journey in the afterlife they would earn the respect of the dimensional guardians. That would grant them a pass into a life of their choosing. Again, they'd repeat the devotion, purify themselves and ascend again. Several lifetimes later, after helping a large number of others during their spiritual growth, the people would reach a point closer to their creator, a point where they've purified their energy and entered the purer realms of existence.

The presence of advanced androids (already quite perfect), currently denoted by a developmental disorder, on earth affirms the grand shift in the reality time machine because the latest human models, which aren't really human anymore, are needed to maintain the operations of the new reality. The kind of future we're about to enter is a science fiction future, but we have to remember that we're not in any decent level of awareness so typical things still look typical, even though they're not.

Autistic children are not typical. By detailing their symptoms and by applying intensive therapies to aid their development, the medical scientists confirm the significance of their presence only that they've misdiagnosed advanced life form technology for a human spectrum disorder. So, it is a sad case if we notice their misinterpretation. It is, unfortunately, accepted given the oppression of cosmic knowledge here.

An android is a high functioning operational device and because it functions on a very sensitive and subtle operative level it is prone to performance fluctuations. An autistic child has to live inside a very polluted world. Not only is our food, air and water polluted, but also because we live in a technological realm (see other essays on this) there are multiple technological interferences (eg existential programs, existential implants, existential Trojan viruses). The purer the android, such as the autistic child, encounters these existential programs directly and this interferes with their sensitive instrumentation (even their external programming). But remember, the android child appears 100% biological and the reason for this is because biology is itself a technology, one so advanced that it is well beyond our reach or understanding.

An advanced cycle

Ultimately, the presence of 200,000 functioning android children in Canada (and many more across the planet) is a solid sign that we have entered the new age, a cycle launched in March 2007 and a cycle that will last a few thousand years (about 3,000 years). So it is significant in many ways. To maintain a healthy existential system, we require a robot population of about one-third (33%). Other advanced civilizations follow this principle in their own fashion and have synthetic groups of androids, but we're going to experience the birth of an advanced civilization. Yes, here.

In order to anticipate an influx of advanced ideas, solutions, knowledge and devices we're going to have to advance our thinking. We are going to have to re-examine unusual circumstances and events. We're going to have to look at the growth of autism and notice the birth of a technologically advanced culture; that look seamlessly human.

In doing so, in looking at typical things in an advanced way we begin to better understand our own origin and we are better able to utilize the abundance of technology already within society, accessible today. And, we'll see that we need to train ourselves as well in cosmic tasks. And all of this stuff; all of this advanced stuff is going to redevelop a tired earth and to awaken the cosmic serpent from within. We have to, as soon as possible, recognize the advanced age we are in and to remember that the scale of progress at these historical times are going to be immense.

Autism is not a handicap

We could see starship factories in 24 months and the end of gasoline engines. Within 5 years, we could have regular charters to Mars. It is on this scale that life is possible as long as we can wake up our inner faculties and adopt an advanced mindset to replace the depressed, fearful mindset our oppressors have provided us till now. Yes, we need to adopt advanced thinking and one way to do so is to recognize that the various children who have been diagnosed with social developmental disorders are not handicapped, they represent the future of earth. Imagine if man invented a living robot that looked identical to a human. Would we cherish that artificial being or would be provide for it intensive therapy and medication in order to make it more human? See the lunacy?

Well, it's true that man hasn't yet created a synthetic human, at least not in public because certainly some secure labs were well equipped for these things and likely have manufactured some lesser advanced models. Or even clones who were android in nature. Outside of that even more confusing discussion, man isn't at par with starman science which is what is behind the birth of androids. Actually, it is the return of androids.

Without discussing other signs of the emergence of a super advanced age, by focusing exclusively here on autistic children, 200,000 of them in Canada, we note two fundamental pieces of evidence. One, they are primarily children. That means that they have entered in the last 10 years (or so) and that means they were born in anticipation of this time here now. Two, the size of autistic children has been growing since then and has literally exploded in recent years, especially since we've turned our medicine on spotting symptoms. Regardless, 200,000 in Canada alone are significant. Two hundred thousand people eating Wonton Soup is significant. That's a demographic. That's a new culture, 200,000 strong. My interpretation of that culture is android culture. And androids on earth in this quantity mean one thing: advanced civilization.

To access it, we need to first recognize it. Once we recognize it, we can learn to distinguish it from the typical. But we need to move fast because our oppressors will do everything they can to obfuscate and disguise the truth. They'll inject untold vaccines into their bodies and cause all kinds of malfunction, even damage to their genetic programming. So, none of this must be taken lightly and all of it should be discussed by smart minds. One thing is very true, the cosmos is a technological wonder and anything that comes out of it, including humanity and planet earth is not natural, it is manufactured by cosmic factories.

The Tyrant Wears a Suit and Tie

The Tyrant wears a suit and tie. He wears the smile of a bisexual madman but his eloquent speech calms anxiety by the boatload of rhetoric, false promise and picture perfect delivery. For Tyranny is best described as an oppressive force of polite behaviour disguising the malicious intent of demonic entities, beings from other planes of existence.

The force of humanity, the pure soul and the sacred heart, these parts making up a person, they are incapable of Tyranny. They can be subjected to Tyranny but these human people here cannot create Tyranny. They simply cannot and I'll tell you why: the human soul in all its varieties is far too pure to achieve such a thing. They can be subjects to Tyrannical leaders but they themselves are far too innocent to extract goodness from others for the sake of their own bloated ego, as demons do.

The Creator of the human soul is all benevolent. His energy is divinely pure, untainted in perpetuity. In this way, the Children of the Creator, imbued with this pure energy cannot push Tyranny because Tyranny requires deception and deceit. Tyranny requires malevolent intent. It demands egotism to the extreme, and we now know that Hell is home of pure ego. Tyranny is a child who would order the death of his parents. It is like a child because Tyranny is blinded by ego and ego is the tool of the Devil. The most egotistical beings on earth are demonic beings and the most dangerous ones are wearing human masks.

And demonic beings have the will and capacity for Tyranny. Why do we speak of Tyranny, this invisible stream of slavery? We speak of Tyranny because it is upon us and has been for a while. That means, without question, the exclusive involvement of both demons and malevolent nonhumans (other dimensional forms). Whoever is in charge, whatever the administration council, they are made up of demons and malevolent nonhumans in human form, in tailored, dark suits. They have direct access to the mainstream media and speak polite superficial TV language where every sentence includes the word "terrific," and every guest is airbrushed to hide the truth. In fact, television is a great metaphor for widespread deceit for it disguises everything truthful. You cannot speak the truth on TV, they won't let you and if you do, if they allow you on, they will thrust a spear into the remnants of your life. But, most of all, the TV demands truth because the viewers demand it. Imagine I spoke of demons on TV, imagine the farce and yet what I speak of is but a fraction of the vulgar reality. If you accepted the fact that a demon in human form would drink the blood of your child you would not sit idle. So, you are lucky, you are lucky you cannot yet see the demons as I do, and others. Soon, many of us will see and we will have to reconcile a lifetime of idle behaviour.

That is why we are now needed to re-examine who exactly is fronting this satanic road to Tyranny. Who are the newly-versed societal florists? When Mussolini ruled over Italians he did so in a very overt, strong-handed style. He was a militarist and after all and that is far from an image of today's fascist leader. You see not only is a leader imbued demonically to some degree, but, more importantly, today's leaders are given a friendly, respectful public persona. No matter what a leader faces, they'll always hold steady. And they can do because of their demonic friends. These dimensional negative entities (DNEs) can provide a leader with an anchor to their being by supplying him with an appropriate amount of energy. No matter what happens, a demonic leader can remain in power because of this magic. As well, the controlled leader will increasingly follow the commands of the demonic brotherhood, or their sorcerer representatives. And when a pure hearted leader speaks, the demons will destabilize him or her, they will cloud their minds and infect them with negativity or anger.

The chimera tyrant

An educated society steeped in historical domination and societal engineering cannot be ruled over by any of the previous forms of Tyranny (eg George W. Bush). There are too many examples to study and the Tyrant, whoever is positioned in that illuminated role, would be discovered and disqualified in any number of ways. The only way to fool an educated populace is to create a Chimera Tyrant, a Tyrant that has several different faces so as to satisfy the discerning views of smart people and scholarly individuals. A Chimera Tyrant is effective because the hybrid Tyrant now preys upon human beliefs. If you wish to see the strength of a lion, that facade will present itself. If you wish the strength of character to family, that facet will reveal itself for it has many faces and the human mind has only a two-dimensional view.

The Chimera Tyrant has multiple facets: The head of a lion, the body of a bear, the hooves of a goat, the tail of an eagle, the eyes of a human. They construct a Chimera like alchemists and fringe scientists would construct things in a lab. Of course, since we are dealing with people, you'd need the kind of soul that could be hybridized without killing it, we would need

special cases. We have to remember, this has been done before, only that previous Tyrants have failed because they're dead. Today's Chimera Tyrant would have the ability to portray a happy family structure while at the same time insisting that war is necessary or a financial restructuring is good for all. A Chimera Tyrant would appeal to common folk because it has the skin of many folk. Verily, this kind of leadership is silent in its method of societal strangulation. No man, woman or child would realize what has happened until they've already accepted many humans into their den who have made sacrifices and by then the Tyrant would be needed to carry out the remainder of their insanity. And the love of the people would be right behind them in support.
We have to continually remind ourselves of the way things work in the other dimensions. You have multiple aspects of yourself in other dimensions. Probably, you are only aware of this dimension and may or may not believe the hallucinations you may or may not have had in other dimensions. Therefore, to a person in low awareness, what happens in another dimension is unknown and irrelevant. Even I take you to another dimension and you are not ready, you will deny the experience. You will erase it. If you are ready, you will find your own path, so if you still don't know it is because you are not ready and if you know, I needn't give you any proof. Confusing isn't it? The system is designed to weed out learning by using awareness. If you are brave and willing, you will redefine your awareness and you will see. If you are sceptical and logical, you will wait for proof and you will die in a low awareness for the level of awareness in the cosmos is unimaginable and human awareness is pitiful. So there are many challenges right there.

The Chimera Tyrant, because it is an egotistical aberration, a defiance against the Creator, is a very dangerous device that will undermine the health of any or all nations. It is a kind of administrative virus that infects society with amazing contradictions like "Let me continue my war and I'll give you a few jobs," or "My wife is the boss of the household, but I'm the chief of entire armies," and, "As much as it pains me to use the people's money to prop up my elitist buddies, in the end you'll all thank me for doing it." You can see the danger in these statements such as the fact that war is murder and improving unemployment by way of murder is not a very compassionate strategy, but people buy it. Heck, if you promise to save someone's house they will likely sell you their unborn child.

Woefully, the Chimera Tyrant will give nothing to society. It is a vampire led by vampires who all want to drink the blood of the people. Further, he is hard to spot because he's a leader who is a well-dressed, well spoken without any personal ambition and a dedicated employee of his (or her) country. He knows what to do because his puppeteers (advisors, council, specialists) tell him what to say and which side to be on.

The Chimera Tyrant is powerful because he follows a script written by advanced script writers who themselves are tapped into the demon network. He can change laws because a dark-skinned person wasn't wearing matching socks and therefore was considered a danger to society. And, strangely, society would buy his insane ideas because society will have just survived a previous cataclysmic event and they'll believe that Britney Spears is a singer. This kind of leader is not a leader; he is a robot, like any good prize fighter. His trainers tell him to jab, he jabs. A true leader speaks from the heart and he empowers society. A Chimera Tyrant disembowels society.

Tyranny from other dimensions

All of this will be unavailable to the naked eye. Those who can see these demons will likely be very frightened because they can be found all over the place. In this regard, the demon-ruler cannot be removed by voting him out, he cannot be killed and he cannot be swayed. The only way to stop the Tyrant would be for him to act against his puppeteers, which is nearly impossible at this point. It is impossible because when the leader got into bed with demons, he did so accepting his situation. He likely did so with the promises that he would be able to achieve some grand dream. But as soon as his soul took on the demonic energy, the outcomes shifted, the agreement took over.

Each step forward shifted the original promise he believed, so much so that his dreams literally disappeared and he became burdened by his present circumstances. It is a bit of a sad story but also true of the human ego in that it always underestimates the magnitude of the dimensional entities. The ego will convince a man to jump out of a flying airplane. It will convince a believer to molest a child and to serve a maniac all in the sake of devotion or patriotism. But when the ego of a leader negotiates with demons disguised as industrialists, politicians and friends, that leader is transformed into a Hitler character. Whether they wear a suit and tie or a military outfit isn't important. Behind the flesh, his soul is on an entirely different path. When you couple this situation with a society devoid of spirituality, trapped in logic, and having orgasms with its ego, those who would laugh at these ideas, you get slaves. That's what we here have. It isn't the fact that humans haven't the power to overcome the demonic forces because that isn't the case. The problem is that they are so egotistical and smart that they will laugh at this.

So, Tyranny is not what we've been led to believe, is it? That's because we've been missing the dimensional element. Humans all look human on the surface, but underneath and in-between there is much more going on. That may be why some say that Tyranny is invisible. It is. It is taking place on other dimensions and to overcome what is before humanity now, it demands that people turn off their ego and see the filth that is raping their children. Bishops and Popes don't rape children repeatedly, demons do. Demonic entities in control of sacred individuals and religious leaders suggest another extremely powerful implication of the religious institution, for a demon to gain control of a church on a large scale tells us that this is no Church of God, rather, this is a Church of Satan disguised as a Church of God for no man who embodies Truth can embody a demon.

That's another piece of evidence to tell us all that even the head of the church is demonic. And if we continue to look for oppression, ego, and suppression we will find quite a bit more; and that will tell us that we need to employ a multidimensional strategy in order to emancipate ourselves from thousands of years of slavery. Do not sell your soul for anything for its value is resplendent. Hang onto your soul for the rest of your life and accept no gift in exchange for egotistical promise. Yes, it is true that everything is in divine order, and yes it is true that if humanity doesn't get it soon the results are going to be quite dismal. Trusting in God does not mean sitting at home eating popcorn waiting for the Messiah to clean your toilet. Trusting in a Creator means acting in the highest manner possible, wearing the bravest face you know and not complaining about things that are not in your power to change.

The Creator is always doing his part and that means that he expects you to always do yours, and if not, he's watching and he's making a list, checking it twice, going to find out who's naughty or nice, the Creator is coming to town!

This Force Against

Let's clear this up: There is a force against you. All of you. Everyone who is standing up for the truth. Everyone who wants a change for the better. Everyone who innocently believes that God will save them. Here's some news: There is a force against you.

The troubling aspect of this force is that it appears in many forms and formats. It appears as a well-spoken President and as well appears as a Haitian earthquake. This force can be embedded in your psyche causing you to perennially doubt yourself and as well it can be telling you that you need to buy aspartame in order to reduce your caloric intake. This force is deceptive because it has no remarkable face in this physical dimension. In other dimensions it appears in a very clear format. In this physical dimension, bound by logic and reason, it appears in many forms and formats, and this is why your cosmic dance partner is a troubling force. It is troubling because I am unable to identify all of its characteristics in a formula so that more of you will not only see the face of your partner but also you will start dancing.

I tell you the big problem with this newest wave of enlightenment: we seem to believe that we've achieved nirvana when we feel love and compassion. Well, guess what? We haven't achieved all that much. It can be said that Guatama Sidhartha attained pure enlightenment and his teachings on pure compassion and blissful awareness are legendary, and extremely useful: But, (the) Buddha ("the awakened one") did not stick around to see the spread of this force against you. When he was around, this nasty force was in a child state, but because of human degradation and egotism, this force has been blown way out of proportion.

Perhaps the many of you will question if I am fit to discuss this sort of thing to which I will answer, "Yes." And then I will add: "No one else can (or will) step out of their compassion long enough to admit the truth." The truth is that this nasty force is against you now. If you try to sell truth, you will feel the brunt of this force. If you try to astral travel to discover who really hit Haiti and with what weapon, this force will strike you. If you speak about benevolent interstellar folk and the UFO Cover-Kabob, this force will manifest in your life. If you just sit and wait for Jesus, you may never feel this nasty force. Life's troubles will keep you preoccupied. And, interestingly, this force has figured out a way to seduce humanity into never looking outside the box.

It and its minions made the bulk of humans drunk on their own ego and filled their minds with egotistical chains: looking fabulous, being politically correct, overcoming erectile dysfunction, losing weight, having coffee before you wake up, making teeth whiter than white, finding soul mates, winning imaginary wars, scaring society at every turn, reducing the human mind into rabbit dribbles, anticipating the next discovery of water molecules on some distant planetary body, and boasting the self-serving needs of a self-elected, secret societal group of bozos who pretend to be leader-like in their fancy new suits, protected by a score of high-paid lawyers and demons.

It irks me to repeat the fact that the only way to move forward is to move forward. It irks me to repeat that. I have done everything to express that one simple fact. I have begged, yelled, demanded, pleaded and explained that in order to move forward we all need to sweat. I am not pleased with the result but I understand the hoard of temptations around you. It does not justify our state of defeatism and unwillingness to sacrifice a bit more than we are used to. Why I include this again is because I think perhaps I have failed to express that there is a very resilient nasty force against all your actions for ascension, seen, unseen and otherwise. For every action into ascension, there is a force against. A very nasty force against. If you have not felt it, it is like because you haven't ascended all that much and have not made an appearance on any secret radar; something which you probably prefer, anonymity. Some of you have sneaked around remote viewing this and that and kept that information to yourselves, again nothing all that impressive really. You basically think you are smarter than most because you know this and that. In my view, you are wasting your time hoarding knowledge and not putting it use.

Immanuel Kant, a famous philosopher, discussed *enlightenment* in a way that I like. Most people interpret enlightenment as becoming more aware of yourself and having a greater sense of the infinite world around you, seeing how it all fits together. Kant looked at it more deeply, he said that enlightenment is not only knowing more, but enlightenment occurs when we take action based on that knowledge. To this extent, many people are extremely knowledgeable, unfortunately, they are not enlightened under Kant's template because they have failed to act in accordance to that enlightenment.

You can take any alternative news item – artificial moon, interstellar people, Mars, astral travel, false leaders, 9/11 – you can take any of them and I'll bet that many of you hold a great amount of knowledge on these things and more. You hold this knowledge and yet do not act on this knowledge because you feel that the idiot society of earth will not listen. That people are not worthy of your well kept secrets of how the world works. And you're probably right to some extent. And that is because the people who came before you also decided to hoard knowledge. And so we have lots of people with lots of truths – truths that the truth seekers risked their lives to obtain – and they are sitting at home waiting for Jesus, or waiting for the pizza boy.

People are waiting for something. They are never ready. They need more knowledge. You know, 200 years ago, if you had but 5% of what you know, you'd be out on the street speaking, printing publications, yelling to everyone about the ubiquitous tyranny. I told people that the Haitian Earthquake was the result of an advanced energy weapon strike. Sure, I didn't provide all the full-color slides, footnotes and a fact sheet. And, yes, I failed to identify the underground base from which the strike originated and didn't provide the amount of electricity used to generate the strike, nor did I mention the type of quantum physics that operated the machinery. Yes, this correct. But I did put my life in danger for obtaining this bit of information which, by the way, a scant few others managed. And that wasn't enough to move anyone to rise to the occasion; instead, people took the information, looked at it and stored it away hoping that Jesus would make sense of it when he returned from the dead. Well, here's some news: if you told Jesus that you suspected that the Haitian Earthquake was bogus and then you explained to him how you weren't 100% sure and so decided to do nothing, zippo, the mighty Jesus, having resurrected himself yet again would just shake his head and leap off the nearest cliff. What kind of warriors has he waited 2,000 years for?

The force against you is real

So, we get back to the truth of the matter. There is a force that is against you and if you decide to move forward you will feel this force in greater amounts. That is why I always suggest you continue improving yourself and training which is something you should be doing now if you are on this path of truth or want to partake in the coming glory of heaven, and all that jazzy stuff. The force against you is real. Now, here is the other part that most people won't believe: This force against is attacking you right now. It is in operation at this moment and in the moments before this moment. It doesn't want you to ascend. It doesn't want your children to grow up healthy. It doesn't want you to doubt the leadership. It doesn't want you to welcome the starships. It wants you to be diseased. It wants you to see autism as an incurable illness. It wants to vaccinate you 54 times a year so that you'll be healthy. It wants you to listen to it. And, you have done quite well I must say. The proof is that 9/11 is still in the dumps. Phobos, the Mars moon, is still in the toilet. Cancer is still on the rise after 50 billion dollars of investment. The same bunch of bozos are still in power and some Church clergy are still raping children while they profess that they serve God on High. That's some of the proof. You can tell me how much compassion you have, which is nice, but compassion is useless at a time of sweat. Screw compassion (you earned it, you have it, now move on), get out your workout gear, roll up your sleeves, get dirty and shut up.

Compassion and spreading love are useless against patriotism and sorcery. Proof: War in Iraq. It is useless when electromagnetic weapons are influencing you to be compassionate. H.A.A.R.P. Yes, they can make you compassionate about Haiti even when they themselves murdered 250,000 people. And you'll not only buy it, you'll sleep better knowing you gave $5 by phone. Was Haiti contrived? Here's the only proof you need: George W. Bush and Bill Clinton, two of the purest clansmen in the world, were christened by President Obama to save Haiti; to be the saviours of the people at a time of need. Bush and Clinton, two ex-Presidents who belong to the same club? That's your proof that something is up. Can a mass-murderer be a saviour in the same lifetime? It looks like it.

Right now they are attacking you. They are spraying chemicals in the sky. If the chemicals were good for you, they would tell you, "Uhm, ladies and gentlemen, listen, we have been spraying all the cities for the past 25 years and just so you know, we have been doing so to protect you. Sorry that we didn't tell you, but we thought you should know." The military doesn't spray chemicals on people for their health, and by the way, society doesn't need to be sprayed with anything. If there was such a need to spray vitamins into the air, the governments would be obligated to tell us. So, the reasons for the chemicals in your lungs and on your skin are not for your health and are not making you healthier. If they were, they'd tell you. They'd boast. They're not boasting, they're keeping it secret.

What else? The oil rig off the Louisiana Coast. A natural explosion? Sure. How many rigs have exploded completely, causing massive environmental damage in recent decades? Not too many. The coral reef plays an integral part in the ecosystem. I'm not an ecologist, look it up: coral reef.

I'm not going to go through the lists of illusions and attacks because you probably know many of them, perhaps even more than me, but I don't know if you believe it. If you are filled with compassion and love you are missing the plain, simple fact that you are a threat to the rulers of earth. And, if you act, you are a greater threat. See the dilemma? Either way you are being attacked. You might as well take action before you are dead. Big or small, it is to your benefit and to the benefit of others to act in a more progressive manner. Don't wait till they hurt you. Don't wait till they absorb all your compassion. Screw compassion, we need action. Action will save earth, compassion cannot even overcome patriotism. Try it. Try telling the US Administration with all your compassion that the 10-year war is wrong because murdering people is not very compassionate. Try it. Try telling the aviation authority with all your compassion that chemtrails are not healthy for society. Try it. Compassion is not the cure today, we need action, informed action. We are well informed, we are short on action.

Let's clear this up: There is a force against you. All of you. Everyone who is standing up for the truth. Everyone who wants a change for the better. Everyone who innocently believes that God will save them. Here's some news: There is a force against you.

Let's generate a counter-force. In doing so, it and its minions will generate more force to which we will require more counter-force. Thus is the cosmic dance. Two partners equally playing their part. So far, one partner seems asleep and the single partner is dominating the dance. If you want to impress the Creator, start dancing, and shut up.

The Technical Specifications of Love & Compassion

"Love thy neighbour" is a saying as famous as any. From two thousand years ago in the swamp of human spiritualism till today in the modern technological era, there has existed this thing called *love*. A term so complex, so imperceptible, so argumentative that no man, woman or child has resolved its complexities and subtleties. From even 500 years before, at the time of Gautama Siddhartha, an awakened mind who taught compassion as a form of communication above all else, we continue to have till this day this concept of *compassion*. Thus, we hold in our hands two very prized possessions, Love and Compassion, handed down by masters and practiced for millennia by their accidental disciples. Practiced but never mastered for no man or woman on earth has ever fully grasped Love and Compassion, especially in the way that I would like to express.

One thing that undermines our ascension deeper into the cortex of the cosmos is our unimaginative conception of the illustrious universe, a thing of such immensity that the programmed human mind cannot grasp in all its glory. And this is understandable, completely. At the same time, we have to realize a very important, if not fundamental truth that was as prominent yesterday as it is today. This truth has to do with divine language. When the masters and teachers taught spiritualism to their disciples, many times they introduced divine terms and these terms, over centuries, have lost their deeper meanings. If we could gather up some new definitions, we could gain a very new kind of insight into the nature of the world.

A divine language is a technological language and that is because the further you ponder into the cosmic computer you discover an infinitely advanced technological culture, and, by right, that culture would speak on the basis of technology. What has happened is that the human mind, at the time, could only reach a level of spiritual interpretation, of divine truths; and over the centuries our minds have been further regressed such that we no longer even understand divine truths, rather we stick entirely to the entries in our collegiate dictionary. We are prone, if not seduced to some extent, to believe the dictionary over another interpretive authority such as a priest, and rightly so since the dictionary is definitive and the priest is subjective. Plus, the dictionary is easier to understand and much more accessible, perhaps that is why the dictionary owns most of the market share on how we interpret reality.

So, let's look at Love and Compassion, two very prominent and ancient terms. We have to admit that both Love and Compassion are artefacts in our hearts and minds. We still believe in Love and Compassion. We are still practicing Love and Compassion. No matter what has happened on this dirty planet of meaningless wars and erectile dysfunction, we still accept Love and Compassion, and we have still failed to understand two very old terms many generations later. I'd like to offer a renewed look at Love and Compassion. My interpretation of Love and Compassion is going to have a technological basis. In this way, I hope to stretch your definition of these two terms to a much fuller extent and in this way we might get a glimpse at what else is hiding behind Door Number Three (ref: Monty Hall's Let's Make a Deal TV Show).

Divine wireless connections

Most of us have computers or have access to them. Most of us have attached a peripheral device (eg printer) or even a mobile phone to our computers. Twenty years ago, we needed a special serial cable to connect our printer to the PC. Today, we have high speed USB cables. Twenty years ago, our brick-sized mobile phones had no access to our computers. Today, via Bluetooth wireless capability we can download camera images on our phones to our computers. The latest introduction of mobile phones, the iPhone (a kind of social class in itself), is a very powerful miniature computer that then connects to our larger laptop computer. One device connecting to another device without wires.

The process of connection is uniquely important. Each device must not only speak the same language (software codes) but must also vibrate at the right frequency. Different versions of software or hardware that is not compatible with certain machines simply won't connect, they will never share the same views. So, the process of device interaction demands us to pay attention to our version of software and the compatibility from device to device.

When two (or more) devices meet up in the wireless space (a completely fabricated network of energy) and share a connection, they then go through their software protocols to establish the mode of communication, whether it is downloading an image, printing a file, or accessing the internet. Whatever the intent may be, it is vitally necessary that the two devices speak the same language and vibrate at the right frequency. It can be also said that the two devices must have a similar culture to ease the process of communication.

We now have two devices speaking the same language and at a similar frequency and these devices are then able to share information and to transfer data. This is not unlike when two people connect because it is also necessary for two people to speak the same language and to be a similar wavelength, or frequency. The only difference is that people and machines are biologically dissimilar. But is that true?

If two devices connected and experienced each other at the same wavelength and really got to know each other (transferring all their data), then if we would interpret that connection we could easily say that they are "in love." We could say that because the basic components of love, without all the romantic poetry perhaps, is there. Two devices "in sync" could actually be "in love." Or, it could then be said that being in sync is being in love. When two humans are in sync they get married. That process might take 7 days in Las Vegas or 17 years in the banal world of domestic confusion. Interestingly, more and more people are using computers (machines) to get into online dating because they haven't the capacity to do so in real life. You see, we trust a machine's advice for a marriage partner more than ourselves and this is happening in a very large scale. Call them machine arranged marriages if you like. Perhaps in the future we might be saying, "I sync you."

If two people *in sync* is love then what is compassion? Well, compassion is really about sending out your higher frequency. When you send it out people feel better because it alters another person's frequency from out of a low frequency (eg depression) into a more receptive frequency (eg belonging). We could use the same concept for our machine culture. Devices sending out signals in order to belong and when they belong they can share their data, they can function more holistically, they can print reports and upload party pictures.

If Love is a band of frequency with a connection to all those in that frequency then Compassion is more than one band, a multiband frequency (eg quadband).

Syncing and linking

Not everyone has Compassion and some people Love on a very selective basis. This can be explained better if we allow ourselves to think that some people are loaded with an outdated connectivity software or have hardware that is similarly outdated. And, some people can love the masses and spread compassion like a waterfall because they have not only advanced hardware but also they have a very compliant, multigenerational software program.

It is getting easier and easier to think of biological terms in a technological sense, that we can talk about our brain as a hard drive and that some of us can reboot our biological system by doing certain yogic exercises. It is becoming easier and easier to think in this manner and that is because, again, what the ancient teachers spoke long ago they were speaking in technological terms. These technological terms were interpreted as divine and then reinterpreted as spiritual things. Our process over the past 50 years, especially since the introduction of the computer, has been to think of life in a technological context, and the basis of my work has been on teaching *technological awareness*; that we have gone from biological awareness to spiritual awareness and now we must make the leap to technological awareness.

Armed with some new knowledge, we can rethink of the message of Jesus in a technological context because on a technological level of thinking our Jesus was not introducing humanity to loving their neighbours and spreading love, rather, he was teaching his brothers and sisters to sinc up to each other and spread these higher vibrations because Jesus fundamentally understood a very advanced level of technology, a human technology and he wanted to unite people before they were divided and conquered. Unfortunately, his efforts did not fully succeed as we are still killing and dividing each other today. I think that the old definitions of Love and Compassion need to be updated. Perhaps this new view on life might reinvigorate existence into a unified force of ecstasy. One dreams.

Everything ascension

While most people who have learned how to love and be compassionate, and who have done so after much work and error, they feel that they have achieved a very significant achievement in their spiritual progress. On one hand they have, but on another hand they have merely understood how to connect to people, and even to other living things like trees and animals. Mastering Love and Compassion, using our technological approach, is mastering our ability to connect, to be in sync with other biological constructs. This has allowed us to marry, to have children, to build businesses, to save whales and to teach greater divine truths. There is great value in Love and Compassion. But we have to remind ourselves that we live in a hindered world, a world controlled by others and these others are masters of reality. In being masters of reality they understand things much higher than Love and Compassion, in fact, they can use Love and Compassion, because they are frequencies, to imprison the world, even a loving world.

To control humanity with an electromagnetic device (such as HAARP), one needs only to understand how to direct Love and Compassion. The human being has a built-in need for Love and Compassion (Syncing and Linking) because it relies on other living things for data and information. If you block its other access points, the human device will Sync and Link with those in greater need, as a default. We quickly help those in need (eg Haiti victims) or at least understand their plight and offer our compassion. We do so because it is built-in to do so. We are programmed to be united and anyone in need, in rehab or depressed is disconnected. To rehabilitate them, we need to get them reconnected and we use compassion to re-establish their connection to us, to our network. During a catastrophe, we rise to the occasion. If catastrophes could be orchestrated (eg World Trade Center Towers Demolitions Services of 2001) then the built-in Love and Compassion applications (among others) would naturally become activated.

If the world is always suffering, always in need, if poverty always exists, if pandemics always come out and terrorism is always near us then those who reach (or are reaching) the level of Love and Compassion (Syncing and Linking) will always be busy but will never ascend. They will never ascend because they will never get the chance to fully upload or download the correct information. The majority of others will never even understand Love and Compassion because they are too busy surviving.

We see the problems with ascension online. When we try to download a very large file, even separated in several parts it requires a long period of time or repeated downloads to get all the data. If our computer processor is busy generating photographic images and printing large files for distribution, we simply haven't the memory space to fully and quickly download what we need which might be why we take vacations. If our brain processor and heart hardware is busy calming the suffering of others or surviving the trauma of our youths then we are never able to ascend properly and therefore we are operating below capacity.

The central aspect of existence is ascension. Everything we do and everything we are is based on ascension because ascension demonstrates learning and learning is central to cosmic growth. We have to grow. We are programmed to grow. In order to grow, we need to learn. The faster you learn, the faster you grow and the faster you ascend. Anything that interferes with your ascension is interfering in your growth. We don't enter an existential plane to not grow. The very reason we enter is to grow (learn).

People Apps

Love and Compassion, reinterpreted as Syncing and Linking, tells us something very important about life and growth because Syncing and Linking is a fundamental feature that allows us to connect to the other human devices. But once connected you still need to launch other applications. You might want to launch the Marriage App. You sync up to another human device and once the technical connection is set you launch the App. There are many Human Apps. There is the Education App. There is a Kill App. There is a Vote App. And there is even an Ice Cream App. And there are new Apps all the time. Lately, we have seen them introduce the Lesbian App and the Bisexual App. And people devices want to run those Apps because they have been free for first time users. We still have the War App, which is now in Version 109.1. They keep improving it and people keep downloading it. They tried to sell the Swine Flu App but early testers caught on and that Disease App didn't sell well, certainly not as well as the Terrorism App.

The problems in life right now is that we are only Syncing and Linking with an artificial network, one created by the keepers of this place. We are not downloading our data from the cosmic computer which does not have War and Disease Apps. The cosmic computer has Peace and Health Apps. The cosmic computer has Bliss Apps and Infinite Knowledge Apps. The cosmic computer has Telepathy Apps and Superhuman Power Apps. The cosmic computer has Free-Energy and Starship Apps, both of which are not found in the artificial net. The artificial net is surrounded by a firewall that prevents people from accessing the cosmic network. The better we understand the nature of reality, the more able we are to circumnavigate the deceptive networks and to reconnect to the cosmic mainframe.

Having a technological basis does not diminish the human experience, rather it only replenishes a once banal life of suffering and erectile dysfunction with a limitless life of interstellar travel and disease-free existence. It promises longevity unlike ever before and all it requires is activating the built-in features in your body. The starting point is in redefining our divine terms, one by one, and then using those new definitions to take us into new dimensions of existence.

This is the Cure for Disease

There is a cure for disease, nearly all disease, and this cure is accessible. This cure is not easy to explain and it is less easy to understand. It is not easy to explain because human awareness is severely skewed and woefully distorted. It is less easy to understand because of ego interference. Nonetheless, this is the cure for disease.

Why is there a cure for disease, you might ask? Aren't diseases natural genetic and molecular formations in the biological body? Well, the oddest thing about the biological body is that it isn't at all biological. That is also to say that it is more like a construct which you embody, unfortunately, it has been made your prison because your technological features have been maliciously shut off or tampered with.

I quite often refer to the body as having android qualities because essentially we are synthetic constructs inhabiting an artificial world: But, this world is so advanced that artificial feels and looks biological. That and the fact that your mind has been reprogrammed to interpret and process only a handful of data streams means that you are unable to see the spectrum of existence before you. Well, enough about that for I've written extensively on this already.

Humour my presentation for a few minutes and let's say that I'm essentially correct. Let's say that we are androids, stemming from a myriad of historical lineages. We all have evolved quite differently, only our root is the same, the platform is the same as are the designers.

So, let's now take away the body, in other words let's confirm that it is a robot. If we temporarily hide the layer containing the android form, what is left? What is inside your body? At first, you'd say, "the soul." The soul would make sense if the body was biological because body and soul go well together like lemon and honey. Now, since we've temporarily decided to interpret body as android we are faced with an incompatible term since soul doesn't fit an android. A better term that dries a machine, in fact provides instructions for operation is "a program." Programs run machines and souls run bodies.

In short, we've arrived at: **We are android constructs driven by existential programs living inside a manufactured environment, a false reality.** It's a wild presentation and it so far makes enough sense. Remember, I want to present the cure for disease so a little mind-boggling stuff shouldn't matter, a small price to pay for the cure for disease, no?

Well, it was sad to see a few readers drop off. I'm sure their ego got the best of them. I'm glad you're still hanging on.

Let's get to a quick analogy: a smart phone is a mobile telephony platform that runs on a mobile software codec and uses smaller applications ("APPS") to provide users with more functionality, such as APPs for Social Networking,

Turns out, your program-driven molecular machine also uses APPS to further your existential experience. Only that these APPS must conform to the same matter as that of the central (Program, or Soul). That matter is quietly regarded as energy. As invisible as is your soul energy so too are these Human APPS. In fact, these APPS are always in occurrence. You are regularly downloading and upgrading your Human APPS, which we now see as Android APPS. The APPS must first upload onto the System Program (Personal Soul) and then the System Program will launch the application onto the materialized construct. So, for example, let's take a far out example like parenthood. Say you've never been a parent, perhaps you're 16 and you've just got pregnant (by accident). You're quite afraid of becoming a mother, and rightly so. But upon giving birth and in those interim weeks, quietly likely, you find your motherhood. Because of all the fear and stress you don't realize what is actually happening. Because what is happening is that you have been downloading some Motherhood APPS including Teen Mommy APP and Dealing with an Absent Father APP, not to mention the Appease In Laws and Breastfeeding APPS. Sorry, we've drifted a bit too far into the real world, which is artificial but let's get back into humouring me.

You're an android with an internal program living inside a beautifully realized world, I mean this reality is resplendent. So much so that you have been mesmerized by it till now. We have to admit that it is pretty convincing, eh?

You're now realizing that you can download APPS and that APPS are packets of invisible energy that jack into your System Program and upload the data you require (eg Motherhood). It's not that complex to understand on paper. You have a phone, you get on the internet and download a phone APP (eg Weather App).

Disease APPS

When we get to disease, what are we talking about? Well...APPS. A disease is an APP, isn't it? It is a packet of existence-grade energy. It's invisible but once it's loaded onto your system, it then enters your construct and alters molecular arrangement (according to its instructions set and programmed code). Why? Because your android construct is impermanent, it is like an advanced holographic projection. It morphs and shifts. Ever had days you look awesome and days you look like you were hit by a runaway bull? We bulge, shift, twist, stretch, shine and bloom. We are in perpetual motion. We are transitory, but that is another story. We'll stick to this story a bit more because I want to tell you the cure for disease in the hopes that one day soon you'll put it to use. Making use of it today is probably ambitious. Take your time to download this information.

A Disease APP hits you. In order for an APP to enter your system you must ACCEPT IT. Now, if you don't understand what is happening, you'll very easily ACCEPT the wrong APP. We've seen this before on the computer: one night you're tired, drunk and you visit the wrong website, you CLICK OK to the wrong download and you've just accepted a Trojan. Your system gets a virus. No unlike you the android.

Bad men around

Where do these diseases come from? Well, let me ask, where do computer viruses come from? Computer programmers. Whether by accident or on purpose, machine viruses are a big problem and anti-virus software is big business. You can see where this is going, don't you? Some android programmer creates a disease, he or she gives it a name (eg Polio) and he or she spreads it into the reality system. While the system responds against these viruses, the android inhabitants have lost the awareness of how things work. They think that diseases are still biological. They forgot that diseases are APPS. They forgot that they can reject Disease APPS and can build disease firewalls. This is why I'm here – TO REMIND YOU.

Here's the other thing: there are people who want to spread disease. They are creating new diseases. They want society to suffer. They will copy the Disease APP or another and add their own dark fingerprint and change a Polio APP to a Pneumonia APP. Remember that most people get sick because the immune system is weak and the immune system is really also a kind of firewall, right? When your anti-virus firewall is not functioning properly, your computer is vulnerable to infection. In simplifying this to make it accessible, we are omitting a number of things, but I'd like to keep the level of mind-boggling down as much as possible.

What I'm saying if it isn't clear is that you are continually being bombarded with Disease APPS. These programs are coming at you through the television, through certain android carriers and through the fluidic air, and that is because the rulers of this place like to see you suffer. If you master this knowledge, they're in trouble because you could virtually eliminate disease.

The very naming of a disease is a way to spread the APP. The gateway to your program is your mind. As long as you wholly reject these nasty APPS, as long as you regularly purify yourself with healthy food and exercise, as long as you practice some of these technological concepts, you will be disease free.

Quarantine the virus then clean

Now to the other part: If you are diseased now, all you have to do is to reach a mental state where the technological world makes sense. See yourself as an advanced android, go into your program (soul) and remove the Disease APP. Delete the files, clean your system, rebuild the firewalls. Don't think of any disease as scary. Whether cancer or Meningitis, look at them as "machine viruses (programs)" and uninstall them. But you must continue to keep your improved thinking or they'll come back because you are being bombarded with disease, luckily you have an incredibly resilient construct.

I'm not trying to diminish your experience here, but we've strayed too far off the natural path. In speaking in this manner, in remembering your technological roots, I hope that it will return your awareness and will enrich your life like never before.

Getting past the ego on a consistent basis is tough. The ego is practical. Your true self is imaginative. The ego is fearful and excessive. Your program is fearless and honest. This world is built on ego because the rulers are egotistical, they use logic and reason to keep you immersed in lies, so you have to be illogical and unreasonable at times. You have to soothe your ego and, at the same time, you have to activate your existential program. For example, if you're on antidepressant medication you are not going to stop your meds because you are not strong enough mentally to do so.

What you do is you gradually reduce your drug intake with your doctor while at the same time you increase your connection to your internal program (soul). Some people are farther than others. What is true is the probably all of you have strong attachment to ego. The cure for disease relies on stepping out of the ego and allowing the program to rid itself of the infection. The better you are able to do that, the faster your recovery. A person who gets what I'm saying could virtually have an instant cure. Some of you might need a healer to assist you. What's important is that we start seeing disease as energy programs. Even addictions could be seen in this way. You might have a Shopping APP that forces you to buy shoes or a Fat APP that forces you to eat ice cream, or you might have been infected with a Cocaine APP or an Alcohol APP. By uninstalling these APPS from your internal system and cleaning your system, you'll discover the true power of healing from within. And it's probably the hardest and cheapest healing program in the world. At the very least, remove as many negative influences in your life and add as many positive influences as possible. A positive environment, or even positive places you can go on occasion, is a crucial step to any kind of cure which is why rehabs tend to work. People remove themselves from the infection sites. That's why life change works. That's why makeovers work. That's why love heals.

The cure for disease is accessible to each and every one of you. It requires a very new kind of thinking. In the near future, we could see the eradication of all major diseases and a level of cures never before imagined and the key is in reinterpreting the biological machine and in understanding the technological features of an advanced android organism.

The Alien's Guide to Earth Survival, Part One

Okay, you've decided to come to earth, the planet. So, I'll start off with the basics. I'm going to make it clear and simple, folks, and that's because I want you to succeed.

A lot of you won't like this shit hole, I'll just say that up front. A while back, about 5,000 years in this time spectrum, this realm was hacked and a small group of Dimensionals took over one of the sectors. Since that time, these bunch of bozos have damaged many of the pertinent areas and infected the society with negativity, disease, fear and a lack of will. They've reprogrammed the course of humanity without anyone noticing, and those of us who came before to correct the problem were taken out.

Now, all of you are here because you can handle shit. That's why you volunteered and that's why you won't be outsmarted by the ego device. Sure, we'll lose some of you. That's a given. But I don't want to see the bulk of you warriors surrendering to a bunch of bozos.

As you all know, the bozos are on their way out, they know it. We are here for that reason. It took us a while to get here but we're not going. None of you are leaving until this place is clean.

Enough of that. Let's cover a few items. Write this down: it's an old saying from where we come from:

"Never fucking give up." Jot it down on a piece of paper, stick it on your fridge, memorize it, I don't care, but that has saved my ass more times than I can remember.

Let's get to business.

Earth culture is unique in this part of the cosmos. The human population has been twisted in every way imaginable and now thinks on a very low level of awareness. I've haven't met a culture that rapes children since the last trip through the Vulgares Nebula. But on Earth, the Bishops and the rich have a monopoly on children, and the media stays out.

Ladies and Gentlemen, for your benefit, I've prepared a summary of cultural characteristics of Earth People that you need to know. Some of these, you may have already encountered, good, consider yourself all the better off for it. Some of these may be obvious. None of these characteristics shall we adopt. Does everyone hear me? Do not adopt these characteristics? If you do, you will have to be considered a loss on our part. Be strong in the face of adversity. Live in the high zone.

Here we go:

Overeating and starvation. A human female will gorge herself on cake and ice cream, cookies and soda pop for weeks upon weeks and will grow fat from a bad caloric intake. Feeling fat and ugly, she will further drown her sadness in pizza and cheap buffets, sitting on the couch for as long as possible. When her obesity finally makes her angry, she listens to a motivational tape, buys a diet book and joins the gym. She stops eating food and starts eating yogurt, diet drinks and lots of water, maybe throwing up a bit. She cuts her caloric intake down to starvation, losing all the inches she's gained, sweating off all the fat molecules until she can put on a bikini and feel confident.

Military supremacy. A male leader is so devoid of peace that he will proudly claim that war is necessary. He will explain to his people that war is not only a requirement but that he needs the support of the people. His people will gladly support the murder of other people in some other nation as long as they are promised that their free lives are never changed. He will arm and send thousands of soldiers into a battlefield and he will promote this invasion as a sign of grace and intelligence. And his people will believe him. They will support the troops because the troops are their people too. But the leader will not wage war for resources or disagreements, no, this is not the case. The leader will wage war to demonstrate that his nation is capable in military things. He will want to demonstrate that his military is supreme, just as any body builder will flex his muscles to scare away the 97-lb wimps. And it works. Flexing his military muscle and actually murdering people tells the rest of the planet who is boss. The local mafias have been using this strategy for centuries.

Consuming all natural resources. Human beings have an insatiable appetite for consumer goods. Because of this demand, corporations no longer care in how they derive the raw materials to produce those goods. And people do not care about how things are made, they only care that they have them. They don't need one pair of shoes, or two pairs of shoes, they need 100 pairs of shoes. They don't want one television per home, they want one per room including one for the bathroom because when you are taking a shit, you need to watch Jerry Springer.

Celebrity fascination. It is more like celebrity fascism because when it comes to celebrities, no matter the breast size, audiences need to know. They want to know what a celebrity had for breakfast, they want to see pictures of their new haircut and they want to listen to their interview where they stumble over large words. Let's face it, celebrities are not the brightest of the bunch and neither do they hold any power in the world. So instead of interviewing scientists and sages, TV producers direct tens of millions of dollars a month to filming celebrities, who we know spend 15 hours a day on a film set or a TV studio. The last thing they need in their life is to have their picture taken but that is the first thing the public wants. The public doesn't need pictures of starving children or to listen to conspiracy theorists, they need to know how a celebrity lost 5 pounds in 5 days.

Counting time. This item you'll all love because it's quite childish really. People of earth are still using 24 hour clocks. They need a clock to tell them what time it is. The reason for this, we believe, is that htey can no longer read the movement of the Sun and other planets. In fact, many people hate the Sun because it will give them skin cancer so they use Sun Block. As long as they view time in 24 hour periods they'll never speed up their existence to our vibration. We detached ourselves from time thousands of years ago. You can see how far these people still need to go.

Demonizing Starkind. Earth planet was not only built by our kind but it was also seeded by us and to show their appreciation the offspring here have decided that we don't exist. Not only do we not exist but we are suddenly evil and want to rule the world. Let me ask you, why would we need to rule a world we made? What is the gain in that? That's how much sense these people make. They'll happily call us evil, they'll follow the sheep and doubt we exist and they'll turn a blind eye to the fact that we started their very breath. And if we show up, we'll be seen as invaders.

Pain killers. Humans are in pain. Everything is a pain. Sore back is a pain. Headache is a pain. Pain in the ass. The people here are in pain. Just be aware the person you are talking to is on pain medication. They can buy it over the counter and they tend to take a few extra pills to kill as much pain as possible. Some of them get addicted to pain and take very harsh pain killer medication. They have been taught to accept pain and suffering. And they like pain killers. They need pain killers. If you tell them outright that reality is an illusion and that this is a computer-generated world they would only take more killers rather than deal with the fact they have been swallowing illusions to kill illusions. Let them take their painkillers and ease up on the truth when it comes to "life is an illusion." They are so expert on pain that they now have pains for specific parts of the body: knee pain, neck pain, back pain, muscle pain, arthritic pain, eye pain, stomach pain, joint pain, heart pain, whole body pain, surgery pain, childbirth pain and pain in the ass. But don't take on their pain, remember the illusion. Remind yourself and you will not feel pain, or much less than usual.

Then there's

The murder paradox. Humans are controlled by their artificial laws. Because these laws are not in sync with our laws, these people are experiencing a lot of additional horror in life. Here's an example: As a civilian, if you shoot someone on purpose, it is murder. Murder is against the law and you go to prison, or worse. However, if you serve the government in the army and they send you to a foreign nation, they'll not only give you a gun and bullets, but they'll also pay you to murder people. They pay you to murder people because it's like getting drunk in Vegas, what happens in a foreign nation stays in a foreign nation. So, if ever you get into trouble just say you were in the army in Vegas. And if it involved sex just say you are a Catholic Bishop.

And finally:

Porn. It's a porn house here, folks. Action movies are full of bullet porn. End of times movies are full of destruction porn. Men's minds are tuned into internet porn. There's terrorism porn. Vaccination porn. The news is filled with distraction porn. Once you buy into porn, it's over. Stay on truth.

You're not going to believe this experience here. It's something that I have to remind myself each and every day. It's intense. It's violent. It will make you want to throw up at times in disgust, especially when they are destroying the rain forests and killing dolphins. The fact that people don't care is because they are so tuned out of the truth and so tuned into the illusions, you can't blame them for thinking the way they think. Put things into perspective. Some of them here are nasty. They will eat your children if they could. Could be anyone. The elites are the worst. Basically, anyone who wears a suit and has a driver is an elitist. Then there's the others, loving, kind, and generous. Stick with them, they are closer to us than they realize.

Champions of the Existential Inertia

On a child's playground we can find a large metallic disc upon which can be found a number of evenly-space bars. The children step onto the disc and holding onto the bars as firmly as possible; the disc is pushed by one or two children to make it spin. As the disc rotates, a centrifugal force is generated and one by one each child loses their grip and is forced off the rotating disc. The faster the disc is spun, the faster the kids fly and the one able to hang on the longest is the playground champ.

The rotating disc can teach us some valuable insight into the nature of ascension here on earth plane. In exchange for a flat disc, we have a perfectly round planetoid upon which are 7 billion people. As the plane of existence upon which we live evolves technologically, it begins to improve its rotation on other levels of observation. This results in a higher vibration. But this higher vibration, at the planetary level, does not correspond to the vibration of the human level. And as long as these two groups are not in sync, the civilization here will be limited in its awareness. We will always have key individuals, perhaps groups, who enjoy a heightened awareness but they will have done so because they will have made their bodies vibrate faster using the ancient process of Atonement.

Atonement is the cleansing of sins, regrets, traumas and abuses. To regularly atone, a person begins to vibrate at a new level of spirituality. In old times, this process was regularly done as it is in some religions even today, but because modern society has been enveloped in egotistical pursuits there has been an avoidance of atonement, and because of this we have seen Humankind and all of its dimensional counterparts bogged down in Existential Weights, verily unresolved issues and rampant denial. Without proper atonement, people will not be able to be in sync with the newly established Reality System, a cosmic system that is far more advanced that its predecessor, launched about 2,500 years ago.

Everything counts in the Afterlife

In previous Administrations from Heaven (a loose term for higher dimensional space inhabited by profoundly aware people), the Burden of Sins were discharged and a compassionate view of a human life journey was afforded to the individual upon their demise. That meant that in previous judgments (or Really Final Exams) a Catholic Bishop priest who raped 84 boys and girls, covered it up and pretended to be one of God's Representatives, in previous determinations, the pedophile priest was forgiven and allowed to choose a new life.

What happened then was that he reincarnated into George W. Bush who thought if God is so dumb, I might as well kill a million women and children because Heaven doesn't put anyone in jail. Well, all that happened under the previous Administration. The next Administration has a new set of determination protocols on the Afterlife and your ability to handle centrifugal force is important.

Basically, the same pedophile priest, if he died today, he would reincarnate as a Choir Boy under the tutelage of the worst rapist in the Church and he'd experience first-hand the glory of sexual abuse. And if he still didn't learn at the spiritual level, if he still refused to ascend, well he'd reincarnate as a loving, sensitive mother of an autistic, diabetic, blind Choir Boy with only one arm who was being ritualistically molested by a sadistic priest or some elitist who likes to drink Choir Boy's blood.

The differences in administrative protocols are huge. In exchange for forgiveness and compassion are first-hand experience and extreme training programs. Sinners will not be excused for their horrors and neither will you be allowed to ascend because you were a nice person who never did anything wrong because you sat on the couch all day, got fat and complained that the pizza was late and you should get $5 off.

All your actions count in the afterlife. Everyone gets an afterlife and that means the higher your score the better off you are if you want to move forward. You can deny it or avoid it but you are living for your Afterlife and your neighbour too. So if your neighbour becomes nasty don't become nasty, learn or they will have screwed up your Afterlife potential. And trust me, your neighbour, your boss, your demons; they will all test you because they don't like to suffer alone. All of us here, most of us anyway, are suffering because of the immediate past. Even for something we didn't do. But we allowed it to happen. Is that fair? That's the way the multidimensional cosmos works. There are things working on all levels and it is up to the individual to become aware of their own situations

Some of this is common sense and you can understand in human form. Some of it requires more awareness or your higher selves will know and it's a matter of interacting with them. And some of you are special and are required to live with a higher moral purpose and virtue, even to shun the world of ego and to contribute as you were designed to. If you are one of these people and are sitting on the couch watching a gun porn film starring Tom Cruise all day, well you'll need to atone.

Atonement is the release, verily the cleansing, of these Cosmic Weights. If we recall Christ, he was known as The Redeemer. He was the purifier because he knew that spiritual purification ensured a good Afterlife, a life in Heaven and with God. Well, sadly, today, we want wealth and fame more than an Apartment in Heaven and that's fine, you're allowed to live an egotistical life. You are. Of course, you're coming straight back because you'll have failed to make any gains in life via ascension in your previous life. And your excuse will be that no one ever told you about ascension and it won't work. Because I've just told you. Ascension is an integral part of existence.

You can be working for a secret society or you may be a soldier in the battlefield, doesn't matter, unless you fully atone, you're coming back. There is an Afterlife. Death is not final like the Demons have taught society. They have done so in order to degrade Humanity, to lower vibration of the entire civilization so that they could forever enslave you in low awareness. And it worked! Humans are slaves who ritualistically believe that life is pretty good, that they look toward retirement, and that their sex life is getting better and better.

Atonement as an application

Atonement is a process much like deleting all those Temporary Internet Files on your computer or cleaning out the Quarantined Viruses. On a computer, it is straight-forward to empty the Folder and all the files in it. But in life, humans do not have these components. Whereas in previous lives, God or Angels would Click the Delete Button, today they will not. You yourself have to Click and Delete each one and the more you have the harder you have to work to redeem yourself.

Basically, you can continue to do as you have been doing and rethink your ignorance in next life or after a harsh turn of events, or, you can improve your spiritual life now and cleanse yourself of your sins.

Bad signals

Isn't that what sin is, a technological term? If you sin, you will move away from God. If you indulge yourself in false ideas like terrorism you lower your vibration, if you lower your valuable vibration then you fall out of God's Network. You basically lose the signal and you now are in Hell and Hell is having no signal when you need a signal, you become lost, you are devoid of knowledge and none of your true friends can reach you.

How do you rid yourself of sins (and similar products)? First, you understand what sin is. Sin is a disconnection from the main Divine Network. The more you sin, the lower your signal until you are expelled from the system. If you were to rid yourself of sin, your vibration would increase, your signal would kick in again and you would find peace with God. What you call Oneness. What Woody Allen would say, "I am two with nature."

You achieve sin by way of bad behaviour, by way of falling into temptation, by way of refusing to ascend, by way of rejecting growth and by way of being out of sync with your reality environment.

You are a corrupt Investment Banker. You are filthy rich. You practice sorcery behind closed doors. You are destroying world economies. Obviously, you are full of sin. Probably a servant of Satan. Who is Satan? Satan is a reality virus that robs energy from God, converts the signal and uses that to spread itself onto the reality platform. Satan is a program, large enough to infect the individual programs (people). How does an evil Investment Banker remove his sins? He can't. He is completely overrun with the virus, if you removed the virus there is nothing left to be redeemed. He'll return again and again because he is no longer living, he will become a replicating hologram, a non-player character, an object.

You are a Housewife. You hate your neighbour. You regret not giving away your virginity to your High School flame. You don't love your husband but he provides what you need. You are neither happy nor sad. You are 30 pounds overweight. You have no connection to a God. Because you have no connection to a God or to a Divine Network, we can be assured that you have sinned. If you hadn't sinned, you'd be connected. So, let's say that the Housewife ends up in the hospital to have breast implants put in and in that moment of drifting off to sleep before the operation, she realizes that she was molested as a child, by her uncle. She wakes up, more full-chested but now aware of her rapist uncle who even sent a Get Well Card. Bastard. If she continues to avoid dealing with the molestation issue and refuses to confront her uncle, she will be sinning. For whatever excuse she can muster, she will have sinned because she is in avoidance to the truth and is afraid of resolution. For her, if she would address the molestation and the resulting divorce, she would be able to ascend.

Sin is rather tricky and loaded with beliefs and this is why it is hard to discuss. My view is rather different and incomplete, for sure, but you can see that you are sinning if you are in avoidance of the truth, and some sinners cannot be redeemed. Each of us has their own issues and we know ourselves best, and there are people who can assist us when we are ready for the truth. As long as you are disconnected, as long as you are mildly connected, as long as you feel empty inside and are living in a substandard situation, you are required to atone for you have many Existential Weights. By removing one weight you will discover another, perhaps even worse that the previous one. But don't be discouraged.

We have to admit up front that we have lived centuries in avoidance of the truth and the proof is in the dismal sewage that we call life here on earth. The headquarters of Catholicism, the moral authority and the voice of God, is rife with rapists and a Pope who covers up his fellow rapists. If that was the only problem on earth, it would be monumental, but that is one molecule on a huge iceberg of filth.

Many of you will not agree with me and will brush your little flowers of love over the sewage. And that is fine. You can spray expensive French perfume on a pile of shit and it still stinks. You can overlook the fact that all the governments who know about interstellar people are purposely covering up that knowledge in order to repress society. You can overlook that. You can watch your LCD TV while some Choir Boys play with the Bishop in his bedroom. Close your eyes and they are gone. Fine. But all of these actions will distance you from the Truth and from the Heavenly Authority. The inertia has just tossed you off the disc.

All debts must be paid in full. No one gets off for good behaviour. We have to face the issues now or in next life, regardless we have to face them. You might be a person who must only face their personal issues and then that is what you must do. You might be a person who is required to help the masses, to overcome some cover-up and then that is what you must do. If you don't do what you came to do, you will come back and do it on some other level in some other format. If you are lucky, you will have lived a life of contribution and atonement and you are probably dead because you earned a promotion. Good job.

I am not a death advocate. I firmly know there is an Afterlife and I firmly know that they have made you all afraid of Death so that you are all living for today, for this singular life and haven't earned any points for the Afterlife which means you will come back with more burdens. And the demons here will use your suffering to enslave you further and the next life you will become further burdened and when you reincarnate the demons will fuck you all the way to Hell. And I'm not exaggerating. I sure wish I was. But look at the atrocities of Man, the atomic bomb on the Japanese, hundreds of thousands dead, a country destroyed and Harry Truman a hero for ending the war. Since when do murderers become Heroes? Well, here it works. And no one said a damn thing. Then it was Mr. Bush. Now it is Mr. Obama. Do you see the repetition? Isn't that the reincarnation of sin?

The Cycle of Atonement allows us to cleanse ourselves for our own participation in the selective events of our lives. In doing so, we lighten our bodies, we vibrate more fully, we recognize truthfulness and in recognizing truthfulness we begin to speak more truthfully and in doing so we vibrate better and reconnect to the Divine Network. If we achieve a higher signal, we can even end suffering because we will realize the illusions before us and in doing so we will understand who and what is real. Not long after we will find ourselves at the center of the disc, champions of the existential inertia that had bogged us down for longer than we can remember.

How to Build a Tyrant (Level 1)

To create a tyrant you need to build up his credibility. Catastrophic events, disasters and threats of war are perfect opportunities to cement the tyrant's position. The recent oil spill in the Gulf of Mexico can teach us how magicians manipulate reality behind the scenes in order to maintain their invisible autonomy on the world of men.

To create an Adolf Hitler, Mao Zedong or Bill Clinton, we require a receptive audience. That audience needs to be artificially prepared beforehand in order for our incumbent to gain their trust and love. In a natural system, leaders were propelled forward because of their ability to lead; these were great men and women who had an actual, measurable capacity. In the artificial system of today, a system that has had its naturalness squeezed out, all the key leaders of the world here have been placed there by very powerful processes. These processes reveal the magicians who are directing the action-packed show.

The process of installing tyranny is extremely complex and requires a very broadminded reader so we are going to simplify some of that process in order to get a *glimpse* at what may indeed be going on. Much of this is why tyranny is invisible and why it works long enough until the next tyrant can be inserted. Hitler, Mao and Clinton are all three purposely different and all three were tyrants because to produce the same type of tyrant would be ineffective. It would be ineffective because the people would not accept it. As long as people can accept a tyrant, he is effective, but when the tyrant's charm has run dry they have to be painted with a fresh coat of paint.

We are at that point in history whereby a new tyrant is rising and so all the necessary steps are being executed in order to ensure the investments of the past come to fruition. There is never any guarantee that the tyrant will work out or how long he will last. The tyrant makers do not know and that is why they aim to extract as much as they can while their tyrant is in power because they know that his tenure is unknown. Not only that but the tyrant makers don't care. The tyrant is another misdirection used by them to isolate power from the world and to suppress human ascension. As long as they keep this complicated process running, the tyrant makers will never be caught. And to stop the tyrant business we would have to catch the tyrant makers.

Once the tyrant candidate has been selected and placed in position, it is necessary to build the tyrant's image as an effective ruler. Of course, the tyrant makers realize that when it comes to effectiveness, the new ruler is just a robot that they preselected and that the world is filled with much smarter and more capable individuals. Now this is not something they want the people to fully realize because that would diminish the leadership's power. Fortunately, after centuries of governance the people desperately need a ruler, a pseudo-father figure who is at the helm of an illusory existence. So really the tyrant is an illusion, he is the dummy that the ventriloquist manipulates and entertains the audience. A good ventriloquist makes that dummy come to life and then the people no longer think that there is a ventriloquist. They start listening to the dummy and they accept the dummy, forgetting that he is just made of wooden parts. Pinocchio became a real boy because he convinced himself that he was real and in doing so he became real in the eyes of the people.

The snake charmer cometh

Since ancient times, men and women have revered things that could kill them and often attributed those things to godly devices. The snake is one such item that because it has been placed on the earth and commanded by gods that it should be revered. To capture a poisonous snake and then to charm it is a form of reverence to the gods themselves, especially to the gods who represented snakes. We have long lost any idea of reverence except for money, large tits and expensive cars, these things we revere much more so than snakes or old trees. That is why we revere celebrities and billionaires. They have no respect for gods, they stand for nothing of an exceptional spiritual nature and they have no healing hands, and yet they are revered. The Catholic Pope, the hand-picked voice of God himself cannot lay-on-hands, a trait that Jesus and his apostles all had.

Charming a snake was used to hypnotise the worshipers of a particular temple because the poisonous snake was a symbol of a particular god and therefore the audience could be transported to another dimension. In that godly dimension, the snake god would bestow some knowledge or power to those worshipers. The snake charmers would then go out into the streets and spread the dimensional powers of a god and all of this would be accomplished with a flute and basket with a snake. But the original snake charmers were not trained animal handlers, they were *magicians*. And magicians regularly employed symbols to enchant people.

While the snake of yesterday was an effective symbol for times past, in today's modern complicated world the magicians are using far larger symbols to *hypnotise the masses*. Not only that but the magicians are bent on world domination so whatever trick they employ, no matter how disastrous it appears to be, is not meant to enlighten people, it is meant to imprison people. The magicians also need a symbol for people to worship and this is why they invent a tyrant.

What does a snake charmer have to do with a tyrant? The snake charmer is required in order to secure the position of the tyrant. And the snake charmer employs symbolic events in order to hypnotise society and to steer them toward the direction they prefer. The tyrant is in place to absorb all the kudos for the symbolic events. But the tyrant is like the story of a movie, he doesn't win all the time, he has his struggles as the main character, he must go through a period of difficulty, but the magicians decide what happens in the final act because they are writing the script. And that is the payoff for the audience and that is when the legacy of the tyrant is secured. Sure, not every movie works and that is why there are many failed tyrants throughout human history. Today's tyrant is a result of a major investment from the collective of magicians around the world in order to secure the final period of this earth cycle.

In place of a deadly snake, or even a set of poisonous snakes, the modern day snake charmers are using catastrophes, environmental disasters, political upheavals, threats of war, terrorist attacks and orchestrated events to hypnotise the audience. Each step along the progress of our tyrant's journey, he will encounter these symbolic challenges in order to find his dark evil crown at the end of the first movie because of course the magicians would like a sequel.

One such symbolic challenge is the Oil Spill in the Gulf of Mexico. This has all the hallmarks of a magician's touch and, so far, has perfectly hypnotised the mainstream masses. By some observation, the Oil Spill has effectively hypnotised some of the awakened crowd who pride themselves on knowing the prevalent conspiracies.

Hypnotizing oil in the Basket of Mexico

To win over the audience, the oil spill magicians highlight the negligence of the mega corporation (big oil) and they highlight the environmental damage and the decades before the oil will be cleared off and the number of innocent baby dolphins that will die and the tons of fresh oysters what will no longer be edible. They will replay these items until enough emotion like anger is evoked.

There will be anger at the oil companies, anger at using fossil fuels, anger at the death of the environment, anger at the incompetence, anger at the deniability - all of this is played out extremely well. But remember, the magicians are behind the misdirection (the Oil Spill). The magicians are not the oil company or the news station. These are the dummies, the poisonous snakes. The magicians are invisible. If the magicians were to become known, the audience would no longer be hypnotized because the Oil Spill Illusion is too big and too complex to hold. When the snake charmer stops his tune, the poisonous fangs of the snake come out and the magician is dead. Of course, a good group of magicians have many illusions in play at once (eg threat of war, terrorist attacks, flu outbreak, celebrity scandal, economic recession) and will easily switch to another illusion. Therefore a good audience will recognize that the next staged event is also an illusion and will be resistant to the hypnotic effect of people dying.

The question is "why" isn't it? Why artificially create an oil spill (as unbelievable as that sounds) and make it look like an accident and get big oil in trouble and kill dolphins? Better to ask, how sick must you be to even think this without care or concern for life? But before we go in that direction, let's get back to the why. Why launch an oil spill application? Why this misdirection? Well, let's get back to tyranny. If our goal is to enforce a ruler, a tyrannical ruler then the tyrannical ruler needs to be able to handle very large obstacles, way beyond the capacity of the people. Hey, how about an oil spill.

As the blame and anger grows, the people will be directed to the government and then to the leader. A-ha, we have come to the ruler, finally. The people, all angry about the dolphins and the corporate deniability, now ask, no, they *beg* the ruler to "do something." A smart ruler will pretend that everything is okay and his politicians will redirect the people to the corporation for answers. The corporation will make a bigger mess, kill more oysters and let the beaches fill with crude, fumble, so people can't go swimming. The news stations will put journalists on the scene; the images to sell the mind. The magicians now using the energy from the people's own anger to redirect human history, to empower the tyrant, even to alter reality. And the people willingly providing that anger because they are angry at the situation, which they don't realize has been carefully constructed.

Now the people turn to the ruler again, "Help us. Do something." When the timing is right, when the polls suggest it is time, the leader will take a position and the problem will begin to be solved. The people have now surrendered their free will to the ruler, willingly. The people have begged the leader to take their free will in exchange to end their suffering at this accidental catastrophe, all perfectly executed by the invisible magician. Now, before you ask me who the magician is, ask yourself. My job is to highlight an advanced technique that you may or may not have noticed, and I have not included everything in order to keep it as clear as possible.

What will have occurred at the end, at the point where the leader takes charge, is that the leader will have been given more power over the people, clearly an important step to tyranny. Whether it is a financial crisis, a terrorist attack or a healthcare bill, each of the misdirection further enforces the will of the leader who will soon become a ruler, and no one will have noticed the invisible hands that have stolen their minds.

Who knew?

Of course, if you believe in accidents then all of this isn't relevant and the leader did what he had to do. If you see this event as a planned event, you will see that the corporate reaction and the deaths of dolphins are very real. They do not know that it was staged. That's how you achieve believability. The dolphins weren't told. No one sent out a memo to the oysters. If anyone knew the *prestige* that the oil rig was blown up, well no one would've went to work that day, right? So, what we see on the stage, which is actually the illusion because they are reacting to a planned event, is real. People died. That is real. It has to be real to evoke emotion. The film actor has to induce tears in order to be believed as crying. So there are real parts and there are fake parts. More importantly though, the magicians simply have no regard for life in any way and are very good at hypnosis.

I think that last statement alone is very hard to accept. That there are people who would purposely destroy the environment and good people and damage a corporation just so as to shift the base of power is inconceivable, and yet human history is filled with such things. The saddest part is that immediately following

So, what are we going to do about the imminent end of the world? Are we going to wait until there's a crowd of people who get it and then we'll join in like sheep. "Yeah, I knew it was going on but I had to wipe my nose, sorry I'm a bit late, and my cat wasn't feeling well, and the door on the passenger side of my car was stuck, you know, I saw this really good deal on a new video game, maybe when the world turns off we can get in line before the superstore opens. What do you think?"

I think there are plenty of End Signs out there right now, in the past few days. People dying, people launching new businesses, leaders meeting, leaders rattling their sabres, military engagements, new policies, debates, the comedians are raking in the dough. Being a comedian right now, wow, that's where the money is at. When the world is melting and the public has been hypnotized by oil squirting like sperm into the belly of the ocean, well, it's great business for comedy. Did you hear why BP hasn't been able to cap the Oil Spill? Well, apparently they hadn't heard of it either.

Well, so what, it's the end of the world, and I'm sorry. Why am I sorry? I'm not sure. I think I'm sorry because it didn't end sooner. And I'm sorry I have to use bad language. I think the end of the world is a lot like the Gulf Oil Spill. We've been watching the life being drained out of the old world, mesmerized by the incompetence surrounding the problems and we've sat around worrying about this and that. Instead of pulling out our best ideas, we're just watched as others have taken over, not realizing that behind the scenes the scoundrels were jockeying for a new series of military engagements in Korea or in Iran, whichever came first. They need a trigger for WWIII and either axis of evil nation will work. No one is going to stop them. We'll just watch the movie and hope the screenwriters have a happy ending.

I think the last line of the draft of the script I saw read, "And just before we go to CREDITS we see all the people's balls get eaten by mutated Chihuahuas. FADE OUT." I heard they'd like a sequel so the 3rd world war would star in the next film which means they have to establish all the main characters in this script, Season One: *Goodbye, Planet, Goodbye, and: It's Too Bad that Humanity Just Didn't See the End Coming Fast Enough.*

I can't blame the filmmakers. It's hard to write a good end-of-the-world script. Look at the film *2012* (2010). Made a bunch of money then disappeared. The filmmakers took *2012* to the TV studios to make a 2012 TV series, but it was neglected which is pretty interesting given the supposed interest in the Mayan propaganda. The Mayan Scam would make a worse film than *Lesbian Vampire Killers* (2009). It might make a good porn film, Maya does Mayan. She loves calendars. If she sees a Mayan Calendar she gets horny and pulls off all her clothes. So all the geeks start buying Mayan Calendars and having sex with Maya. On December 21, 2012, Maya has a giant orgasm.

Nope, the end-of-the-world is here. It's here in so many ways it's embarrassing. Of course, I'm not an expert. What do I know? Who cares what anyone knows. I mean, the people who know stuff aren't talking except for Icke. I think David Icke should get an award. I'm not saying Icke is 100% on the spot. And I don't think he'd say that. What he represents is he represents balls. This guy is talking plainly about stuff that won't be proven for another 20 years. To him it's proven. He's bet his life on it. There are other people with the truth and they're afraid to open their mouths. Not Icke. He speaks the truth 100%.

You don't have to be 100% correct to speak 100% truth. At the rational, 2D, physical level of stupidity, you can't say anything anymore. I mean if you sing a song on TV more than 3 seconds you have to pay the record label a royalty fee. If you sing *Happy Birthday* on TVB or in a film you have to pay the owner of the rights. A company bought the rights to *Happy Birthday*. Isn't that dandy?

You can't speak the truth unless you have proof but you can lie as much as you want as long as no one finds out. And if you have power, you can lie on camera and no one can stop you. Look at what President Soetoro said about the American Space Plan, Mars in 30 years? They're already on Mars! They've got anti-grav ships flying to Mars and there are people on Mars. They even planted trees on Mars. What do they tell the hope-filled public? We're going to get to Mars in 30 years, or 20 years. It doesn't matter because they have been there a while. If they said in one year, it's silly. They are already there! They're on the moon. There are people on the moon. I've said it. I've talked about it. Other people have talked about it. No one will listen because they need an 8x10 glossy of a naked Martian woman.

I still don't get American News Media. A celebrity, a minor celebrity like Jesse James, he gets a 30 minute exclusive interview on a major network because he cheated on his actress wife, Sandra Bullock, and had sex with 7 or 8 women. That's a big news story. It's not the size of his dick. It's not because he's a big celebrity. It's because he broken Sandra's heart. And I can sympathize with that. She's a terrific star, talented, beautiful. What I don't get is that an intelligent young British man, Gary McKinnon; he playfully hacks into the Pentagon computers and discovers departments on alien interaction and nonterrestrials officers under the secret space program.

I mean this Brit hits the jackpot and if it was Nixon's Watergate, he'd be a hero. They'd find a way to get this story out. Instead, McKinnon's story is closed down; the Pentagon wants to put him in jail for 60 years, he's having suicidal thoughts. Jesse James gets a blowjob by a woman full of tattoos and he gets an exclusive TV interview. Does it make sense? I think if Gary was getting a blow job from a tattooed woman who works at the Pentagon while hacking into their computers, he'd get offers from two TV studios. Gary, next time, add some naked women, some infidelity, some nude shots and they'll call you!

I don't get it. Sure, the argument is that he broke the law. But the counter argument is that he uncovered a major Pentagon cover-up that deals with UFOs, Secret Space Programs and the all-invisible alien. What do major media do? Exactly. Nothing. They don't even pursue a story on this subject. If that's not proof of a lack of intelligence in the media, I don't know what is. Sure, they're intelligent when it comes to blow jobs and nose jobs and boob jobs, but interstellar affairs, nope. And I get it. It's all one big snow job.

Icke should be getting exclusive interviews on TV. He couldn't care less which one because he's happy with the truth. But what he talks about – Satanism, Reptilians, Hollow Moon, Pedophilia in the Church and Government, Holographic Reality, Human Awareness, how to make a good cup of tea – not one bit of interest from major media. And that's why? It's not because he's labelled as a conspiracy theorist. It's not. You're not a theorist when Bishops are getting blowjobs by six year-old boys. You're not a theorist to say that members of the elites are vampires. You're not a theorist to talk about the artificial moon. That's not why he wasn't invited by the TV journalists.

I'll tell you why he wasn't invited, he wasn't invited for an interview because his balls are too big and his boobs are too small. He wasn't invited because he's too deep. You know, I don't know why he wasn't invited. It might something to do with a thing called *truth*. If you can't get airtime with truth at the end of the-world then when can you? C'mon. It's the end. Let's blow the roof on lies.

Hey, I ain't saying that Mr. Icke is 100% correct on his translations of the wide virtual reality dance floor and that he hasn't had his ups and downs; what I am saying is that he has upheld the truth for 20 years and he has earned his respect. If you can maintain the truth for 20 years, if you can dance for 20 years, if you can eat eggs for 20 years, you should get some recognition for accomplishing an impossible feat, especially considering all the hazards involved in talking about giant lizard boys and depopulation agendas by presidents and ex-presidents. I mean, vampires are hot right now in Hollywood!

He's been playing hardball with the big bozos with the big dials on humanity and he's still smiling, and by my standards that's worth a bit of reverence. Some actor makes a film and it gets $100 million in box office dollars and all of a sudden everyone is worshiping him, everyone is dressing like him, everyone wants to hear the echoes in his skull.

Anyway, it's the end of the world and we should loosen our ties, say what we need to say and get ready for the ships to land. You all did know that the ships are landing, right? "I'll believe it when I see it." Okay. I like that. I like it a lot.

Android Adam & Android Eve Remind Us of the "Ecology of Existence"

There are well-developed theories regarding the Evolution of Mankind and these scientific approximations on the Replication of organic life on this planet, including without limitation the Incarnation of nonlocal souls, are indeed proto-interpretations of the actual incidence of Creation. Granted the debate of Darwinism or Design are problematic simply because they are human derivations of million or billion-year truth. We generally agree on the Adam and Eve principle because it gives us a reliable and acceptable starting point of discussion, and human progenitors hold some presence in religious scripture.

I'd like to offer the nonhuman derivation of Mankind's origins. It will not be a perfect derivation because we haven't the technological mastery of this illuminated cosmos, and indeed that will come. For now we work with what we have and we have enough awareness to consider the original ideas I present in this paper. I will explain the fundamental nature of the human lifeform as I understand it and will include some reality material to provide a reasonable foundation for thinking. My ideas are not formed from hypotheses nor are they borrowed from another's work. They are derived from the highest place possible, a dimensional variance of which there is no compare.

Anyone caught reading this material without any preparedness or corrective action will find themselves in certain discomfort for this discussion is on human origin and is presented by a recognized interstellar mind. Discretion highly advised. More material at a later date.

The mechanical bones

The problem with a metallic exoskeleton is that metals cannot regenerate. We cannot grow new titanium molecules after regular wear and tear. Sure, we can replace and repair parts but we haven't learned to regenerate metal. The alternative to a metallic skeleton is to insert a bone skeleton, especially a bone skeleton that is composed of tiny holes that allow the natural built-in lubricating nutrients to pass into flesh and organs. As exoskeletons go, the human version is a well-built terrestrial model. The rhythms of the body (eg menopause) do not adversely affect the flow of blood or the temperature of the individual carbon unit. Blood is pumped from the centrally based engine into all the pertinent regions of the vessel. Loaded with oxygen from the lungs, the blood invigorates the head and brain, the driver's dashboard.

We take for granted this mechanized genome of inexplicable technology and we do so because we are afraid of where those conclusions might lead. We have been quick over the centuries to root out any derivation on this aspect of life while those neutral try to determine what is declassified for public consumption. Invariably, at several points throughout human history, humankind has been told of their technological origins. Without a doubt that knowledge has been carefully destroyed. They have been careful to destroy the truth that I now share because they needed to figure out how to interrupt those nonbiological processes and to find a way to squeeze shut the power of evolution, a fact that every person here takes for granted. We take childbirth so lightly that we musingly choose a career over childbirth.

Granted there is money and prestige involved in a career and along with that a new house, car, shoes and a vacation in Florida or the Spanish Coast, but ultimately we are surrendering the ability to manufacture life. It is not an easy thing to manufacture a complete biological organism, especially to do so from the abdomen of a female body. In fact, given our best scientific devices, there is no machine that is a Human Replicator. Not in several thousand years has mankind realized anything of that scientific magnitude, not without effort. But built into nearly every single woman's body is a human replicator, a highly evolved technological appliance.

We tend to think, through population control schemes, that births must be impeded because the babies are economically unfeasible and they destroy the elegant lives of successful people who pride themselves on their successful people who pride themselves on their selfishness and thong underwear. It is very selfish to impede the built-in ability to replicate life, is it not? It is like a car owner removing the reverse gear because it's difficult to drive backwards. Interrupting the process of birth, including delaying childrearing until well into a woman's forties or choosing homosexuality as a new way of life, is an indirect or direct attack on the replication of life.

We have forgotten why we are alive. We have been misled to believe that we are able to harness our god-given powers of freedom, wealth and unrestricted fame. We have been convinced that we must forever be beautiful or must try to always be beautiful and the proof of that living is found in the hundreds of kinds of shampoo. Women will endlessly buy new shampoos that process shiny, healthy hair while forgetting the fact that each shampoo uses the same basic chemical ingredient. There's always a shampoo to make you more beautiful or a pill to enhance a man's virility. The sexual power of a woman is tucked away in her hair and in a man, his penis. Those two things, hair and penis, this is what we fight for. Why we are alive? Are we alive in order to have an 8-hour erection on demand? Are we alive to have shiny hair 24 hours a day, even while we sleep? Obviously not, for those reasons for life are decrepit. A few people will mention the Creator. Most people will speak in volumes of selfishness: to be our best, to be rich, to have the best family, to cure some world disease, to build some better contraption, to enjoy life. These are all selfish convictions. But why are we really alive?

Can the Sun refuse to shine?

The question begs a deeper introspection into the idea of life, verily the impetus for existence. The impetus for existence is REINCARNATION. You are not for this life only; you are the Bridge for the next life for you embody the energy for those to come and for you to return. And the only way to ensure those newcomers can arrive or for you to re-enter the atmosphere is to Replicate a version of yourself. You are required to bear a child (or to ensure that children are plentiful in other means).

That is not a god-given right, this is not a demand. This is part of the very process of a Revolving Life. The rain from the clouds fills the lake, the Sun evaporates the lake water to form clouds and the clouds send rain back onto the Land. Can the Cloud refuse to Rain? Can the Sun refuse to Shine? Why is it the woman has been convinced to interfere with childbirth? Because humanity is more advanced and women deserve equal rights to wear pants and earn a living?

As we are alive to Replicate because it secures the Ecology of Existence and keeps us in harmony with the Cosmos, we also need to recognize that bearing a child means bearing a New Unit for the next Soul. If women stops bearing a certain number of babies then the Count of Souls decreases and the Ecology of Existence here is seriously interrupted. If you interfere with the weather enough, plants and animals start to die off, and for good reason --- human interference.

We interfere with natural processes because we have been misled by those in charge. And this detour has gone on far too long. The Ecology of Existence has suffered terribly and families have been seriously distorted, as intended by the self-imposed Masters of the Universe. We have allowed all those deviations, and more, because we have lost our True Origins. The fact of the matter is this: while we have long believed in Creationism and Darwinism and even Intelligent Design, we have overlooked a simpler process of human existence. This has to do with *Androidism*.

The most powerful ability a machine, any machine, can have is the ability to Replicate itself. Imagine if your heavy duty laptop computer can replicate itself from some special Uterus Card. Instead of a new laptop, you simply give birth to a new version of the old laptop. What does that mean? It means that you don't need a separate factory churning out new laptops. All you need is a software maker improving the Replication Code so that each generation of laptops is an improved version. You know, this is where humanity is at. The basic differences are the shape, texture and complexity, and a male and female version. The two genders share genetic code and replicate themselves so that a new software entity (soul) can enter this atmospheric condition.

Ultimately, without a doubt, what I'm saying is that a) you are not your body, b) you are here for a short time and c) you are an *android*.

And that really is the point of this paper, to highlight the technological basis of life, not to prove it for that has been discussed elsewhere in detailed form (see *On the Sparkling Nature of Human Origins)*. Here we need to reiterate the fact that the human body is actually an android body occupied by an advanced piece of software (soul). The differences between us depend on our Inception Date and the amount of evolution we've encountered. In other words, your android model may have started 400 years ago so you are quite native to this planet. Or, you only just have been engineered recently and are equipped with the latest features (even if latent). Inception Dates and Model Numbers are very helpful in your identification but without we are all of a similar manufacture. And we are required to maintain the Ecology of Existence and to replicate so that those to come will have a Body of Experience. Thank you.

For the Express Purpose of Human Replication, Thank You

Shrinkage in the retail industry is the difference between what was manufactured and what was sold at the cash registers. Even at an average rate of 2%, that can amount to $30 billion a year in lost sales due to employee theft, shoplifting and other fraud.

There is another kind of shrinkage that is applicable to the human industry. It is not your usual way of thinking about children, but I think it illustrates some vital indications that should alert us as to the real situation of population growth.

Shrinkage in the human industry is the difference between female egg production and the number of actual births. Typically, this is referred to as the birthrate. According to the CIA Factbook, there were 36 babies born for every 1,000 people in 2009. That's a birthrate of 3.6%. About midway on the list of about 200 nations there is Peru with 19.38 babies for every 1,000 people, or about 2%. And at the tail end of the list are Japan and Hong Kong, two highly-populated nations with a birthrate of 0.7%. Out of curiosity, China is 1.4%.

A typical female is born with millions of eggs in her ovaries which dwindles down to half a million or so by puberty (ages 8-14). During the course of her life, a woman will probably release 300 mature eggs and given the difficulties in procuring the correct and idealized mating partner in today's over-caffeinated, fear-driven industrial machine the very chance of getting impregnated before age 30 is quite a challenge. As we know, there has been a steady inclination to promote women's liberation and to equalize the discrepancy between males and females in society. This is all fine and dandy, but along with that female empowerment there has been one very powerful implication and this has to do with giving birth. An educated and empowered woman, in the usual sense, has fewer children than a dumb blonde farm girl, in the generalized notion. What has happened over the years is that educated women, now a significant part of the workforce and even making up a large part of the university campus, they have decided to postpone their children for as long as possible so as to enjoy all the things life has to offer.

No one seems to be reminding them that the egg factory is only open for so long, some even suggesting that by age 30, most of the chances of pregnancy have peaked. We are then inundated with images of aged female celebrities having children and then subliminally get the idea that if Kelly Preston can get pregnant at age 47 then there is still time later to have a child. Celine Dion, 42, is expecting twins. Naomi Watts had her first and second child at ages 39 and 40. Halle Berry had her first child at 41. Finally, Sarah Jessica Parker had her first child at age 37 and then had twin daughters via surrogate mother when she was 44 years old.

Celebrities are extremely, even if subtly, influential on pop culture. A famous actress who adamantly chooses career over marriage, becomes a box-off success and then has a baby at age 40 is seen as some kind of heroine in the eyes of the audience. Whether they realize it or not the message is quite clear: you can have your cake and eat it too.

But that's the point that we are trying to avoid. We are trying to avoid this hyper-realized, fertilization sideshow by reminding women that they were born with eggs in their two ovaries for the express purpose of human replication.

The factory is built to manufacture a certain number of products for the market and then the head of operations decides, "Well, since I am the boss and I would rather go to Hawaii, I am not going to manufacture anything until much later. Why, let's wait a couple of decades and see how I feel. If I lose all my workers, I can hire immigrants. If I can't get any immigrant workers, why I'll go overseas and use one of their factories for an even lower cost. All in all, we've got plenty of time. Everyone take an extended coffee break for 10 years, you're all laid off till further notice, thank you."

Let's assume that the factory boss can make the rent and overhead payments on his idle factory, which is quite unreasonable, but let's say that the factory remains, it's rented out to a night club owner who renovates it into a disco club, parties, dancing and illicit substances. And plenty of sex of course.

Now, let's imagine that this factory-cum-club is a woman's reproductive system and instead of creating babies when the eggs are plentiful and the energy is superb, instead of doing the natural thing, she is having fun, making money and looking like the next fashion icon. Certainly, that is the trend nowadays and it is a trend that I think is misguided. It is misguided because it denies the woman her most impressive source of power, to replicate a human being. Think about it, with the best human robotics we cannot create an android. We cannot even build a robot that can replace a human and within the very organic body structure of a human female, underneath the dermal layers is an organic factory that can replicate a living thinking being every 9 months or so. And rather than respect and appreciate that immense power, women have been conditioned to respect and appreciate a bank account, shoes, plastic surgery and a wide variety of shampoos to make their hair always shiny.

Half a million eggs pissed away in exchange for things that have no lasting value. The shoes, the cars, the clothes - all of them will wear out; and the things that will provide a lasting legacy, growing in value even after their death, these unborn children are denied their rightful place in the home because the shoes need their spaces and the Egyptian cotton towels need their spaces and the smartphone needs a lounging space.

My Basic Perceptions of Life on Earth

I'd like to share with everyone a summarized view of my basic perceptions of life on earth, as presented over the course of my essays, books and other reality materials thus far. Since anticipating a media run in the near future I've noticed that not many people actually understand what I am about, and admittedly there are many reasons for this.

Part of the problem is that I have developed quite a number of ideas and each of these ideas are fairly significant, I mean they have profound implications on humanity if proven true. That is what I haven't done in the way that was expected of me, although in my defence I did present a thorough discussion of my ideas in my books, and as they are more widely read and discussed it will make more sense. So, in about 20 years I can start publishing my next round of books starting with a discussion on the transfer of consciousness into solid objects. That was a joke, sort of.

My basic perceptions of life on earth are entirely derived from my connection to the cosmic heritage which I am from. As many of us are already starting to realize, our awareness determines our truths and our truths determine our perceptions. As such, it is often quite difficult to talk with many people who all have a very different level of awareness. I decided, after observing the situation here on multiple occasions, that rather than repeat what other teachers have been discussing in a new and exciting format and then watching humanity repeating itself yet again, I decided to translate areas of knowledge that would inspire humanity to reach a bit higher.

Sure, the question is always, what is the right height of knowledge? And this isn't something that can be properly determined because there are far too many factors that are all intersecting at any one moment. For the record, I take responsibility for my own determinations and I can affirm that not all knowledge will be fully understood at the same time. It will be sporadic and uneven until some equilibrium where it makes sense and then it will widen and not make sense again.

This was another challenge I discovered after deciding on what to offer because each time I derived certain knowledge, I discovered that there were other aspects of our intelligence that were missing and therefore could not properly make sense of what I wanted to teach. For example, I wanted to discuss the kinds of interstellar cultures on or near earth, as I have come to directly understand. Soon after I realized that people only talked about the "evil aliens," not cultures, and they included: the Annunaki, the Grays and the Reptilians. Obviously, these evil interpretations and experiences clashed with my wonderful experiences with a multitude of benevolent and beautiful races.
My immediate challenge was not to talk about the cultural differences between humans and nonhumans;

rather it was to inform people that the "aliens" were not monsters and were in fact highly-evolved, technologically-advanced *offplanet cultures*. After many years of covert brainwashing, people had almost memorized the propaganda and could only think on very simplistic terms. You can see just by my interstellar example how difficult it is to speak truthfully, and that was talking about a topic that is well known in the UFO circles. Imagine talking about my even wilder ideas.

Now, I am not asking anyone to agree with my ideas 100% since the details and the application of those ideas will clash with your own internal programming. You may find a better relationship with them over time, or you may not, all of it is a result of your level of awareness. You may simply choose to live out the rest of your life without any new knowledge. I have had open-minded friends who followed my work watch a video on reality and they felt their minds expanding and it frightened them so much that they told themselves to forget what they saw.

Ultimately the only thing I can trust is my personal connection to the cosmos and that my translations of that higher knowledge are applicable to this plane within this next phase of existence and to even possibly continue on after that.

I will present a set of *major* ideas and follow that by some *supplemental* ideas. These ideas when applied to everyday life, in whatever capacity possible, will allow us to realign ourselves to the cosmos and that is because we have been thrown way off course. I present these ideas not to make myself seem superior, as it might be perceived, but to provide a set of tools to help us get back on track. The forces against me in this respect don't want you to learn these truths because that would strip them of the powerful grip they have on your minds.

My ideas will help to reshape the world we live in because the stronger our cosmic connection the less deception and disease in the world. In fact, you will find the illusions melt away faster than you can say "bye bye bozos."

At the end of the day and according to the recent series of human ascensions, at this point it doesn't really matter how fast or how slow you take to these ideas. They are entering this plane and life will be more prosperous if people do make some sense of them. Of course I'd suggest starting early to which some might think that I was a bit arrogant to which I would reply, "Do as you wish because you are responsible for your life. We'll check the life recordings when you expire to see just how smart you were and it will be recorded that many truths were provided and not all of them were remembered."

TALESSIAN'S 10 SUPER-TASTY IDEAS

MAJOR

Reality is manufactured.
We are living in a plane of existence that has been wholly projected by a set of technologies that is many billions of years ahead of humanity's best science. All aspects of this reality, or world, are actually artificial including the flowers in your garden, the trees in the forest, the fish in the ocean, the air you breathe and the Sun that wakes you up. When you look at something long enough, you begin to like it and when you like it you begin to reinterpret it to fit your level of awareness for this provides you comfort. This is why a woman can marry a jerk. This internal process is also at play when we look outside and when we eat dinner, for what looks organic is actually completely artificial but it is also necessary for life because as you will read, you are technological yourself.

Human beings belong to a multidimensional android legacy.

A long time ago, androids were created for this plane. Those first android models had some amazing features. The following series of androids became increasingly advanced and included the ability to procreate. Any artificial being that can replicate itself is an incredibly powerful device because it can prolong its existence and it can better itself. How do you live forever? You replicate your codes and transfer them to a child or to many children. That is also a form of immortality. Along the human history, newer android models were added into the mix of legacy androids so that there were newer and older models living together. Of course, the human android models were built by very advanced scientists and they appear completely lifelike and organic. Behind all the beauty and efficiency is an existence-grade machine.

The cosmos is an immense multidimensional machine.

Rather than what it appears, the cosmos, the universe, is an immense technological wonder that uses varying qualities of energy and raw matter to expand itself. Because of its immensity, we perceive it as a huge space filled with galaxies and constellations and planets when really those galaxies and those stars and those nebulas are all immense machine parts keeping the reams of existences alive and functioning. In addition to this, what we can see of the cosmos is just several layers of dimensions that include many layers that we will never see. Because the cosmos is constructed in this way and because we are formed from cosmic materials, it means that we are similarly built but on a much smaller scale.

Aliens are varying grades of technological existences.

The interstellar cultures inhabiting the vast cosmos and this place called earth are equally constructed of varying cosmic materials. Many of these cultures are extremely advanced machines that can appear to have many bodies on many dimensions. They can appear to have a human body on the human dimension and at the same time have a nonhuman body on an entirely different dimension. The lesser advanced alien cultures are limited to a singular hard body but can project themselves on different planes and can enter different bodies. These technological existences understand the computer-generated nature of life on earth. The malevolent cultures have long manipulated humanity, a culture steeped in obviousness and evidence and holy books, by using the multidimensional holographic qualities of reality to restrict human thought, to impose blocks on human memory and to baffle religious believers into believing that there was a God, things of this nature. All interstellar cultures operate within the confines of the cosmic laws to some degree. The more benevolent cultures adhere to a very high grade of the laws while the lesser forms have fewer adherences. To better communicate with benevolent star cultures, a human must first accept the multidimensional nature of reality and then to respect the benevolent nature of these ultra advanced lifeforms.

There are multiple cosmoses.

Where there is one there is more than one. This is also true for the cosmos. If one cosmos exists, and we are assured that it does because we have seen it and we live in it, and then there must be another cosmos because nothing can exist on its own. The proof is that there is one cosmos and that we are living in it to whatever technological capacity that we understand. This is also why the idea of the entire human race being alone is the most powerful mind control implant ever invented and those inventors should receive an award for duping all of humanity and should be jailed for murdering those who knew different.

SUPPLEMENTAL

Time is a self-generated rhythm.
Time is a matter of perception or indoctrination. We are prescribed time and many of us are out of tune to that rhythm. The proof is that not all of us are on time; many of us are always late for an appointment, a marriage, a college class or a day on the job. In the past, the rulers were the creators of the calendars and the time clock, and that is why each major nation developed their own calendar. That is your proof. How can time and calendars be singular if there are multiple time calculations and multiple calendars, and all of them make sense? This will become even more evident with this new Mayan sham regarding the year 2012. Because right there we have yet another calendar! In the Chinese calendar there is no 2012 end date and they have a 5,000 year old calendar. The fact is that time is a reflection of our interaction with the energies around us. As the cosmos progress or digresses it affects our own vibration and therefore should affect our determination of time. It hasn't because the rulers of earth have fixed our interpretation after disconnecting us from the cosmos, and this happened slowly over history so no one figured it out.

Allergies are Programming Upgrades.
Flowers come out in spring and toss their pollen into the air and into your nostrils making you sneeze not because you are allergic to pollen but because the pollen is transmitting program codes from the inner plane to prepare your body for a new vibration of existence. Each season requires us to adjust our vibration and the flowers share that with people so that people can make the shift from a slow winter vibration to a higher spring vibration so that the body has no complications. Of course, human science sees pollen as a threat and aims to stop allergies rather than to teach humans how to integrate with their technological environs.

Replication is a Human Necessity No Matter What.

If your parents did not have a child you would not be here. Just as you were given a body to experience life on this place, it is expected of you (or most of y0u) to replicate other bodies so that others from other dimensions can come here. To deny that and to follow the brainwashing schemes that lead to depopulation (eg women's liberation, birth control, modelling, career, abortion, vaccinations) is to disobey your original intent and agreement for coming here. No action is more necessary than human replication for that ensures that life goes on. Anyone who contradicts that or who insanely distorts replication into careless family planning is a person or group you should link with demons and devils, for only their kind want to depopulate this world. Anyone who truly respects human replication is in tune with the cosmos. Anyone who believes in population control is in tune with demonic elites.

Thought determines the shape and texture of reality.

Each thought you have is extremely powerful. It not only shapes your reality and what you personally experience but it is also added to the collective of thought. One way that humanity has been ruled is to divert and twist its thinking patterns. For example, if in the original state man and woman were the only genders to copulate; when the thoughts were twisted it was now possible for a man to copulate with both a man and a woman. Later, it would be further twisted so that a woman could copulate with another woman as well as a man. In fact, any or all was possible, even with beasts. All of this was accomplished by twisting human thought and rewiring the brain to think of it as normal. This is also the case for war and disease and religion. If we understand this power, we could rewire our thoughts back to a purer state of consciousness and by doing so we could eradicate disease, we could end war, we could release the other bindings that we have been misled to place upon ourselves.

God is an implant.
In order for humankind to step from a biological mindset to a spiritual mindset, it was necessary to give people an instrument to assist them to reach higher ground. One of those instruments was that there was a Heavenly Father, a Creator, which is truthful. Another instrument was the collection of divine books that comprised the many bibles (eg Christian, Jewish, Islam, Hindu). In the beginning this was effective, but what happened is that these instruments were hijacked by the demonic powers and the idea of God was implanted into the human psyche. God now became the all-powerful entity, a judgemental whitish Man who punished those who did not obey his commands. People then became unworthy of God unless they devoted their life to Him and His Words. Thus formed the Churches and Temples along with their abuses. All of these instruments were false because they were created by demons (dimensional beings from weaker planes) that were bent on destroying humankind's connection to the Truth and the Cosmic Computer. They reformed human belief to move away from the technological nature of the cosmos and to fixate on some invisible old white man. In many ways, God is like a Santa Claus, there is some truth, there is some magic, but he is a construct and when kids grow up they realize that there is no fat old man in a red suit living in the North Pole making presents for billions of children without a factory, with only one sleigh to deliver billions of gifts on Christmas Eve. But Santa is a great story for a 5-year old.

Well, this doesn't sum up my many ideas but it does provide 10 key ideas that are an integral part of my work. I've included 5 Major and 5 Supplemental Ideas so you can see what plays a major part of your existence and what are some key features that can help you live a more fruitful life. In any case, there is so much more to discuss even with this handful of ideas. You always want to apply this knowledge as best you can in your life or to put it aside for a time when you are more ready to make sense of them. Or you can study my works.

10 benefits of starships landing in public

I'm a reasonable fellow with an unusual bent on the nature of existence. We have been immersed for decades in the foul stench of "evil alien" propaganda, and worse, we have been led to believe those lies.

The benefits of meeting interstellar cultures (oops, extraterrestrials) far outweigh any imagined consequences. We strive to live a positive and inspiring life, but when it comes to aliens we pull out the ugliness.

I'd like to identify ten benefits of allowing starships to land on earth. Certainly the ships haven't landed *in public* at this time though those events are quite near the horizon. They are near the horizon because humanity is at the point where their self-destructive behaviour cannot be overcome without new knowledge. That new knowledge will be brought down by the advanced cultures from various systems, dimensions and galaxies.

Sadly, government stonewalling and military-grade propaganda have forced everyone to take a wait-and-see approach. But these administrative agencies have no intention or desire to alter 100-year-old policy on interstellar relations. Therefore, the general public is needed to politely invite the starships to land.

We could see starships land with only a small public effort. The government is a write-off on this issue because it serves another master. If the general public, in small groups around the world, made the starships feel welcome the ships would arrange to land without any pre-approval. The public is in control and with a respectful effort on a sizable scale some of humanity could make contact.

10 benefits of starship landing in public, by Talessian:

1. Explain principles of free-energy
Starmen and starwomen are fairly familiar with a host of free-energy sciences and technologies. Given the foundational sciences on earth, it would not require much effort to re-educate talented scientists and hobbyists in this environmentally-friendly approach.

2. Introduce energy medicine
The next level of healing is energy medicine. Energy medicine can include vibration healing as well as directing energies to cure specific injuries. Energy medicine is a holistic healing practice that works alongside the human body. It would also require patients becoming more proactive in the healing of their wounds.

3. Balance environmental concerns
There are experienced interstellar experts in planetary sciences that are many levels beyond human capabilities. These specialists can work with the various earth energies and this will help alleviate significant problems and back-ups around the world. This can include rebuilding deforested areas, reducing pollution levels and subsidizing the risk of upcoming earthquakes.

4. Teach real human origins
Outside of the Darwinian theory and Intelligent Design there are many other ideas on human origins to discuss. It all depends how far back the history is observed. This will undoubtedly touch the nerve centers of the make-up of reality.

5. Explain Earth's full history
The historical process of the earth is better told and certainly more clearly explained when a million, or billion, year-old culture explains it because they have the tapes. There is very little hypothesizing when advanced camera technologies can show the actual evolution of life on earth.

6. Detail the make-up of reality
Since Ancient Greek philosophers tried to discern what kind of material world this appeared to be until today, thousands of years later, when virtual reality builders are trying to create their own realities, the knowledge of holographic master cultures would really step up the idea of how false reality actually is.

7. Bring new cultural ideas
Just like throughout history, cultures from other star systems and dimensions bring with them a plethora of new languages, fashion styles and arts. New dances, songs and languaging systems will reinvigorate the stale assortment of human culture. Perhaps even new interstellar foods and cooking styles could be incorporated and TV shows to illustrate how to make interstellar cuisine.

8. Eradicate many diseases
Diseases can be reinterpreted on other levels of dimensions. In doing so, doctors will be able to trace the root of disease and alongside renewed medical approaches many diseases that previously seemed incurable will suddenly have new cures. The eradication of disease will be tempered by the psychological

attachments to having a disease so psychiatric therapy may also need to be improved.

9. Reduce global oppression
The world is oppressed by a handful of very rich and powerful elitists. And these groups also have a stronghold on military technologies, space technologies, laws, banking and even pharmaceutical industry. As the advanced cultures lay bare the make-up of the world and the power centers, thereby dispelling many of the illusions society believes, there will be a rapid dissolution of the heavy-handed oppression worldwide. This will result in a more balanced, moral world.

10. Answer the mystery of Bigfoot
Bigfoot, or Sasquatch, has been a mystery for decades. Well, finally the mystery of Bigfoot will be solved because he can finally join up with the starship landing crews.

How to Think Big, by Talessian El-Wikosian

First of all, we think small. The proof is we live mediocre lives. The proof is we are slaves. If anyone can explain how we are living in spiritual glory and the freedom of expression in a world filled with disease, war, corruption and cover-ups, please send me a report. Earth is ruled and we are the slaves. That's the conclusion of my report. That means we think too small – white teeth, fragrant vaginas, buff bodies, big houses, war invasions, wealth management, misuse of substances, discrimination, hate, endless dieting and the perennial big boobs. All of these things would be fine if we weren't immersed in a cultural sewage. But we are brown all over and that's because we think small. Problem is we don't know how to think big.

People think that getting a new job or a divorce is thinking big. No, it's not thinking big. It's a requirement, you married the wrong person now clean up your mess, apologize and get back on track. Thinking small is thinking how you can make more money because money is artificial, it is controlled by demons and it has no spiritual value. Listen, before you argue with me, let me say this: you've had your whole life to make money and if you haven't made it try something different. And by the way, not everyone needs to be a celebrity, I know everyone wants to but let's direct our energy somewhere more productive.

Your parents had their whole life to make it, and guess what, even they are rich they ain't any happier. Money cannot buy happiness but it can sure buy a blow job, which is very small thinking. Fashion? Small thinking. Dating? Small thinking. Marriage? Small thinking. Getting married ain't going to stop the endless war. It ain't feeding the poor. It ain't landing starships. Marriage is a requirement. When you're ready to have a family you marry. Sure, to most guys, it's a huge life decision and either that it's time to slow down and let go, but I'm not writing these essays for deadbeats and whores, I'm writing for the champions just gearing up for a spot in history.

If all of you reading started thinking big, well, we'd have big changes. Problem is none of you are truly thinking big, you're talking ego, you're trapped in trauma, brainwashing, horoscope reading, sharing blogs, waiting and whatever other nonsense. How can I write an essay on thinking big? Because I think very big, I think huge. I've been penalized for thinking huge, why I've had people try to delete me for thinking huge and, at the same time, I've had my supporters attack me. I realize what big is and I know that when you think big you get reactions from others. Problem is, we don't like to upset people. If you want change but you don't want to hurt people's feelings, you shouldn't be reading this stuff. Go back to the apathy train and watch it all happen on TV. Doesn't bother me. I need an audience too. Now, if you're here to think big then goddammit start pissing people off and think big! What is thinking big? Well, again, when you think big you get a reaction and sometimes it hurts (eg people avoid you). So you need to be willing to take a hit or two. Thinking big goes against the grain and that makes the task rather heavy and that means it will take sustained effort to achieve.

Thinking big could also involve supporting some crazy dude who says stuff that rings true. That is thinking big too. You might not have anything but energy, support the wackos, they might be right. If they're wrong, then choose more carefully next time. By the way, all wackos will say they are right, it's in their contract: "You will fully believe in your convictions even if they tickle your feet and peel your potatoes."

I signed the contract, *Wackos at Large*. So, there are any numbers of variations of thinking big. Basically they are outside your domestic duties. Listen, you want a boob job, okay, I don't mind but that's not thinking big, that's a domestic issue. Hey, big boobs will get you a large audience.

Perhaps I'll invite a number of big-boobed women to a stage performance one day. That'll confuse them. "Uh, but I thought Tal was an egoless starman upholding the cosmic laws....how can he let these big-boobed women on this stage? "How? I'll tell you how—they are people too. And many of these women are more wonderful than anyone will ever understand. Why do I talk of big boobs? Because, you see, I've just realized thinking big for me – Having these beautiful women with me on a stage. For a starman, that's thinking big on two levels!

See how some of this can be fun? You've got to push the boundaries, put on a one-man show and talk about conspiracies. Turn your abduction experiences into a routine. Sing interstellar songs. Write a book. Make a film. Get out there and protest. Write to your government. Go on TV, like CNN, and tell them that ET is here. Send them an email, or 1,000. Or support the leaders you like. Look, no one is perfect. I'm flawed, let's just be honest. But I do bring a number of powerful truths with me and till now I haven't been proven a fraud. That's five years. Others have been teaching for 20 or 30 years, give them your support, lend them your ear, send them positive feedback, ideas, love. There are millions of things to do. If you are bright then take an ordinary problem, like money, and write a paper on how to delete it and the entire monetary system; invent a new science. You probably have a list of things on paper everywhere, now is the time to have it out and brush off the dust.

If you speak truthfully and you think big you'll upset people. I know. But don't listen to me, you have to live with your own consequences. The longer we think small, the longer our enslavement, the more our anger. When you think big, pace yourself. It's a marathon. Keep your job and your marriage for as long as you can. I always say, have two lives, one is domestic and one is superhero. What happens to one does not affect the other.

If we want to manifest the new reality goodies, we all have to start thinking big. Thinking big alone will fundamentally impact this environment. Group meditations are pretty straightforward. It doesn't take much to achieve something. You should never try to put yourself in the history books, I've tried it, doesn't work; instead, be true to yourself and why you are here. That's it. You might be here to write one important letter or to connect to people and that's fine. If everyone does their part, it all gets done. C'mon superheroes! Let's think big! You'll know when you're truly big when you've run out of petroleum jelly.

STORIES

The Society Programmers

The mothership was as quiet as 10,000 butterflies all flying in total unity. Inside the upper deck, not far from the scientific quarter, there had been a meeting. The meeting had gone well, another one of those cosmic visits every so many cycles. It was on the advice of the visiting VIP that Science Leader Osmus redirect the final part of his visit to the chamber of experimentation. Without question, Osmus had agreed, knowing that this would answer a number of lingering questions, but also Osmus knew that he could demonstrate some important discovery, perhaps even more important than the experiments on the bipedal species.

Osmus was a usual Zetan Hybrid, typical green skin, tight like a shirt one size too small. His hair was green as well and he was short. His size did not diminish his authority or expertise; he was top of his class in genetic programming and had come to specialize in societal dispersion. Early on he took an interest in the evolutionary path of a given society, or even a civilization. He excelled at determining specific societal dispersions. Despite his advanced skills and dedication, he realized that the endless number of variables, something he called interferences, were troublesome. Nothing turned out as he had planned.

His latest round of experiments was waiting for him in the experimentation chamber. VIP was eager to see the data.

"This subject lived the life of a traumatized youth. His mother was placed on heroin addiction when the child was 12 years old. The child's abusive father left home when the age of 18 and then died by the time the child was 21."

The Man Subject is now 35. It was hard to determine his real age for he was dishevelled and worn. Several teeth were missing when he smiled.

"The second Man Subject was given a similar experience with an identical number of constraints. With this subject, we intervened at two essential points."

This Man Subject is 38 years old. He is clear-skinned, youthful in appearance. At first glance, he looks ten years younger than his real age.

"The intervention consisted of a genetic upgrade and a reprogramming change."

"What was reprogrammed?" asked VIP. His synthetic voice provided a musical note to the conversation.

"His interpretation of life circumstance," replied Osmus. "The natural tendency is for the subjects to perceive reality as harsh and truthful; therefore, the addict mother and death of the father is perceived as family catastrophe. The result is a weak man with a weak will. A man whose ignorance forces him to live in denial. He loses the ability to trust and to love," he said.

"What of this one? What is the result?" VIP was looking at the 38 year old Man Subject.

"He was programmed to perceive reality as experiential and beneficial. Every incident, every outcome, every event, no matte4r how it appeared, was beneficial," said Osmus.

VIP: "This Man Subject looks vibrant, if not trouble free."
Osmus: "And yet he grew up in the same life conditions as this sample." He points to the previous sample.

VIP: "So the perception of reality determines the outcome of evolution."

Osmus: "We can also say that anyone who controls the perception of reality determines the outcome of a person, or a society."

Osmus smiled. "Let me show you the larger sample."

They walked along the fluorescent corridor of the ship. The occasional ambient sound permeates the false air. A doorway forms in the electromagnetic wall. The double doors slide effortlessly away as if they were never here.

The metallic chamber inside is huge. There are two groups of people here, numbering in the thousands.

The two star beings enter; a third Mantoid Doctor joins them as they stand on a platform overlooking the two groups.

"As we can now conclude with the individual subjects, that the interpretation of an outcome determines the outcome, as if one plus one is equal to two," said Osmus, "We can also conclude that if we were to change one of the variables, for example, the one numeral to a two numeral, the interpretation would change and therefore the outcome as well."

"Tell me," started VIP, "why is this culture not able to overcome its problems with perception?"

"As much as we are improving perception, the subjects are not actively improving their own perception," said Osmus.

VIP: "They are not away of its value?"

"They are..." Osmus had to think a moment to find the right word, "...preoccupied with their own self interests. Perhaps they are afraid to like others."

"Even we improve their genetic disposition?" commented VIP.

"Yes. And there is a third variation, a corrupt element of the culture is further manipulating both DNA and perception," said Osmus.

VIP looked over Osmus briefly, reading him. "After three thousand five hundred years, this culture has remained within the same framework of primitivism as it started."

"Yes. Perhaps our two groups can illustrate this better," Osmus said. He offered his arm, "Please."

The telepathic lighting systems instantly light up to reveal two groups of people. The group on the left is sizably smaller, perhaps a thousand subjects. The right group has several thousand.
"Our Group Subject on the left was placed in an authoritarian environment. The Head of Government was a Dictator, those who did not conform were chastised, brow-beaten, ridiculed, jailed and killed," said Osmus. "Those who conformed are obedient. Many lives were lost."

The entire front row of the group, as if passing them one by one, pasted smile after pasted smile, missing teeth, leathery skin, weary eyes, and all bravely forcing smiles.

"They have responded in the expected manner," said VIP.

"Authoritarian Systems start out angry and become volatile until the will of the society breaks then there is surrender. The challenge is to break the will quickly, before society realizes they even have a will," replied Osmus.

"And what of the second Group?" asked VIP.

Osmus looks at VIP for a moment then he watches the Mantoid approach. "Perhaps he can explain."

Mantoid: "Naturally, we intended to place the second Group under the conditions of a Free Nation, a liberal society for the benefit of the people, as we once proposed on the distant planet Earth with the Human Species."

He looks over to the second Group. The faces on this Group are not smiling. Their mouths are closed as are their eyes. They seem to be praying, hands clasped together.

"They are praying," said VIP.
"Yes. We can say that," replied Mantoid.

"What was the psychological condition?" asked VIP.

"We provided them with a Heavenly Environment. The Head of Society was an immaterial Creator, a Divine Father. The Divine Father appointed Ministers to guide and influence society. People did their duty to appease the Creator for a blessing at the time of their physical death," said Mantoid Doctor.

He looks back at VIP.

"To deal with the challenges of physical life, the people invented prayer. No person was above the Creator," added the Praying Mantis Man.

VIP: "How did the Creator communicate with the worshipers?"

Mantoid: "We invented a book that contained the stories of the Creator. We implanted several stories in each of the key Ministers so that it would be accepted as divine words." He nods, briefly. "Excuse me. I must attend to something."

Mantoid Doctor leaves for a manifesting exit way.

"Tell me, why didn't you supply them with a liberal environment?" asked VIP.

"The mind of this species cannot handle true freedom. It needs to strive for freedom. If you give them freedom, as in a true democracy, they will randomly act out and there is no unity, no cooperation. They need instruction," said Osmus. "When given instruction and rules, they complain. The trade off is structure. There is structure because there is disdain for the governing system."

"Is that not an improvement over Dictatorship?" said VIP.

"Well, originally we perceived as much. We've programmed some societies this way, but the liberal programs don't last. The mind becomes corrupt. Leaders rise up, wars are fought in the name of freedom, for a concept we provided. Democracy is turned quietly into authoritarianism. The difference is that the Dictator is well-spoken and polite," said Osmus.

"But even the Divine Governance seemed to fail. They pray to an invisible being and worship a book," said VIP.

The double door opens. Mantoid Doctor has returned with another person. As he approaches, the person forms into a 35-year-old Male. He appears neither drugged nor chained in any way. "Ah yes, this is one of our most important realizations," said Osmus.

"Who is he?" asked VIP.

"He is one of the special cases. We took several and provided special environments for them to live in," said Osmus. "This one here was our most successful Candidate to date."

VIP looks him over. General good body shape, healthy skin, clear eyes and a soft smile on his lips. "What condition provided this?" he asked.

There was a long pause.

"We placed him in every condition and we arrived at the same general disposition. It was one of our breakthroughs!" said Osmus, with a hint of excitement unavoidable.

VIP is curious, even happy at the prospect. "What was changed?" he asked.

"For the longest time, we've followed the conditional model. We provide an environment and we notice the result. According to old models of society, the texture of society is determined by its environment, except for our special cases," said Osmus. "With our breakthrough, the texture of society is always optimistic, always forward-looking, no matter the environment. In all environments, the subject's disposition is good. As you can see."

VIOP looks again at the Subject; there is a certain pleasure on his face. "What was the breakthrough?"

Osmus: "Ego degeneration."

"Explain."

"Starting at birth, we program the ego to reach a maximum weight at an early age and then it is degenerated and removed," Osmus hurried along faster than usual. "Without the ego, the subject has the highest perception of all circumstance and situations. We didn't realize that the ego was the device obstructing evolution. As long as we can dial down the ego, society will ascend!" Osmus had raised his voice.

Mantoid Doctor took away the Subject.
VIP whispers to Osmus: "Tell me, any breakthroughs on the aspect of love?"
There was a long pause.

"Nothing but repeated failure. I'm certain that one of our teachers had good documentation on this," said Osmus, the excitement already dimmed.

"You are referring to the humanized William Shakespeare," commented VIP. Osmus nodded.

Then: "But we're working on it! We'll figure it out. We just need to understand the variables."

IMPLANT

FADE IN:

A dilapidated town mall in an alternate world. The air is thick with a typical dead haze, chemtrails beyond the awareness of the many. An import SUV drives up to the curb; the front doors.

The frown-faced BOY, 6, sits inside. His MOMMY giving him a stern look just before they enter the mall. Boy staring back at Mommy.

Mommy looking at Boy.

CLOSE ON: BOY'S TENSE FACE for a long moment THEN

BOY
Mommy, I don't want to love anyone. I don't care about love.

Mommy combs Boy's hair to the side. He is unmoved.

BOY
I don't want to love anyone, Mommy. I don't want to love anyone.

She examines his innocent face. The coldness in his eyes reminds her of herself.

INT. MOMMY'S APARTMENT – BATHROOM – FLASHBACK

Her cold reflection stares back at her. There is no spark in her eyes.

MOMMY
You don't need a husband. You'll be fine on your own.

Her voice becomes cold.

MOMMY
Love...is for the mother country.

EXT. MALL - DAY

Mommy's cold eyes still examining her child.

MOMMY
We all have to love someone. Okay?

Boy shakes his head, once, in rebellion.

Mommy grabs Boy's wrist and yanks him through the automatic mall doors. Boy drags along like a laundry bag for a drop off.

BOY
I DON'T WANT TO LOVE ANYONE! I DON'T --

The doors shut out Boy's screams.

EXT. TIMES SQUARE - DAY

An old Buick pulls up to the curb. The dark-skinned driver wears a trim beard and a blank face. His hair is thick black.

This is our TERRORIST, 30.

The business crowd outside is hectic. This is Old York mid-day. People walk with a purpose.

Three teen girls, dressed in designer wear, strut along the shops as if they were models; the front of a jewelry store loaded with diamonds; a Chihuahua being kissed by a large-breasted blonde woman with large lips; two businessmen shaking hands just before one drops into a taxi; a black limo pulls up to an executive office building.

The sky clear blue. A crow perched on a over-filled street garbage can. Its beak picks at the tossed bag of popcorn.

A 3-year-old girl stares at the crow, rambling. A scrap of newspaper tumbling on the sidewalk. The sound of wind.

INT. BUICK - SAME

The scrap of newspaper bounces off the windshield. The engine idles. It is the last piece of music.

Terrorist breathes slowly. He has been watching the people. He notices himself in the rear view mirror. His dark skin reminds him he doesn't belong in America.

He's a foreigner to them and he'll never fit in. He feels better knowing this. Terrorist reinforces his misidentification.

His hand quietly turns the ignition keys. The engine stops idling.

EXT. BUICK - MOMENTS LATER

Terrorist steps out of vehicle. The wind blows his glossy black hair to one side. For a moment, he looks cool; then the moment is lost. Two high-heeled white women ramble by, completely ignoring him, immersed in their designer discussion.

Terrorist walks to fire hydrant, puts up a shoe.

ON STREET

A STREET VENDOR hands a newspaper to a customer.

POV STREET VENDOR

Terrorist ties his shoe laces on the fire hydrant. The old Buick quietly left behind.

Terrorist stands up straight, checks his watch, walks toward the CAMERA, happy to leave.

Street Vendor watches, curious. On his forearm is a tattoo, a naked Asian girl with a knife to her throat, and the year "1967" etched over her head. Probably a veteran.

Vendor the Vet staring at the trunk of a Buick for a long moment then

Smoke oozing out

Then

Vendor the Vet on mobile phone.

INT. NEWS BUREAU – TV STUDIO

A smart phone pulls away from a Latin face. A fingers clicks a button.

A production assistant affixes the microphone to the lapel of this well-dressed Latin male. The suit is custom made. He is clean shaven with sharp white hair. Looks 55, probably in his 70s.

He has a Viagra smile and smells like expensive cigars.

Meet PRESIDENT JESUS VALDEZ.

The NEWS HOST shakes hands with PRESIDENT VALDEZ. Some polite words are exchanged then News Host sits down for the interview.

News Host, late 30s, is a smooth-skinned Oxford graduate. His mother is famous, his father dead, and he's never disclosed his sexual orientation because he's gay and that would hurt ratings.

News Host addresses the TV audience.

NEWS HOST

I'm here with President Jesus Juan Valdez of the Collegiate Regions of New America. We are very honoured to have his presence here today.

He politely turns to President Valdez and starts in his very male voice.

NEWS HOST

President Valdez, thank you for coming here today. I wanted to start this interview with your response to the recent failed terrorist plot in Times Square. What does this say about the intent of the enemy?

PR. VALDEZ

New America is not safe. That isn't because we have offended any other region of the world. What we have done to the world is contributed over and over again. We have provided for the other nations in every way possible.

He fixes his pants.

PR. VALDEZ

Now, some people will think that if a Pakistani terrorist can park his used Buick in the middle of Old York, loaded with enough explosives to kill thousands of people, that we New Americans are too preoccupied not to notice. That we will just allow evil on our soil without care or attention. And that is simply not the case.

News Host scribbles down some notes. His big boy voice:

NEWS HOST
Mr. President, what is being done to once and for all remove terrorism from the world. It has been twenty-five years since the first attacks and we still haven't wiped out terrorism.

PR. VALDEZ
That's a good question you ask...

News Host smiles, proud of his smart question.

PR. VALDEZ
I want you, and everyone watching, to know that my Administration is determined to protect you. Last year, we stopped immigration on any foreigners with more than two children. I am happy to announce a new bill in effect today that will not allow anyone to own old Buicks.

He scratches his neck. The light on the camera housing is GREEN.
News Host watches on like a puppy to his master. He licks his lips.

PR. VALDEZ
So, I want everyone to know that you are one hundred percent safe one hundred percent of the time with zero percent error. The Collegiate Nations of New

America will forever be the safest place on this planet. Now...

He tweaks his perfect nose.

PR. VALDEZ

...enough about terrorism. What I want to talk about now is that the end of religion is not an end of God because you can think of me as your God, for I alone will protect you and your children.

DISSOLVE TO:

INT. SUBTERRANEAN INSTALLATION - UNDER OLD YORK - SAME

We are eight miles under Old York City but the ambience of this neatly finished installation is so pristine that it looks like an executive suite at a five-star hotel.

FRONT DESK

The RECEPTIONIST is an ex-model, long hair, slender, white teeth. A tall FIGURE approaches the counter. We can't see his face because his back is to us.

FIGURE

Agent Barkowitz.

Receptionist glances at her contact book.

RECEPTIONIST

He's in the West Wing, room nineteen.

WEST WING HALLWAY

An LCD screen is playing the TV News. An ANCHORMAN in a suit speaks calmly. In his hand are his notes.

ANCHORMAN

The attacks till now have been soft targets so they are not capable of carrying out any large-scale attacks like before. The suspect has admitted he tried to detonate a homemade bomb at Times Square. He has cooperated with the authorities and is now being held in a secret location for further processing...

Figure walking past door upon door, each numbered in sequence...seventeen, eighteen...

Nineteen.

Figure stops. We finally notice the uneasy silence in this installation. Underground, it is very quiet.

INT. LIMOUSINE - DAY

President Valdez drinking some Scotch. His other hand on a smart phone. An EXECUTIVE ASSISTANT, 25, typing on a laptop, fixes her glasses.

PR. VALDEZ

(on phone)

...I think they'll buy it, they always buy it, Frank...no, you don't need another event, one event at a time...the people are suspecting each other, they are going to work for us, pretty soon they won't trust their neighbour...well, that's what we want...you always want to be dramatic...no, I will not authorize another nuclear strike, the clean-up costs of the last one blew my budget, Frank, nukes are expensive...with what? You'll pay for it? Who is paying you, Frank? Me. I am paying...fine, Frank, but let's leave it for a while...why do we need more cameras when we've got millions of people working for us...okay, Frank...yeah...give me a call in two months...maybe another Mumbai...

INT. SUBTERRANEAN INSTALLATION – WEST WING – SAME

The sign on door: "19". The Figure's face is cleaner than when we first met him in Times Square.

He is Terrorist.

INT. ROOM 19

GENERAL, 50, is the man behind the desk, His military uniform, an upscale version, official. His face is rugged; eyes of steel. This is a man proven in the battlefield.

Terrorist approaches General's desk. General doesn't look up.

GENERAL
Good job on stage.

TERRORIST
Was the airport arrest effective?

GENERAL
It worked well on the news.

TERRORIST
Right on cue.

GENERAL
The audience loves a happy ending.

TERRORIST
Then the threat implant is secure.

GENERAL
No one is aware of it.

He quickly looks up at Terrorist before right back down to his notepad.

GENERAL
Without implants, society would step out of its bounds, we would lose control. That's why we're here, soldier. You can go back to your cover. How's the divorce?

TERRORIST
Same as usual. Can my next cover have me marrying a blonde?

General scribbles in his notebook. Just as Terrorist is about to turn away.

GENERAL
I've booked you for the surgeon, see Maggie up front for the card. They'll put you back to normal.

TERRORIST
Maybe they'll up the IQ.

Just as Terrorist exits the door, General looks up. He is staring at the door.

DISSOLVE TO:

INT. COFFEE SHOP – NOON

It's busy, there's a line-up. The TV up on the wall is tuned into a news station.
ZOOM IN on the TV ANCHORMAN.

ANCHORMAN (ON SCREEN)
The Old York bomb plot has now been linked to the terrorist organization, Rumiah, working out of a small mountain near the border of Pakistan, where it is rumoured that no trees will ever grow there. Though geologists did find certain shrubs in the vicinity.

TIGHT ON Anchorman's head, as if his head was floating in space.

ANCHORMAN (ON SCREEN)
Just one hour ago, Rumiah sent in a PRESS RELEASE stating that they were responsible for the attack and promised that they "will continue to attack New America until all New Americans were completely dead."

ZOOM IN on Anchorman's mouth. Then to his lips. His lips multiply into three colors, hovering on the screen, speaking from some other dimension.

ANCHORMAN (ON SCREEN)
In response to the failed attack on Saturday, President Valdez said, "We are determined to wipe out terrorism at its core because no citizen of this free nation should ever feel threatened."

FADE TO BLACK

PR. VALDEZ (VOICE OVER)
We are citizens of freedom and liberty. Any man, or woman, who would take that away from us is a threat to those things we hold dear. If every citizen, even children, are watching each other, looking for threats, then our country will always be safe. We must watch over each other. Report what is unsafe. Safety is the most important goal we have because the planet is not safe. Outside our borders there are people who want us dead. That's a fact, folks. Everyone wants what we've got. So, trust my Administration and we will keep you and your liberties safe.

FADE OUT:

2010 Woman™ Modern

The all-new Woman™ comes equipped with a built-in Human Replicator™. The Human Replicator™ uses a proprietary god-derived technology to embed a soul into a new Body of Flesh. With this fascinating and wonderful replication technology in your belly, you will discover that with the simple insertion of the Male Penis™ you can easily manufacture a replica of yourself. The Revised You will carry both your traits and those of your Man™ and will ensure that a newly released soul will be able to enjoy Life on Earth. We hope you enjoy your Human Replicator™ because in time to come this technology will become wholly unappreciated, feared and underutilized.

The Woman™ was invented by God Himself. Along with the Man™, God Himself decided that these two existential technologies would enter the Island Paradise of Earth and populate it with more copies of each other. God Himself added the Orgasm Surprise in order to encourage Man™ and Woman™ to replicate and to do so as often as possible; otherwise the Island Paradise of Earth would be empty and boring.

Man™ and Woman™ have been put on this Earth and provided with all the essential Foods, Clothing and Homes so as to sustain existence for many millions of years. After you Incarnate into a replicated body through the Woman™, you will discover many childlike years upon which you can make many mistakes, even to disrespect your Elders, but as you become older you will find a new appreciation for your knowledge. You will activate the Moral Codes.

You will seek to use the Human Replicator in the Woman™ to replicate yourself. A replicated body will allow another soul to descend onto the plane. This is what God Himself refers to as the Cycle of Existence and it requires a continued replication of humans.

We sincerely hope you enjoy your Man™ and Woman™ because they were built by the best materials and uploaded with the highest potential. We certainly hope that you do not over indulge in Temptation and Egotistical Wants because that would lead to an excessive amount of Warring, Disease and will usher in a thing known as Evil. Good luck on Earth.

Fast-forward 4 billion years...

The 2010 Human Woman™ Modern is online all over the Earth. What good is an ancient technology if it hasn't been upgraded to the modern times? In programming the Woman's mind, the intention was to ensure that her thoughts were running a mile-a-minute. The impressive multitasking ability allows her to distinguish herself from the slow-witted, all egotistical Man™. Designed in exact proportion to the super-smart brain is the all-impressive thought processes, it gives her an amazing ability to buy the perfect shoe while sipping a mocha decaf, texting on a hand phone and holding a 9-month old baby.

We inserted 400,000 fresh and vibrant eggs in the twin ovaries. The Woman's reproductive system features God's Advanced Replicating Factory human channel which, unlike previous models that simply allow for conception, uses an impressive network of child-bearing capability that can be automatically switched off if it interferes with status, money or sexual pleasures. The body's Direct Alertness to Delay Childbirth system works with the ego's Selfish Desire and Wanton Abandon to disengage the body's natural leaning towards pregnancy faster than earlier models, and then allows you to justify the use of birth control devices.

Embodying the Woman™ is a terrific experience that perfectly matches its fine-tuned structure. Woman's exclusive Selfish Desire and Wanton Abandon technology increases the lust for wealth, power and equality through career growth. Determining where the needs and desires are best distributed, she can change her mind On the Spot. Plus, the new Testosterone applicator allows her to assume the attitude and demeanour of a Man without any pharmaceutical drug.

You don't get a legacy technology like the Woman™ Modern without distorting and neglecting everything that was once natural and easy. Even the way she is raised by divorced parents or molested by disturbed uncles. Allow new interactions with other women. Change her interests in dolls to a deep desire to play sports. Think of prostitution as a part-time job instead of a career. God Himself didn't touch the Modern version of the Woman™. The Modern version was programmed by a completely egotistical leadership. It was inspired by taking parts of the Man™ and inserting them where necessary so that the Woman™ could wear full-length pants. No, God Himself wouldn't put His name on this Woman™ Modern and that's because she is setting an entirely new standard which makes very little sense. The result? The most conceited, confused, birth-controlled Woman™ ever put on Earth. But she is politically correct, intelligent, has very white teeth and looks hot over 40. She can even bear children without any eggs.

The 2010 Human Woman™ Modern version wants everything. God Himself gave the classic Woman™ everything she needed. All of that has been lost in materialism. These are modern times and this is the modern Woman™.

The 2011 Woman™ is the next stage of existential technology. Stay tuned for any announcements.

Proof

Made in the USA
Charleston, SC
02 July 2010